D1412676

TEXTILES OF CENTRAL AND SOUTH AMERICA

TEXTILES OF CENTRAL AND SOUTH AMERICA

Angela Thompson

THE CROWOOD PRESS

First published in 2006 by
The Crowood Press Ltd
Ramsbury, Marlborough
Wiltshire SN8 2HR

www.crowood.com

British Library Cataloguing-in-Publication Data
A catalogue record for this book is available from the British Library.

ISBN 1 86126 826 2
EAN   978 1 86126 826 6

Photo Credits
All diagrams and photographs by the author, except for the following:
p.44, 66, 101: copyright and from the collection of Birmingham Museums & Art Gallery
p.26: copyright 1946.43. Cambridge University Museum of Archaeology and Anthropology
p.176: Fringes and bobbles decorate a selection of woven and knitted textiles from Bolivia. Bob Challinor
Frontispiece: Mid twentieth-century double-weave poncho, from the Cuzco area of Peru. Angela Thompson.

Cover photograph: a selection of knitted caps and woven textiles from Peru. Bob Challinor.

Typeset and designed by D & N Publishing
Lambourn Woodlands, Hungerford, Berkshire.

Printed and bound in Singapore by Craft Print International.

Acknowledgements

Special thanks are due to my son, Timothy Thompson, who accompanied me on my first journey to South America and whose expertise and advice on photography and computer technology have proved invaluable. Also to Alison Davies, my travelling companion in Mexico and Guatemala, for her reliable and cheerful support at all times and to Pauline Milnes for her enquiries on my behalf into Guatemalan and Mexican beadwork and the purchase of contemporary beadwork items.

Thanks to Colin Squire, for his patient assistance as my weaving tutor. I would like to thank all those who have helped me in my research by providing information, back-up material and/or the loan of textiles for photography: Anna Adcock, Jeri Ames, Betty Ballard, Jane Davies, Dr K J Hill, Jenny Parry, Herta Puls, Liz Thornton.

My grateful thanks to Wendy Brown, Museum Administrator and to Tabitha Cadbury, Curatorial Assistant for Anthropology of the Cambridge University Museum of Archaeology and Anthropology, for guiding me round their exhibition of pre-Columbian textiles and arranging for photography.

Special thanks to Christopher Wingfield, Curator of the Ethnographic Department of Birmingham Museums & Art Gallery, for showing me the reserve collection and to Haydn Hansell, Picture Librarian, for arranging new digital photography of the chosen items.

Finally, to Bob Challinor, for his group photographs of items from my collection.

Angela Thompson, May 2005

Contents

Introduction

The pre-Hispanic countries of Central and South America are linked by a culture of woven textiles – used both as practical garments and as status symbols – which often took the place of monetary currency. This textile tradition, which has developed and adapted to varying circumstances through the centuries, is in many areas still part of everyday life. The introduction of embroidery, and knitting and associated techniques, has added richness to an already prestigious textile heritage.

Many of our Museum collections contain superb examples of historic textiles from South and Central America, but an example of weaving exhibited in a showcase cannot give a full and rounded explanation of how it was used or how it was worn, however accurate the accessories, models and display background. The way a fabric drapes around the human body in motion, the deportment and attitude of the person wearing it and their reasons for choosing that particular garment, are an intrinsic part of the understanding of any textile. They cannot be viewed in isolation.

An even greater understanding is possible through a practical knowledge and application of the various textile crafts. Even at the 'beginner' stage, the feel of the fibres and the way they react to one another gives a message from the fingers to the brain that is never forgotten. An understanding of what is and what is not practically possible in any particular textile craft helps not only with identification, but also gives an appreciation of any difficulties that have been overcome and the limitations imposed by the technique on design possibilities. Even more important is the link through a shared common knowledge with people from other places and from other times.

Those who are lucky enough to be able to travel and experience other cultures for themselves know how light can affect the colours of textiles worn in any particular geographical location, and tourist treasures brought home to a different environment can look wrong, wherever you live.

Merchants, sailors, and conquering armies – all have had an impact on the design and production of textiles throughout the years, but paradoxically, the advent of modern tourism has both saved and helped to destroy many textile traditions. It is natural that young people exposed to a global culture should wish to conform to contemporary ideas in fashion and dress, and many are abandoning or adapting their indigenous costume.

Tourism is an important part of each country's economy and while traditional costume is still worn in remote areas, tourist versions of costume, some more freely adapted than others, are used in dance demonstrations and festivals. Embroiderers have discovered that the general tourist is less discerning when it comes to the level of workmanship. They have to a certain extent, downgraded technique, but fortunately retained a fair standard of design. Throughout history the use of textiles – their construction, design and the reasons for use – has continued to evolve. Even if traditional costume is not worn every day but only for religious festivals or family celebrations, the patterns and techniques are being kept alive.

Although an interest in textiles of all types had already prompted me to form a collection, it was an exhibition in 1985 of Peruvian textiles held at the Commonwealth Institute in London that was the catalyst that led me to a desire to learn more and travel to far-off lands and see for myself how and where these wonderful textiles were made.

I shall never forget the Peruvian man who, leaving his village on the shores of Lake Titicaca for the first time ever, had come to London to demonstrate knitting for the Exhibition. He was making one of the traditional knitted caps, using very fine steel needles to knit a complicated pattern in a choice of two colours to each row. The wool was tensioned by the passing of the yarn over his shoulders, with the ends hanging behind his back. If this man had the courage to come to London, then surely in return I could go to Peru and visit his country.

My chance came the following year, when together with my son, I joined a South American tour, visiting Colombia, Peru, Bolivia and Brazil. A prime reason for making the tour was to go to Machu Picchu, Lost City of the Incas, which my

OPPOSITE PAGE:
Machu Picchu, 'Lost City of the Incas', rediscovered in 1911 by the American explorer, Hiram Bingham.

Reed boat and floating island on Lake Titicaca, the highest navigable lake in the world.

late husband had always wanted to visit. Although it was one of the important highlights of my trip, it was the woven textiles that were to change my life. They were everywhere – weavers had set up horizontal looms by the wayside, or leaning against an Inca wall, wove braid on a back-strap loom, tensioned on the big toe. I bought knitted caps from Pisac market, a poncho and other woven articles from Cuzco and later in Bolivia, more weaving, but of a different type with design elements echoing the stone carvings on the temples.

A few years later I had the opportunity of joining a weaving tour of Guatemala. I was already familiar with the brightly woven textiles though Tumi, the firm who had organized the Peruvian Exhibition, and through articles in the *National Geographic* magazine. However, nothing could have prepared me for the riot of colour, the intricate brocaded patterning techniques, the charm of the people in their traditional costume, worn on an everyday basis.

Our group was lucky to take part in a two-day weaving course under the instruction of a Guatemalan family in Aquas Calientes, near Antigua Guatemala. It was Maria Lopez, the mother, who with great patience instructed us in the art of back-strap weaving on looms set up the previous day by her daughters. It was not easy and our admiration for Maria's expertise increased hourly. In villages along the shores of the volcanic Lake Atitlán we were shown warping methods and soon became aware of the different weaving types that varied from place to place. I needed to understand more about the weaving methods so, on my return home I enrolled in weaving classes and after four years of general weaving, spent a year on supplementary weft techniques.

A more recent visit to Mexico has reinforced my realization that the peoples of Central and South America cannot be divided and sub-divided into politically arranged boundaries. They are basically of the same stock and share weaving and thread preparation methods, often having similar types of clothing. They have long used weaving as a form of wealth, to be bartered or given as gifts.

Even the people who inhabit the hot and humid tropical regions, and who therefore have little use for woven garments, share a surprising similarity in design techniques, whether these are used to decorate pottery, baskets or as painted patterns on the human body.

It is intended in this book to explore these similarities, rather than to deal with each set of people or each modern country separately. The only problem is in deciding where the region begins or ends. The entire area has been under Spanish or Portuguese influence since the time of the Conquest, but in relatively recent times Northern Mexico was sold to America to become the states of New Mexico, Texas and California. These states now have more in common with the indigenous North American population and are not part of this study.

The Spanish brought new crafts to these areas. They introduced knitting, lace-making and surface embroidery, which is not the same as embroidery on the loom. They brought new ideas and a new religion that was grafted onto the old, more or less successfully. Long before the

Spanish Conquest, these countries all had a history of war, trouble, strife and the continual shifting of loyalties and political boundaries. For over two thousand years the people have endured barbaric cruelty, slavery, genocide, religious persecution and torture. They have survived the intrusion of invading armies and the destruction of cities, homes and farmlands. They have been forced to accept alien cultures and beliefs, the desecration of their temples and monuments and complete changes in lifestyle and dress. Yet through all this, the people, with an indestructible sense of self, have preserved their identity – they and their culture can never be completely subdued. It is an identity that manifests itself through the continuing tradition of their symbols and designs, their weaving, pottery and crafts. Long may it continue. This book is intended as a appreciation of their achievement and an expression of my gratitude for being allowed to take even such a minor part in it.

1

Historical Background

Pre-Hispanic Conquest

Throughout the pre-Conquest years the history of the region, both north and south of the equator, is like a repeated pattern in a kaleidoscope. Cultures rise and fall, wars and tribal forays alter boundaries, the conqueror is enslaved – but his descendants rise to conqueror yet again. Crops fail, areas are devastated, cities are moved and rebuilt. It is as though the actors in a play are continually replaced, while the script remains the same.

Most authorities agree that nomadic tribes crossed from Asia to the American continent about 35,000 years' ago. During the Ice Age the sea level of the Bering Strait fell, thus joining the north-eastern tip of Asia to what is now Alaska. It is believed that the nomads came in small groups, possibly over a period of time, to seek better hunting grounds. As hunter-gatherers they moved gradually southwards continually extending their territory, following their prey during seasonal cycles of migration.

Over the millennia they were to populate the entire regions of North, Central and South America. There is a possibility that Polynesians may have sailed their rafts across the south Pacific to land in the area of Chile or Peru, but there is no definite proof of this. Migrations were not only southwards – some long established tribes in the southern part of the continent eventually moved back northwards, either in search of better land, or to take part in tribal warfare.

Climate changed and the era of the hunter-gatherer gave way to agriculture during the Neolithic period. The central part of America, known as Mesoamerica, covers the lands from Mexico down to Panama and it was here that many of the early cultures flourished, linked by a common view of the world connected with fertility and the natural elements. A settled agrarian society was able to develop weaving, pottery and

twined basketry and there is evidence of looped netting, both here and in the southern continent.

The Olmecs were the first people in the Mexican region to develop a high-culture society about 2000BC and their influence was gradually felt in the rest of Mesoamerica. The Olmecs are named after the latex jungle area on the eastern coast facing the Gulf of Mexico and were thus known as the 'rubber tree people'. Their religion, based on an astronomical concept, required a high degree of mathematics for calendar calculation. Sadly the climate has not been conducive to the preservation of textiles, but stone carvings and wall paintings on the pyramid temples give a good idea of the sophisticated level of costume worn by the priests and rulers.

The inhabitants of the central Mexican plateau formed a civilization round the city complex of Teotihuacán and ruled from the early classic period, AD300–600, but gradually declined in the late classic period of AD600–900. The ruins of the Pyramid temples of the Sun and the Moon are a favourite tourist attraction today, massive testimony to a society that once had a ruling class of priests and kings served by a vast slave population from the surrounding territories.

They were followed in the late 900s by the Toltecs who were ancestors of the Aztecs. The warlike Toltecs destroyed Teotihuacán, created a capital at Tula and took over the temple complex at Chichén Itzá, one of the most important of the religious sites, which had been founded by the Maya in about AD400. The Toltec ruler Topiltzin, who introduced the serpent cult, was known as *Quetzalcóatl*, meaning 'Plumed Serpent' and was probably regarded as a god. Although Toltec textiles have not survived, the stone figures and temple carvings indicate a well-established hierarchy of elaborate ritualistic costume.

The Aztecs appeared late in the pre-Hispanic era, from around AD1237, and gradually conquered or gathered in neighbouring tribes including the peoples of Oaxaca, who lived on the western side bordering the Pacific. They were descended from the Zapotec and Mixtec civilizations, builders of magnificent temples with patterned brick friezes depicting geometric motifs and serpents. These

OPPOSITE PAGE:
The carved stone figure on the 'Gateway to the Sun' at Tiahuanaco, a sacred site on the Bolivian Altiplano, high above La Paz.

The ancient city of Teotihuacán. View from the Pyramid of the Moon looking down the Avenue of the Dead, with the Pyramid of the Sun on the left.

same patterns can still be found in modern textiles woven in the area today.

The other important civilization that flourished at the same time was the Mayan. Nobody knows exactly where they originated, but it is thought they were connected to, or influenced by, the Olmecs. The Maya were brilliant astronomers, architects, artists and craftsmen. Evidence of a high level of weaving technique is shown in depictions of looms and clothing in the few codices or picture chronicles that survived the Spanish conquest. These picture chronicles, which were produced by the Aztec and Mixtec people as well as the Maya, were mainly historical and astrological records. The Mayan religion was based on a continuing confirmation that the state of the heavens would remain stable – that the sun would overcome the darkness of night and rise each morning, that the seasons would rotate to order and the solar eclipses perform correctly. This required complicated mathematical calculations and whenever necessary, the ritualistic sacrifice of blood and life.

About 1,500 years ago the Maya settled in the highlands of Guatemala, but later formed a federation of states and gradually moved to other areas, including western Honduras, Belize, as well as Chiapas and Tabasco in southern Mexico. They eventually moved back northwards to the Yucatan Peninsula in south-eastern Mexico where their descendants are still living and the women wear their traditional costume

on a daily basis. During the classic period, from about AD200–800, the Maya flourished. Their society was based on a feudal system in which the rulers and high-ranking citizens enjoyed a superior standard of living provided by an agricultural and artisan underclass.

There is an exception to every rule and one group of people resisted conquest and, until recently, conversion to a different religion. These were the tribes, known in the past as the Kuna Indians, who once populated the mainland area of the Panamanian isthmus in village settlements along the river borders. They were eventually driven to the eastern coastal strip of Panama and finally, during the nineteenth century, to the outer band of the San Blas islands, in 1987 renamed the Kuna Yala. The Kuna women today are famous for their reverse-appliqué *mola* (cloth) blouses, a relatively modern phenomenon dating from the mid-nineteenth century. Their ancestors, who lived in a tropical region, had no need of woven clothing apart from bark cloth and the decorative use of feathers, seeds and vegetable fibres. They also practised the art of body painting and in time these symbols may have been transferred to designs on the *mola* blouses, but this is open to debate.

Kuna beliefs were based on a different concept of the universe, one where all natural objects – whether plant, animal, mineral, geographic or celestial – were governed by a series of spirits that inhabited different layers. This concept of layers may have influenced the construction of the *mola* blouse panels – it is not always the top layer that is the most important. The Kuna believed that a person not only had a physical body, they also had an internal and an external spirit body, or several of them – all copies of, or similar to the original. There were good spirits and bad spirits or simply mischievous spirits. All had to be appeased, preferably by the chanting of songs by the shaman or chief, thanking the great Mother and the great Father for all the gifts of Nature. Anything that upset the balance or any intrusions from outside were to be avoided at all costs. This is probably one of the main reasons for their resistance to religious conversion, together with a complete incomprehension of any faith based on cruelty and bloodshed.

The tribes who inhabited the isthmus region were great navigators, taking advantage of the complex inland river systems and seacoasts stretching on both sides of their land. Using dugout canoes they traded with neighbours and even ventured onto the coastlines of Columbia and Venezuela, south of the isthmus. After the Spanish conquest this area was to become a haven for invading ships and was continually harassed by marauding pirates.

It was this contact with the 'outside world' that gradually introduced the Kuna people to different ideas regarding costume and craftwork. Eventually cloth garments were worn and the importation of brightly coloured trade fabric, Spanish steel needles, scissors and even thimbles, spurred the women to decorate their clothing. Over a period of time their reverse appliqué embroidery techniques were to evolve into an art form and recently, many examples have found their way into museums and private collections.

Carved stone masks on the façade of a Mayan temple at Kabáh in the Yucatan peninsula.

Paracas Textiles

The chain of mountains that form the High Andes stretches from the southernmost tip of South America, northwards through Chile, Peru and Bolivia, finally reaching Ecuador and Columbia to form a continuous chain of volcanic peaks on the western side of the subcontinent. In the northern area, the narrow coastal strip of land between the sea and the mountains has little rainfall and was occupied by many of the pre-historic tribes who left evidence of their civilizations in the ruins of their temples and burial grounds. The dryness of the climate and the methods of burial for the priestly class, which included mummification and the dressing of the corpse in numerous layers of woven clothing, have provided us with an unique opportunity to study the textiles and methods of construction. The fact that copper artefacts such as tools and little bells were included with the burial, has also helped with the preservation of the textiles. This was due to an advantageous reaction to the chemicals produced by the verdigris, which form on the copper as it slowly decomposes over the centuries.

The science of modern archaeology came late to the area. During the years after Peruvian independence in 1824 the new government welcomed foreign, but not Spanish archaeologists. In the early years of the Conquest graves were systematically looted, but later the Spanish ordered excavations where government officials, although more often it was priests and friars, took meticulous recordings but then destroyed much of their findings in an effort to efface any traces of idolatry. During the early eighteenth century after the death of the last Spanish Hapsburg king, his French Bourbon heirs, who to a certain extent held a more enlightened view, made changes. Unfortunately, the

graves had been continually targeted by treasure hunters in search of gold and silver articles many of which, as offerings to the Gods, were of superb craftsmanship. The gold was melted down both for the value of the basic metal and to avoid detection, thus destroying a cultural heritage of irreplaceable worth.

The textiles meant nothing to the treasure hunters, who discarded them together with the bones and skulls and scattered them indiscriminately across the desert terrain. Archaeologists were thus unable to match the textile remnants with the bones and were unable to determine whether the fragments had belonged to a male or a female, or link ornaments and artefacts to a particular burial. The few burials that remained intact have been a valuable source of information.

When the excavations of the burial sites on coastal areas of northern Peru were first carried out there was little upon which to hazard a date for their construction or to what they could link the various textile types. Cultures were named after the places where the excavations took place, as there is no written history. In more recent times radiocarbon dating of the bones has given us a much fuller picture of the prehistoric or pre-Initial period. Although the dates are only to within a hundred years or so, in a timescale that encompasses several thousand years, they are vital evidence of an era that produced such beautifully designed and intricately woven textiles.

Many scholars have endeavoured to form a time frame for the various cultures, but the one with the greatest acceptance is that of Professor John H Rowe. As this is based on the first evidence of pottery, about 1200BC, it does not apply to any of the textile fragments that pre-date this by several thousand years. Evidence has been found of woven textiles imprinted into the ears of dried corn, possibly from some kind of container or sack. The first nomadic tribes had settled eventually into the coastal area when the climate changed. Among the crops was wild cotton, possibly brought from the Amazon region, which in time they cultivated as their primary textile fibre, so that into the third millennium BC their textile tradition was already established.

There are many famous textile examples on display in museums and in private collections. There are painted cloths of the Chavin culture, dating to 900BC, but prime importance is given to the Paracas culture, which lasted from 700BC to AD1100. Many graves were found on the coastal area south of modern Lima. Those from Pachacamac, a temple-citadel dating from about 500BC, are particularly fine and examples can be seen in both the Pachacamac site Museum and the Archaeological Museum in Lima. The weaving is superb and the mantles in the 'embroidered' technique date to about 600BC. The designs, which often depict little figures apparently flying through the air, probably have a religious connotation. By the ninth century BC, herds of llama and alpaca had been

A late twentieth-century tapestry rug from Peru continues the ancient tradition of depicting priestly figures.
(Lent by Betty Ballard)

domesticated and mixtures of cameloid fibres were used in the woven textiles, replacing the fibre and hair of earlier times.

The other important culture was that of Tiahuanaco near Lake Titicaca. The main temple site, on the high tableland of the Altiplano near La Paz in Bolivia, became a ceremonial centre with a great influence on the surrounding area and had connections with another highland culture that also featured flying figure motifs. The Huari, sometimes referred to as the Huari-Tiahuanaco culture, lasted from about 600–100BC. Tiahuanaco is famous for the stone-carved Gateway to the Sun, which has a central figure with a face surrounded by serpent heads or sunrays. He is dressed in a typical tunic and a belt, also with a snake's head, carries two staffs and is surrounded by smaller figures with bird-like heads and wings. These motifs are repeated on textiles,

'Gateway to the Sun', temple complex, Tiahuanaco.

ceramics and other artefacts, almost as a Peruvian insignia. They even feature on modern hotel wallpaper.

Weaving and loop-stitched techniques from 400–100BC were found at Nasca, famous for the Lines incised into the desert sands. The motifs of the Lines, which can only be truly appreciated from the air, feature the same animal and bird outlines found on the textiles. Finally the Chancay culture, from 100BC to AD1200, refers to the valleys of the central coastal region where textiles of superior design and construction were found. Many of these geometric-style patterns are echoed by those on pottery, basketry and on stone carvings.

The Atacama Desert area in the north of Chile, described as one of the driest places on earth, was once part of southern Peru. Here, similar temple complexes and graves were found and artefacts and textiles are exhibited at the Archaeological Museum in Arica, once an important port in northern Chile for the export of the mineral saltpetre. Chile is a long, narrow country sandwiched between the Pacific Ocean and the chain of the Andes mountains, stretching from the Atacama in the north, down through tropical and temperate zones, finally ending in the spectacular glaciers of Patagonia. The original people became farmers and sea-fishers and traded with neighbouring tribes across the mountain divide, Argentina in the south, and Bolivia and Peru in the north resulting in a cross-fertilization of ideas and a sharing of a religion based on nature. The Aymara Indians of the Atacama Desert migrated east into Bolivia, further reinforcing this cultural exchange.

At first, the Inca tribes, whose subsequent empire was founded by Manco Capac in about 1200BC in the Cuzco area of Peru, were not particularly important. Their initial expansion was due to tribal wars but, as dictators used to controlling a feudal society, they gradually took over and subjugated the adjoining coastal empires, even expanding north into Ecuador. They were a people with strong religious beliefs based on a worship of the Sun as giver of life to their universe. They did not impose their religion on conquered nations, but rather accepted other gods and adapted them to their needs. In the same way they welcomed gifted craftsmen from subservient tribes, thus building up a hierarchy who served the Emperor as workers in precious metals, pottery and the spinning and weaving of cloth.

Of special importance were young girls with exceptional looks and intellect who were allowed to become one of the *chosen women*. They were trained in the weaving of decorative cloth and other highly esteemed domestic arts. As 'virgins of the Sun' they might be ordered to make the ultimate sacrifice and give their lives to the glory of the gods. The favourite method of despatch was strangulation.

The Inca leaders kept a tight control over their subservient population. A system whereby overlords were responsible for large areas, which in their turn were governed as several smaller districts, then sub-divided into sections, enabled the authorities to implement orders and changes efficiently. Over the years the population increased substantially, making ever-greater demands on the land. Although forced labour was used to make irrigation canals for agricultural expansion in order to feed the several million people of the Empire, crops failed and an eventual decline led to internal quarrelling and civil war between rulers even before the advent of the Spanish invaders.

Spanish Conquest

The story of the Spanish Conquest is one of adventure, prodigious greed and of courage in the face of all kinds of adversity. It is a record of horrific torture and brutality, of the subjugation and mass genocide of millions of the indigenous population and a grim determination by the Conquistadors to succeed at all odds.

In 1502 Christopher Columbus only narrowly missed landing on the coast of Guatemala on his fourth journey in search of a new route to Cathay. On discovering the islands of today's Dominican Republic and later of Cuba, he had decided these were islands situated off the coast of China and in 1493 lost no time in sending news of his discovery to his patrons, King Ferdinand and Queen Isabella of Spain. They in their turn, fearful that neighbouring Portugal would take advantage, persuaded the Spanish-born Pope to issue a papal bull stating that all lands to the west of a demarcation line some 515km (320 miles) west of the Cape Verde Islands should belong to Spain.

Naturally the Portuguese king objected and the line, re-drawn some 2,900km (1,800 miles) to the west of the Cape Verde Islands, was ratified in the papal Treaty of Tordesillas in 1506. This granted lands to the west of Brazil to Spain and eventually the Spanish empire stretched from the north of Mexico way down to the middle of Chile. When the coast-line of Brazil was discovered by Pedro Álvares Cabral in 1500, it was annexed in the name of Portugal in accordance with the terms of the Treaty and the hinterland became part of the future Portuguese South American Empire.

Mexico

The Aztec ruler Moctezuma II (or Montezuma) became ever more powerful as he expanded his Empire during a reign that started in 1502. But it was not until 1519 that he was told that strange white-skinned men with bearded faces had arrived on the eastern shores of his territory.

Hernan Cortes, a 34-year-old officer, was not the only Spaniard to land on the Yucatan coast of what is now modern Mexico. When Columbus reported the finding of gold and silver treasures, many a young adventurer or escapee from some indiscretion or criminal act joined in the search for riches from the new world. Cortes, who had first come to the island of the Dominican Republic in 1504, became a landowner in Cuba in 1517. In 1519 he landed on the Yucatan Peninsula with ten ships, canon and twelve horses. Moctezuma, thinking that Cortes could be persuaded to leave and return to his ships, made a mistake in sending gifts that only served to reveal the country's wealth. To prevent his men returning home with their newly acquired treasures, Cortes resorted to scuttling nine of his ships and returned Moctezuma's generosity by slaughtering 500 of his subjects. On discovering the factions between the various tribes, Cortes bribed them with the promise of gold and finally took the Aztec capital Tenochtitlán with no resistance. After setting up a new capital on the site of Tenochtitlán, which eventually was to become Mexico City, Cortes went on to conquer Oaxaca in the west and the Yucatan in the east, killing and torturing many thousands of the indigenous population in the process.

The southern Mexican state of Chiapas, which features high mountain ranges interspersed with fertile valleys, at one time included part of the highland area of northern Guatemala. In 1524 a Spaniard, Diego de Mazariegos, persuaded the already conquered Aztecs to join him with their allies and take over the rest of the Chiapas area. Long before the conquest the Aztecs had grown cacao on the coastal mountain slopes and later coffee was introduced at higher altitudes as well as wheat and cattle in the north-east. The Spanish founded a Royal City, Ciudad Real, which became the religious centre of the highlands and formed a link between the Mexican Maya and those of Guatemala.

Guatemala

By the time that Columbus first sighted the coast of Guatemala, the Mayan civilization was already in deep decline, temples and cities having been abandoned and reclaimed by the jungle vegetation. Continuous battles were waged between neighbouring tribes and there was no single power to bind the warring factions together. Several of the Mayan tribes had moved north to the Yucatan peninsula where they erected many of the temple complexes that are part of Mexico's cultural heritage today.

In 1523 Cortes commissioned one of his officers, Pedro de Alvarado, to go south with 800 Aztec warriors and conquer the areas of southern Mexico, then into Guatemala and El Salvador. Alvarado, who was notorious for his cruelty, took advantage of the differences between the tribes to subdue the populace, although resistance continued for many years. In 1534 he set up his own capital at Iximché, near the volcanic Lake Atitlán. Over the centuries the area was beset by earthquakes and a new capital was built at what is now called Antigua Guatemala. The modern Guatemala City was founded on higher ground some distance away when a final earthquake struck the former capital. Antigua Guatemala was re-built and remains a charming town featuring the usual Spanish plan with a grid of streets surrounding a main square on one side of which is the Cathedral Church.

Panama, Columbia and Peru

The Spaniards had made a series of exploratory expeditions to the area of the Panamanian isthmus, but it was not until 1513 that a group, led by Vasco Nunez de Balboa, discovered the Pacific Ocean on the other side of the mountain divide. One of the members of this group, Francisco Pizarro, was determined to explore further, found sponsorship and eventually after several unsuccessful attempts, landed on the Pacific coast of Columbia. He was accompanied by a Spanish priest, Hernando de Luque, and his friend Diego de Almagro who had served in the Spanish Navy. They were spurred on by the discovery, on a native craft that plied the coast of Peru, of woven fabrics and gold and silver objects.

In Panama, Pizarro had a ship built which was then dismantled and carried in pieces by native porters across to the Pacific side. Later, two more ships were added. In 1531 he landed at Tumes on the northern coast of Peru. Although he had only 180 men, the 37 horses that survived were to prove invaluable in frightening the Inca people. Never having seen a horse before, the combined horse and man appeared to them as one terrible monster. In an event that was to change

the history of South America, Pizarro met the Inca Emperor Atahualpa (also spelled Atahuallpa) at his warrior-camp at Cajamarca. Atahualpa had recently fought and won a disastrous civil war against his brother Huáscar who had declared himself Inca Emperor in the Inca capital city of Cuzco.

Pizarro could not have arrived at a better time, as Huáscar's army had been annihilated thus plunging the entire country into a state of chaos. Through emissaries, Pizarro persuaded Atahualpa to meet him. When Atahualpa arrived bearing gifts accompanied by an army of up to 30,000 men, he was not impressed by Pizarro and did not consider him to be a threat. However, Pizarro spurned Atahualpa's gifts like other Conquistadors before him, massacred his unsuspecting troops and imprisoned the king. He was promised release only if one room was filled with Inca gold and two with silver. Although the Incas did as they were bid, Pizarro ordered Atahualpa to be strangled, fearing his status as ruler.

Finally, Cuzco was taken when Almagro brought reinforcements from Panama and eventually the entire Inca Empire was subdued in the name of the Spanish King. Manco Inca, a half brother to Atahualpa and Huáscar, was crowned as Emperor but served only as a puppet ruler until

The ruins of Iximché, founded about 1470 by the Cakchiquel Maya and taken over by the Spanish as their first colonial capital in 1524.

he in his turn met an untimely end. Lima, the capital city on the coast, was founded in 1535 and built on the usual Spanish chequerboard plan. Pizarro was assassinated during 1541 and replaced by Diego de Almagro who had already made expeditions into Ecuador and Bolivia. At about the same time Sebastián de Belalcázar went northwards from Peru into Columbia where he was joined by Gonzalo Jiménez de Quesada who had approached from the Caribbean coast in the opposite direction.

The Amazon Basin

It was in 1500 that a Spanish fleet commanded by Yánes Pinzón first discovered a vast expanse of fresh water to the west of the Cape Verde islands. Although they made a tentative exploration of this vast river mouth, they found no evidence of gold, so abandoned the enterprise. It was not until the expedition of the Spanish soldier Francisco de Orellana in 1541 that the exploration of the Amazon River began, when he travelled for two years down the river from the Peruvian Highlands to the Atlantic. He is said to have named the river after the mythical Amazon women of Greek mythology after encountering tribes of fierce female warriors.

The vast area covered by the Amazonian basin includes the greater part of Brazil and Peru, parts of Colombia and Ecuador, plus a lesser area of Venezuela. The indigenous tribes who had inhabited this area for thousands of years are divided into two types: the Canoe people who lived along the river banks, and the Forest people who inhabited the inner rainforest and encroaching savannah areas. The Canoe people had established an empire of settlements along the riverbanks, forming a highly organized society with a high degree of artistic attainment in the sphere of decorated ceramics. The Forest people could not afford to live in one place all the year round, as they were hunter-gatherers and continually on the move. Their culture was expressed in woven basketry which, although their only method of transporting goods, had also been raised into a high art. Their culture shunned the plain undecorated object. All must be linked to the spirits of nature by incorporating and copying the patterns around them. Their art was also expressed in the feather work and feather headdresses that formed part of their tribal rituals. All this was lost on the invading missionaries, who regarded them as simple savages and did their best to destroy the native pattern of life. Thus, the accessible Canoe people were the first to disappear and, unable to adapt to an alien culture, died of disease and work in the new plantations.

Guiana, sandwiched between the Spanish settlements to the north and Portuguese lands to the south, remained a no-man's land for many years, settled by various European states. British and Dutch navigators had explored the coastal area during the initial years and by the early seventeenth century, trading companies had been set up by the Danes, Dutch and the French. This became known as the 'Wild Coast', inhabited by groups of warring natives and quarrelling colonists.

Chile and Patagonia

During 1540, Pizarro had already sent an army into Chile led by Pedro de Valdvia. Valdvia crossed the Atacama Desert, gradually working his way down through the central fertile area of the Mapocho Valley. As sedentary agriculturalists, the indigenous people offered little resistance, being intimidated by the horses and superior weapons of the Conquistadors. The people of the mountains and of the southern lands offered far more resistance. Even as late as the end of the nineteenth century it was an area unsafe for white settlers or even for the *Mestizo* people who were of dual parentage. Many of the original Spanish horses had escaped and become feral, multiplying over the years. These were tamed and bred by the Mapuche who had learned to ride and used the horses in their guerrilla warfare. The horses thrived on the rich pampas grasses of Argentina and their riders are the antecedents of the Gaucho people of today.

It was during the 1860s that an uncharacteristic type of colony was set up in the wastelands of Patagonia in southern Argentina. A group of Welsh people, unhappy with conditions in their homeland elected, by arrangement with the Argentinian Government, to settle in the Chubut Valley area. The original pioneers, who came from Bala in north Wales where they still hold an annual festival to celebrate the first landing, left Liverpool on the tea-clipper *Mimosa* in 1865. The group was composed of ex-miners, railway men and their families, with only one farmer to help contend with a desert landscape that was barely able to sustain any type of agriculture. In spite of this, a second wave of immigrants arrived and gradually, with the help of engineers, an irrigation system was set up and the land became productive. Eventually this was to become one of the most fertile agricultural areas in Argentina.

The history of the Latin American area is a complicated one where no single country can be regarded in isolation from its neighbours. Each event in sequence had an indelible impact on those that followed. These events shaped the people, the way they think, the way they react to outside influences, even the very clothes they wear.

The Spanish Conquistadors faced incredible hardships, they travelled through dry deserts and searing heat, they hacked their way through almost impenetrable jungle. They

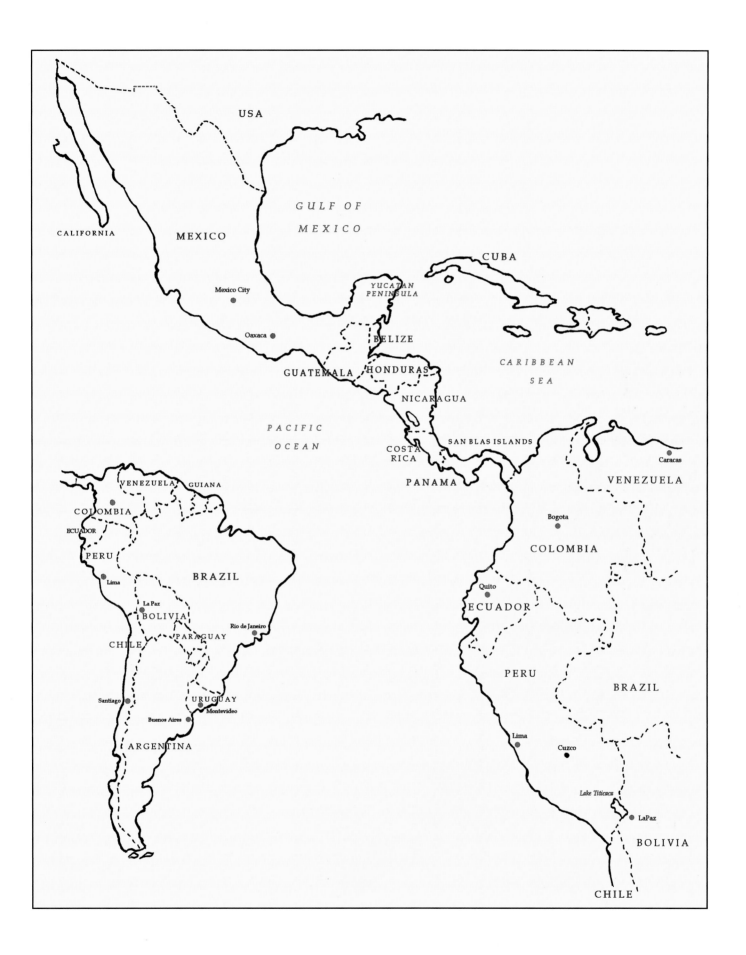

survived malaria, near starvation and the constant fear of death. They climbed mountains, battled through snow and forded countless rivers. It was their tough resilience and a complete belief in their own invincibility that allowed them to become victors against incredible odds.

It was inevitable that once each conquered country was settled, they would marry or find mates among the indigenous women. The resulting mixed caste, called by different names in the various lands, came in time to outnumber the original Spanish population. This aided the assimilation of Spanish ways and acceptance of the Catholic religion.

Restrictions Imposed by Conversion to Catholicism

The conquering Spanish troops were quickly followed by the Catholic priests whose sole aim was to convert the entire population of their newly acquired Empire. Although the Mexican tribes were accustomed to the Aztec system of dominance and the payment of tribute, at first they resisted changes to a life and religion they had been following for hundreds of years. The result was that the priests resorted to force and thousands of Maya suffered death by torture rather than submit to conversion. Those who managed to survive were exposed to the European diseases brought in by the conquerors. The entire indigenous population, both north and south of the equator, was decimated by smallpox, bubonic plague and a whole raft of other infections to which they had no in-built resistance.

The patterns of traditional life were completely changed. Villages were razed to the ground and the inhabitants moved to newly built towns or settlements based on the Spanish grid system. Sometimes families were divided, the men sent to other areas so that they could work on construction, in agriculture or in the mines. Even names were changed. There were restrictions in dress and the people were forced to comply with the imposition of Spanish clothing, although this eventually ended in an amalgam of both native and Spanish costume. In the areas to the south of Guatemala there was little gold, but the indigenous people were conscripted as slave labourers to work in the newly formed plantations where recently introduced wheat was grown together with the local cotton and sisal. Indigo and cochineal were exported as profitable dye products to the Spanish homeland, together with textiles and the plantation crops.

At first, the Conquistadors and the Spanish settlers who followed them were allowed control over groups of the native population in the *encomienda* system where forced labour was extracted. This was abused to such an extent that thousands of the native Indians were to die in the mines or working in the plantations and later the system was rescinded in favour of the *hacienda*s. These large farm estates, which were under control of the colonial government, unfortunately resulted in even more land being confiscated from the Indians.

Although the friars and priests had resorted to acts of atrocious cruelty in order to convert the native population to the Catholic faith, they were also responsible for the education and welfare of their converts. It helps to put things in perspective if ones takes into account the equally barbaric tortures instigated by the Spanish Inquisition in the homeland. Spain, at the same time that Christopher Columbus had first discovered the New World, had only just thrown off the yoke of 800 years of Moorish occupation. A fiercely evangelical reaction was probably a natural response to what was considered to be the heathen faith of their late conquerors.

Meanwhile, the majority of the indigenous population of the whole of new Spain had accepted the Catholic faith, probably in the same way that their ancestors had incorporated the gods of other tribes into their own religious pantheon. The friars had the sense to substitute their own saints for many of the pagan gods. Today the population practises a devout form of Catholicism, enlivened by many saints' days and religious festivals. At the same time, they have not completely abandoned their animistic and shamanistic rituals. This dichotomy is tolerated by the Church and at times the two faiths run in parallel like different sides of the same coin.

In Guatemala, the Church set up a system of religious brotherhoods, called the *Cofradias*. Those Christian saints whose names had been exchanged for the original pagan gods were entrusted to individual *cofrade*, each one responsible for his own particular saint whose image would be on display in his house. The position of the *cofrade* was one of honour and he and his family were looked up to, his wife also regarded as a member of the *cofradia*. He was responsible for the Church processions and was consulted on important matters by members of the community. He was closely connected to the local shaman who acted as a pagan priest, casting spells, divining the future and making sacrifices to the ancient gods.

There are several examples of the phenomenon of dual belief. The best known is that of Maximon, an idol that is found in the village of Santiago on the shores of Lake Atitlán in central Guatemala. For many years the villages have worshipped this pagan idol, a figure, less than life-size, wrapped in many layers of cloth, in a series of coats and jackets and draped with various brightly coloured scarves. Several hats surmount the carved wooden facemask and there is always a cigar planted in the hole that forms his mouth. Every year the idol is taken to a different house that belongs to one of the brotherhood in charge of Maximon.

*Lake Atitlán in central Guatemala is part of
a large volcanic crater.*

*The family of the Mask-maker perform their ritual dance near the
pagan shrine of Pascual Abaj at Chichicastenango, Guatemala.*

At one time the image was hidden in the rafters of the house and only taken out in Holy Week when the idol was to be paraded, but nowadays the idol is on display not only for the villagers, but also for the tourists. An array of thin candles is placed on the earthen floor in front of Maximon to provide a dim light in the crowded room while the villagers make offerings of coins, cigarettes and other small items. The cigar placed in the figure's mouth is lighted and the smoke wreathes upwards above the idol's head, mixing with the smell of burning incense.

The interior of this enigmatic creature has never been divulged and is as shrouded in mystery as in the many layers of covering cloth. There is a possibility of a link with the coverings of the Paracas-culture mummies wrapped in prestigious woven cloths. The fact that the climate of Guatemala has not preserved similar coverings does not mean that the practice did not exist. Maximon is re-dressed every year for the Holy Week parade and carried to the chapel next door to the Catholic church. Here the idol is ceremonially hanged with a rope. Maximon is probably a substitute for Judas Iscariot – the practice of hanging an effigy is common to other Guatemalan towns in Holy Week. There are similar instances in several religions and even our own Guy Fawkes, who narrowly failed to blow up the Houses of Parliament, is burned as the 'bad Guy' but resurrected to suffer a similar fate the following year. In the same way, Maximon, resplendent with a new cigar, returns to be re-housed in the village and start the cycle once again.

In the same country in the mountain town of Chichicastenango, regular services are held in the Cathedral on the square where the famous market takes place. Everyone dresses in their best for special services, which sometimes include multiple weddings. Small children are part of the family group attending worship, never chided but gently

re-gathered every time they wander off. These people, who seldom show emotion, appear to obtain a spiritual satisfaction when taking part in the services, however drawn out – for they are also translated into the native Quiche dialect, obviously filling a need for those who come from outside the town.

Nearby, at the top of a steeply wooded hill, is the pagan shrine of Pascual Abaj, while the house of the 'Mask-maker' stands below. He and his family members dress in fantasy costumes with ribbons, feathers and elaborate headdresses, and dances are staged for the tourists, similar to the ones performed in the religious ceremonies. This light-hearted entertainment contrasts with the place of sacrifice on the top of the hill where, amongst scattered rocks, the charred remains and the occasional feathers of what was once a chicken provide evidence of pagan rites.

In South America, as in the other countries of Mesoamerica, the Catholic churches and cathedrals decorate and dress the statues of the female Saints and the Virgin Mary richly. Although many of the people in the villages are poor, living not far above the poverty line, they are happy to help contribute to the riches of the church and delight in offering ever-greater riches to their chosen saint.

One such example is in the little town of Cocapabana on the Bolivian shores of Lake Titicaca. The cathedral is an amazing white wedding-cake of a construction, contrasting with the dirt-track roads that serve much of the town. Here the Virgin of Cocapabana is accredited with the power to perform miracles and heal the sick. Many discarded crutches and other medical aids are left at her shrine, bearing testimony to her curative powers. The statue to the saint is dressed in the richest and finest clothing that the money of the faithful can buy. Cloth of gold, decorated with jewels and embroidered with gold and silver threads, helps the gown to stand out stiffly and make the statue appear even more important. The altar beneath is encased in solid silver and glints in the soft light. These garments are changed several times a year, according to the religious festivals. There are echoes from the past when the Inca Chosen Women wove especially rich fabrics for the priestly class.

It is not far to an equally famous site from the past, that of Tiahuanaco high on the Altiplano that stretches at an altitude of over 4,000m (13,000ft) for several hundred kilometres. No one knows the exact date when the first people came here and started to build the temple complex, but the archaeologists were excited when they discovered the sunken courtyards with a series of gargoyle-like little heads protruding from the walls. Here on the high Altiplano, the air is crystal clear, making the sharp outlines of the little heads appear much nearer than they actually are. This is the place of the Gateway to the Sun with the statue of the priestly figure carved above the lintel. It is not known what type of religion was practised here, but it is a holy place and it is said that each person who visits, brings their own religious experience with them.

This emotive site was in complete contrast to the market in La Paz, capital city of Bolivia. At over 3,600m (12,000ft) this is the world's highest capital. It sits in a basin between the mountains, shadowed by the sacred Mount Illimani, which for most of the year is capped with snow. Only the rich can afford to occupy the lowest part of the basin – the higher the altitude, the poorer the housing. Many of the

poor of the city and its environs work in the copper mines. This is extremely dangerous and the miners often resort to magical spells and potions to protect themselves, as well as making offerings to their particular saints.

The market is a hubbub of activity, where women sit in groups on the floor, wearing full skirts and bowler hats. They sell a variety of produce, ranging from green vegetables to grain and pulses, together with fresh and naturally freeze-dried potatoes, as well as the occasional crate of captive guinea pigs – a welcome addition to a protein-starved diet. At the end of the market is the Street of the Witch Doctors where a variety of stalls are set out with an amazing assortment of cures for every conceivable illness or unhappiness. The witch doctors are not always men and occasionally, a smiling, brown-faced woman with dark hair neatly parted in the middle can be found dispensing remedies. Little images of various body parts in unfired clay are combined with unsavoury scraps of dried llama foetuses and bundles of herbs, all tied together with brightly dyed pieces of un-spun wool. The miners buy from the witch doctors before they go down the mines, not necessarily as protection for themselves, but rather as offerings to the gods in order to prevent accidents.

Textiles are often associated with miracles. One example, very similar to that of the Turin Shroud, is that of the Virgin of Guadalupe near Mexico City. Ten years after the Conquest in 1531, it was here that the Virgin Mary appeared to a poor man, a native convert. No one would believe him, so

ABOVE: *Bowler-hatted women gather in La Paz on market day.*

RIGHT: *A smiling woman chooses magic potions from her stall display in the Street of the Witch Doctors, La Paz.*

ABOVE: El Castillo is the Spanish name for the ziggurat pyramid that dominates the once-sacred Mayan city of Chichén Itzá.

RIGHT: This stone snake head, situated at the entrance to the ball-court at Chichén Itzá, is the symbol of the serpent god Quetzalcóatl.

he prayed to the Virgin again who told him in a dream to look at his blanket when he woke up. The next morning, he discovered a portrait of the Virgin imprinted onto the cloth. To mark this auspicious event, a shrine was erected and today the Guadalupe Basilica stands on the spot. A special building now houses the relic, in front of which a moving walkway slides, taking both pilgrims and tourists past at an even pace. Out in the square, the faithful parade, going round a number of times before they enter the shrine, carrying banners and chanting. Some are dressed in local costume, but the majority now wear modern dress.

On the other side of the country, at the far tip of the Yucatan peninsula, twice yearly a different set of pilgrims and tourists gather at the once-sacred Mayan city of Chichén Itzá. This most important site was wrested from the clutches of the invading jungle to reveal a vast temple complex, now famous for the high temple of *Kukulcan* also known in Spanish as *El Castillo*, a ziggurat pyramid that towers over the area. It has steps and sides adding up in a calendrical manner to the days of the year, weeks and months. On each of the four sides steep steps lead up to the top chamber, with open windows overlooking the surrounding landscape. Carved serpents frame both sides of each stairway, with their ferocious heads pointing downwards. For a long time their significance was not appreciated until it was discovered that on the afternoons of March 21st and September 23rd, a shadow is thrown that gives the impression that the convoluting serpents are slithering down from the temple. Thousands of people gather to see this phenomenon, which has even been re-created by computerized artificial lighting.

A second pyramid was discovered inside the larger one. Although it was the habit of the Maya continually to rebuild a temple when a new ruler came to power, it is thought that both may have been constructed at the same time, the outer temple dedicated to the Sun and the inner temple dedicated to the Moon. A claustrophobic narrow stairway inside the structure leads up to a small room containing a statue of Toltec origin, called the Chac Mool. The reclining figure is dressed in a tunic and wears a cylindrical helmet on his head. He is holding a stone platter over his middle, once believed by scholars to be the receptacle for the blood and heart from human sacrifice, but according to Aldaberto Rivera, in his book *The Mysteries of Chiché Itzá*, it represents that most important of symbols, the disc of the Sun.

Spanish Influence on the Indigenous Weave-Oriented Culture

The Spanish were impressed with the amazingly high standard and quality of the weaving in all of the New World countries they had conquered. They soon channelled this expertise to serve their own ends. The women were forced to weave cloth for export and blankets for the slaves in the plantations and the mines. At first they were almost worked to death, but the Jesuit priests pointed out that the overseers were destroying a valuable source of income and that the women would work better in their own homes, rather than being herded together in an encampment.

It was natural that the Spanish would dictate different patterns and colours to suit the tastes and fashions back in their home country. They also introduced the European frame loom – one that stands with four posts at each corner and supports an upright framework to hold the shafts that lift the alternating threads that form the warp divisions.

ABOVE: Reed boats on Lake Titicaca would only last one season, so needed constant renewal.

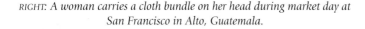

RIGHT: A woman carries a cloth bundle on her head during market day at San Francisco in Alto, Guatemala.

In each country before the Conquest, the back-strap loom together with a simple horizontal loom had been all that was necessary to produce even the most sophisticated of brocaded patterns.

In the past, the precious metals, gold, silver and copper, had been regarded not as money to be exchanged for goods or services, but rather as a means to make superbly crafted offerings to the gods. Only a few of these remain, most of those found were melted down and cast into ingots. The offerings were buried with the dead in order that the gods would give them a safe passage to the after-life. In special ceremonies they were cast into the deep waters of lakes and into rivers either as thanks for favours already granted, or as an offering to placate the gods after some natural disaster and ensure that there was no repetition. The indigenous people must have been astounded when the Conquistadors demanded ever more of these golden artefacts, but as they had regarded the foreigners as some type of god in the first place, their description fulfilling certain prophesies, they acceded to the demands without question.

The original economy was one based on the woven fabric. The more complicated the patterning, the finer the hand-spun thread and the longer it took to make, the greater was the value given to the cloth. Some of the very best examples would never be used, but kept for their worth alone. Gifts of cloth were given to the ruler and to the priests. They in their turn might give gifts of cloth to those who had served them well and needed to be rewarded. These gifts would be displayed as prestigious status symbols, and kept as heirlooms. The ruler would demand pieces of cloth from his subjects as tribute and these were stored in a separate building in the same way that gold or money is stored in a bank. Weavers with special talents were held in high renown and occupied an elevated position in their particular strata of society.

How and Why Woven Textiles Were Worn

One of the reasons why the woven textiles were so important was their connection with the varied geographical areas that ranged from tropical jungle to the high peaks of the Sierras. The horse was unknown, either to ride or as pack animal, and the wheel had not been invented. Goods were transported either by canoe along the rivers, by reed boats in the upland lakes, and by rafts and outrigger-canoes or boats along the coast.

Inland, it was a man or a woman who became the pack animal. Those people who survived harsh conditions and diseases in their infancy grew up to become hardy adults. Shoes were seldom worn, even in the cold of the high mountains. Paths were etched along the contour lines of the mountains, often combined with aqueducts or irrigation ditches. In swampy jungle areas, causeways were built to connect one centre of population with another.

The easiest way to carry anything was in a piece of cloth. The easiest way to hold the bundle in place, or provide a carrying strap, was with a length of woven braid. A large square of cloth, made from narrower strips joined together, could be used to carry potatoes, firewood or earth or dung. The cloth is used to take goods to market where the bundle is slipped from the shoulders, laid out on the ground and opened up, with the cloth thus becoming the market stall. In colder weather it is worn as a shawl, at night it is used as a blanket. In Peru this cloth is called a *manta*, but it has existed in one form or another since the art of weaving began and is found as a basic item in most weave-oriented societies.

For the women, there was nearly always the baby. In many other parts of the world children are still carried on their mothers' backs, even up to the age when they can walk unaided – it is only the shape of the baby carrier that changes. As soon as a Peruvian infant was strong enough to hold up its head, the child was wrapped in the carrying cloth, with the corners tied diagonally across the mother's chest. This left her arms free for domestic tasks, to work in the fields or to spin with a drop-spindle as she walked along. The way the cloth is tied may vary from country to country, but the basic principle is the same, the baby is always close to its mother. The child is imprinted with views of the locality and at an early age becomes aware of the common tasks that will shape its future life. Most important of all, the baby can be fed on demand when the mother reverses the ties of the shawl.

Lengths of cloth were used to make clothing such as the basic tunic, and each country had its own version of cape, poncho or serape. The fabric joins of these outer garments were more complicated than those used for the simple square of cloth. Bags for carrying things are found everywhere. Bags might be large, even replacing the *manta*, with a strap to go over the forehead when carrying heavy loads. Small shoulder bags in South America were made to contain the day's supply of cocoa leaves. These were mixed with lime and chewed at intervals to stave off hunger. The bags were decorated in all kinds of ways, including embroidery and beadwork. Woven bands and braids were of particular importance and apart from the obvious bag handle, were used as belts, headbands and to tie things with. Waist purses and small moneybags were woven as an entity, or constructed from narrow braids, with the ends finished with woollen tassels and fringes.

Textiles as a Badge of Identity

The early textiles found in the graves at Paracas and the other sites are of the finest quality, clearly intended to maintain the status of the wearer in the afterlife. Only the rulers and priestly class would be allowed to wear items with this

At Pisac Sunday market in the sacred valley of the Urubamba River, Peru. Cloths, generally used to transport produce or carry the baby, are spread out to sit on.

complexity of weave construction and decoration. The few remaining codices give a mere indication of the finery of the Mayan and Aztec peoples, but it is obvious that there was a definite hierarchy in dress.

We do not know how any of the rulers would have used the prestigious textile pieces. They may have hung from temple walls, covered royal beds, or been used to decorate a throne. The gauze weaves were most likely made as curtains. A single piece in turn could have fulfilled all of these uses, we can only guess. What we do know is that they were held in such high esteem that they were wrapped in layers round the corpses of the elite and buried with them in their graves. Wherever their spirits went to in the afterlife, we are the richer for sharing these textiles with them.

2

Designs and Symbolism

Symbols as Ideographs in an Oral Culture

The pre-Columbian inhabitants of Mesoamerica – the southern half of modern Mexico, together with Guatemala, Belize and areas of El Salvador and Honduras – shared both a geographical region and a common culture. Although the terrain included areas of dry deserts, high mountain ranges and hot and steamy jungles, there was a surprisingly high exchange of ideas, agricultural products and trade goods.

In spite of tribal warfare and internecine feuding, this cultural exchange led to an overall unity of thought that bound the area together. This was apart from but reinforced by a shared religious concept of the universe. According to the Maya, there were thirteen heavenly layers above the earth and nine layers of underworld in the ocean beneath. It is possible that there may be a link between this Mayan concept of layers and the Spirit layers of the Kuna people in Panama. The Maya believed that the movements of the planets and stars were governed by the gods and that the order of the Cosmos could only be continued by performing the appropriate rituals – the letting of blood and human sacrifice – on specific dates which necessitated accurate astronomical calculations. These were recorded by the priestly scribes who developing a system of writing in the third century BC which lasted well into the seventeenth century.

OPPOSITE PAGE:
Double cloth textile fragment with pattern of stylized pelicans. Late Intermediate Period, Central Peru.
(Accession No. 1946.43. Cambridge University Museum of Archaeology and Anthropology.
Dimensions: 57.5 × 33cm (22½ × 13in))

Although other civilizations in both Central and South America had devised systems for recording numbers or had used signs and symbols to express certain ideas or for use as talismans, none of these can be classed as writing. A dictionary definition of a symbol is: 'something visible that by association or convention represents something that is invisible'. The definition of a sign is: 'any communication that encodes a message'.

A traffic road sign may have a symbol representing an elderly couple. Those who are familiar with the *Highway Code* know that the sign advocates driving with caution as elderly people may be crossing the road. This is quite different from the highway sign that contains the letters 'STOP'. These letters combine to form a word with each letter being a symbol for a sound which, when spelled out, gives us a meaning. Anyone unable to read would have difficulty in understanding this sign, but would probably guess the implication of the symbol showing the elderly couple. Similar symbols may have different interpretations, in the same way that various languages use equivalent letters to indicate different sounds.

Today, various symbols are used as a badge of national identity, or to represent different bodies – whether they are private, commercial or charitable groups. This was equally applicable in the past and many of the symbols used on the woven, painted and embroidered textiles have a common link throughout the regions. As the majority of these symbols are derived from natural sources – animals, birds, reptiles and fish, as well as plant-life and the elements – it is understandable that they are repeated in each area, but with differences according to the particular geographical location. Some motifs are connected to the written symbols, while others are variations of the pictographic signs that were the pre-cursor of actual writing.

Many new symbols were incorporated from the culture of the Spanish invaders and adapted to local needs. Sometimes

Woven belts from the floating island communities on Lake Titicaca incorporate symbols of little houses, fish, birds, animals and flowers that tell a story according to the order in which they are represented.

these new symbols were changed in such a way that their origin became obscure, while others – especially those of a religious nature – were taken over without alteration. The true meaning of many of the ancient symbols has been lost over the ages. In an oral culture, where designs are passed on without resource to drawn or written patterns, it is not surprising that with constant repetition many of the symbols have become unrecognizable. At times the only clue to the meaning of the origin of a symbol is in the surviving descriptive name given to it by past generations of weavers, artists and craftsmen.

In some areas the symbols are used either to tell a story of something that has already happened, or to depict something that might happen in the hope of influencing an outcome for the good. Occasionally symbols might express a train of thought and by their combination pass on a message that could be understood by anyone familiar with the visual vernacular. This is not the same as symbols used in picture writing to convey a message, in which case the picture stands for a particular sound or a word and does not transmute. To complicate matters, a single symbol could stand for more than one object, or it could replace the emotion or feeling that a certain sign evokes.

Mayan Writing

In order to work out the dates for their religious ceremonies, the Maya created a calendar with varying cycles of 260–360 days, plus five odd days, resulting in a fifty-two-year-round cycle. The Mayan astronomers had realized that

calendar dates and the movement of the heavenly bodies do not necessarily coincide, but that eventually they would do so in a given cycle and recur in subsequent cycles. Time had magical properties and was considered to be an unending series of these cycles, each cycle having its own particular god.

The Mayan writing system is mainly hieroglyphic, that is, one that uses picture symbols. At first, twentieth-century scholars thought that each picture or sign represented a whole word or logogram, but during the 1950s it was discovered that the writing also contained phonetic signs, each one representing a syllable. A sign could represent a single word pronounced in different ways, or a picture stand for a word with different meanings. This complicated system of writing meant that both logographic and phonetic signs could interchange, making decipherment extremely difficult.

Until the middle of the twentieth century, the content of the inscriptions found on the Mayan temple buildings was only partly understood. At first these glyphs were thought to be a record of religious events and rituals, but later developments showed that they also listed historical dates, genealogies and the lives of the ruling families. Examples of the writing survived because they were carved into the temple walls and pillars, the *stelae* or standing stone slabs and the door lintels. Many inscriptions were inscribed onto pottery and others included in the few codices or pictorial manuscripts that remained after the Spanish Conquest. These books were constructed on a fan-folding system with the pages made of deerskin or fig-bark paper and occasionally of agave fibre. Jaguar skin was used to enhance and protect the outer covers.

The Mayan hieroglyphic writings were priestly records of the astronomical calculations. They included lists of tables to foretell the dates of the eclipses as well as the synodical period of Venus, a planet of great importance in their religion. It is not known how many of the pictorial manuscripts existed, as the Spanish priests destroyed most of them believing them to be pagan works of the devil and only a few survived. The Dresden Codex, a copy of an earlier third-century work, dates to between the eleventh and twelfth centuries and is so called because it was acquired by the Saxon State Library in Dresden. The practice of producing these records was not confined to the Maya, as there are examples of Aztec and Mixtec codices.

The value of these books cannot be overstated. They give us a picture of the life of the people as well as of the ruling classes. The pictures show us the regalia of the emperors and priests, the accoutrements of the warrior class and the dress of men and of women. It is a cross section of Mayan life, portraying the gods and monsters, as well as slaves and conquered foes. A later, but equally important document was the *Popol Vuh* dated to the 1550s. This manuscript was discovered in Chichicastenango, Guatemala by a Spanish priest who translated the original Mayan Quiche text, which had been written using the Spanish alphabet. This gave the history of the Quiche people and the lists of their kings, an invaluable source for the dating and linking of archaeological and textile finds.

Other Systems

Although the peoples of the southern continent had no formalized writing system, they did use symbols as ideograms in order to communicate or record information, using a variety of media. It is believed that symbols incised into, or painted onto stones may have been used in an astronomical context. Portable stones have the advantage that they can be re-arranged, facilitating mathematical calculations or with altered sequence, magical forecasts and predictions. The practice of painting symbols onto stones is one that is found in several other parts of the world.

In a textile context, the system of knots used by the Incas to record and transmit messages is unique. The *quipu*, which is the Quechua word for 'knot', was formed of a number of coloured strings or cords that varied in length. Each cord could be tied into a series of different knots with each type of knot having a numerical quantity assigned to it. Early in the twentieth century, the archaeologist L Leland Locke determined that all *quipus* had knots forming units with the numerical base ten, as the Incas understood the mathematical concept of the number zero. This system could be used to record the numbers of animals, amount of produce or number of slaves in a society dominated by imperial bureaucracy. The *quipu* keepers, as accountants

and historians, were subject to official inspection and information was sent from one area to another by a series of runners. There is much debate as to the extent that language could be registered by the *quipu* as some believe that it was used to record oral history and the official recorders continually referred to their *quipus* in the same way that rosary beads remind the faithful of their prayers.

More recent computerized research by William Burns Glynn indicates that the numbers could stand for a symbol or motif that corresponded to a consonant in the Inca alphabet. Thus each string might have a number of knots tied into it, which when translated, spelled out a word. Several lengths of the string would be needed to make a sentence. These individual knotted strings would be tied in the correct order onto a firmer cord that could be tied around a person's waist. A knot-encoded message could be sent to distant parts of the empire by the series of runners who passed the *quipu* from one to the other, like passing the

A system of knots used to record the numbers of animals, amount of produce or number of slaves in a society dominated by imperial bureaucracy.
(Pachacamac site Exhibition)

baton in a relay race. Unlike the variable motifs in weaving patterns, it was necessary to standardize the knot system, otherwise it could not be read by its recipient in some distant province. In a formal context, it has been suggested by William Burns Glynn that the knot ciphers could be transmuted into motifs on the woven cloth and thus understood by anyone familiar with their meanings.

The picture writing of the Kuna peoples of the San Blas Islands off the Panama coast has been the subject of much discussion between experts. The words 'picture writing' are in fact misnomers; the pictures are more of a complement to a memory-based oral tradition and do not in themselves portray anything that could stand for a written word. The early pictograms are drawn in colour onto balsa wood and depict figures, animals, fish, boats, flags, flowers as well as a great diversity of other shapes. Later pictograms are drawn in lined notebooks and express both ideas and scenes, many based on the island life.

In 1910 a Spanish Jesuit missionary named Gasso, who had undertaken to convert the Kuna to Christianity, linked the pictures to a long-lost tradition of writing – a view still held by some people today. It was the fieldwork of E Nordenskiöld, a Swedish ethnologist, that in 1928 laid the foundations of new research. Over a period of time he collected many of the chants and incantations, working with the help of the Shamans. He tried to understand the relationship of the chants with the pictures and deposited his notes in Göteborg (or Gothenburg) Ethnological Museum, Sweden, which remain an invaluable reference source. The Shaman priests are keepers of an oral history that is passed on to their initiates. These young men learn many spirit legends by heart. They also learn to use the pictograms as a memory aid to fill out these legends that may take many hours to recite. Thus the pictures are a type of shorthand that the initiates learn to translate by asking questions of the Shaman, which helps to fix the names and events in their minds. In no way can they be classed as writing. This is only a brief summary of a complex subject that is fully covered in a paper by Carlo Severi in *The Art of Being Kuna*.

Any type of pictograph, symbol or motif that has its origins in the historical traditions of the people can be of more value than the written word. With time the intrinsic meaning of words may change but the original concept behind the symbol remains.

Motifs as Magic Talismans

Any motif or symbol connected with the heavens or with the gods was believed to have magical properties. Auspicious symbols were included in woven articles intended for special occasions such as religious and priestly rites, festivals and the marking of the solstices. They were worn on costumes and were part of regalia, used as insignia and carried into battle. On a down-to-earth level, they played a part in the celebrations of marriages, births and deaths. They were considered of great importance to protect the souls of the dead on their journey to the afterlife and as well as being included in the woven patterns, talismans were featured as designs on other funerary goods.

Astrological Symbols – Links with Religious and Mythological Beliefs

Although weavers adapted patterns to their own needs or inclinations, the symbols with sacred connections were part of their cultural heritage and have thus remained comparatively unaltered. Symbols are of particular importance in a religious connotation, the same symbol often serving different faiths. This is especially true of the cross, which was used as a religious symbol in the Americas long before the Spanish brought Christianity to the New World. The Christian symbols were adapted by connecting the various Christian

A mola or cloth picture used on the blouses of the Kuna women of Panama – late twentieth century. A winged mythical beast is formed from a series of fabric layers.

saints with local deities, thus gaining a greater acceptance of the new religion.

In the Mayan pantheon, four gods ruled the heavens and nine ruled the underworld. The earth, which they considered to be a flat rectangle, was balanced on the back of a huge sea-monster that floated on the ocean. The Sun was regarded as male, connected with hunting and music. The Moon was female and worshipped as Goddess of Childbirth and Weaving. According to legend the Sun courted the Moon by disguising himself as a butterfly while the Moon sat in a courtyard, busy at her weaving loom. This may explain why in some weaving patterns the sun motif is represented by a butterfly surrounded by a circle. Another legend substitutes a hummingbird for the butterfly, but the motif is almost identical.

The late-Mayan period site of Chichén Itzá on the Yucatan Peninsula of Mexico has always been an enigma. The founders of this temple city, dedicated to the cult of the Sun, possibly came from the ancient city of Tula. Chichén Itzá was built as a vast religious college where initiates had to perform various tests, which included taking part in a ritualistic ball game, before reaching a level of inner spirituality. There are several examples of the ancient ball courts in various archaeological sites throughout Central America. The rectangular court had a stone hoop fixed on either sidewall, through which the contestants had to deflect the latex rubber ball with knee, hip or shoulder, but were not allowed to touch it with their hands or feet. At one time it was believed that the losing team of seven-a-side were all beheaded, but stone carvings on the walls of the ball courts showing decapitations are now thought to be merely symbolic.

This important site of Chichén Itzá served as a religious centre for the whole of Mesoamerica, with initiates drawn from the various regions. According to Rivera's writing in *The Mysteries of Chichén Itzá*, the Sun was the 'symbol of the sacred fire, the giver of life, the fire that transmutes and transforms energy and all things material'. In his opinion, the Chac Mool figure holding the dish over its middle is the symbol for divine fire on earth and the disc indicates physical and mental control of divine energy.

In Peru it was believed that the Inca – the word originally meaning the emperor or religious chief – had a divine connection to the Sun and was himself a god. This was only an extension of a much earlier sun worship. Like any farmer throughout the world whose life depends on the successful growing of crops, the original agriculturists were at the mercy of the seasons. If they could capture the Sun, preferably at the time of the solstices, this would ensure the Sun's benefice for at least another year. The accompanying ceremonies were performed at some sacred site with the erection of a stone, an archway or the careful positioning of a hole onto which the sun's rays would strike at the magical moment. The Hitching Post to the Sun at Machu Picchu and the Gateway to the Sun at Tiahuanaco were of prime importance. Similar sites were common throughout the world: the Egyptian tombs in the Pyramids and the Heelstone at Stonehenge on Salisbury Plain, England are but two examples.

The Sun

The sun symbol was held in such high esteem that consequentially it features in one way or another on many of the woven textiles. *Inti*, the Andean Quechua word for sun, eventually became synonymous with the actual woven motif.

Dad-ibe, the sun motif, is shown as a face surrounded by five triangle rays set within the heavenly firmament – late twentieth century.

In several parts of Guatemala the women's *huipil* blouses have a circular neckline that is decorated with a sun motif. The length of woven fabric is worn folded in half at the shoulder-line, but when this straight piece of cloth is opened out, the circular sun-motif is seen as a disc with decorative points radiating from the centre. The design around the neckline is embroidered on top of the weaving, going across the vertical stripes of the fabric. Examples of these sun-embroidered *huipils* can be found in Patzun and Chichicastenago. Sun motifs included in the weave construction are more difficult to decipher due to the geometric limitations of the design, especially when disguised as a butterfly. In some instances the sun motif is shown as a circle surrounded by triangles that symbolize the sun's rays, similar to those carved onto the Aztec calendar stone, which was discovered in the main square of Mexico City during 1790 and is now in the National Museum of Anthropology.

The sun, called *Dad-ibe* by the Kuna people of Panama, is shown on the women's *mola* blouses as a central disc with protruding rays encased within a five-pointed star, which itself is flanked by crescent moons. The sun-disc has a small face embroidered in the middle while the background surface of the *mola* is filled in with tiny triangles, representing the starry firmament. In *mola* design it is important not to confuse other circular representations with the sun motif. Sea urchins, a corn mill or even the steering wheel from a boat with radiating spokes can look very similar.

The Moon

Many of the legends were intended to explain the waxing and waning of the moon.

The Mayans thought of the moon as a goddess who sat in the curved shape of the crescent. In some of the codex pictures she is depicted holding a rabbit in her arms – an image probably derived from the shadow shapes on the moon and which are vaguely similar. Rabbit motifs appear on many craft items such as pottery and spindle-whorls as well as in weaving and embroidery. Because the Moon had been unfaithful to the Sun, her light was diminished and she was banished to the Underworld where she travelled across the night sky, only giving way to the sun when daytime came. As the darkness of nighttime was identified with the Underworld, the passing of the moon across the sky assumed great significance, being in control of the gods who must be appeased so that the Sun, as Lord of the daytime over-world, would reign supreme once again.

The moon is not always shown in crescent shape; in some areas of Guatemala a circular fabric disc is applied to the *huipil* blouses. This is said to represent the moon and is often positioned at the base of a neck opening. Four circular discs, positioned at the neck front, back and on the shoulders indicate the four phases of the moon. These appliqué discs also represent the four points of the compass – north, east, south and west – which form an important part of the Mayan cosmos. The moon symbol may have been worn as a talisman as the moon was also regarded as the Goddess of Childbirth. The full moon is shown as a plain disc, distinguishing it from the orb of the sun motif, which generally has protruding rays.

The moon played an important part in Kuna mythology and the picture writings show Moon sailing in a canoe across the night sky, accompanied by mythical creatures, stars, people and animals. According to the legends of the chants, the area between heaven and earth was divided into two distinct territories, presided over by many spirits. Another traditional *mola* blouse pattern shows two crescent moons facing back to back, placed centrally and flanked by two five-pointed stars. Once again the background fabric has been decorated with tiny triangles representing the star-filled heavens.

Venus

The planet Venus was easily visible with the naked eye long before the invention of the telescope and being prominent in the night sky, was regarded with importance. In the Mayan cosmology the planet Venus was male and thus connected with war, so the morning and evening star phases were calculated astronomically and battles timed according to when the planet rose.

The Aztecs identified the original Feathered Serpent god, *Quetzalcóatl*, with the planet Venus. As god of the morning and evening star, he symbolized both death and the birth of life. One legend tells us that *Quetzalcóatl* offended the other gods and was expelled from the night sky. He wandered down the sacred coast in the east where he lit a fire, enveloped himself in the flames and sometime later re-emerged as the planet Venus. It was believed that in a certain year he would return from the east and appear on the Atlantic coast. As this coincided with Cortes landing on the Yucatan peninsula, it is understandable that the Aztec ruler Montezuma assumed that Cortes and his men were ambassadors from the gods.

Venus has always been revered in Peru as the morning and evening star. As in other countries, the different phases of the planet were used to determine the best dates for the sowing of seeds or harvesting of crops. With the help of their Shaman priests, the agriculturists believed that through the correct reading of the various portents, it was possible to predict the annual rainfall.

In weaving, the Venus star motif takes the same form in many countries across the world. It is not known if this similarity of pattern and motifs is part of the limitation imposed by the weave construction, or whether there is some other type of symbiosis, for these shapes pre-date the Spanish Conquest by several millennia. The symbol looks rather like a cross or a lozenge with indentations on each border that can vary from one to four or more. This design is found on Asian carpets, as well as on embroideries from Europe to China.

A single-faced brocade woven huipil *or woman's blouse from San Juan Cotzal, Guatemala c.1990.*
A variety of geometric motifs include the 'Earth' diamond, as well as a 'Tree of Life' at the base of the neckline.

The Earth and the Sky

In several Central-American religions it was believed that the sky was supported by certain gods called the Skybearers. According to the Maya, there were four of them, one to each direction. The heavens were a place of mystery, beyond the understanding of human beings, regarded with both awe and suspicion. The sky is associated with bird symbols, which include the harpy eagle and the horned owl.

The Earth symbol is often represented by a square or a diamond shape. In the Mayan cosmology the four corners of the earth were of great importance. The Earth sign stood for the Middle-world of mankind, sandwiched between the Over-world of the sun and the Under-world of the moon. At each corner, the four directions were represented by colours as well as trees. The green centre was surrounded by the four colours: white representing north, yellow for the south, red for east and black for the west. These colours are said to represent the colours of the different strains of corn, indigenous to Guatemala, which formed their staple diet. Another Earth symbol was the maize field, for the growth of the crops was synonymous with Creation.

A Peruvian symbol called the *Alpaka*, meaning secret earth, takes the form of a rectangle divided by a saltire cross. Pacha Mama was the name given to the Earth goddess, while Pachacamac, the ancient temple citadel on the coast near modern Lima, is synonymous with 'Earth Creator'. On the Island of the Sun in the middle of Lake Titicaca, the Aymara people still sacrifice a pure white llama to Pacha Mama. A specially constructed reed boat will take the sacrifice to the island, where the fresh blood is sprinkled on the Earth Mother, in the hope of good crops in the year to come.

In most parts of Mesoamerica the majority of woven cloth contains a diamond pattern of one kind or another. The diamond, sometimes used as a variation of the Earth symbol, could also represent the universe and is depicted on a *huipil* blouse from the ancient Maya site of Yaxchilan, as well as being an important motif on many present day *huipils* in Mexico and Guatemala. Often used as a repeat pattern, it can cover the entire surface from selvedge to selvedge, or be included as a separate motif or a series of motifs interspersed with other symbols. The pattern is easy to achieve as only one half of the motif, which is itself mirrored, is needed to form the pattern repeat.

While the Mayans believed that the earth floated as a sea monster on the waters of creation, in Kuna mythology a spirit being was thought to hold the earth on his head. This spirit must be placated with ritualistic chanting, as the slightest movement would produce an earthquake. This legend is depicted in a narrative manner on a *mola* blouse, possibly a female echoing of the male preserve of picture writing.

The Wind

In Mayan mythology the Wind god was synonymous with 'breath' and considered to be the embodiment of the soul. He was depicted as a handsome young man, generally in profile with a sharp, straight nose, considered by the Mayans to be an attractive attribute. The god is shown with a floral motif placed on his brow and with the sign '*ik*', which is the symbol for wind, etched on his cheek or ear. Aromatic flowers were also regarded as symbols of scented breath and although they had connotations with female iconography, were by association confirming the beauty of the god. The number three, when spoken, had a sound that was similar to the word for 'breath' and so at times this also was connected with the Wind god.

ABOVE: *A double-weave cloth belt shows the spotted Jaguar with a curved tail, accompanied by smaller monkey, rabbit or hare motifs – early twentieth century.*

BELOW: *A modern version of the jaguar motif on an embroidered yarn picture, or* Paño *– from Guatemala, 1994.*

Animals, Birds and Reptiles

In a society that relied on agriculture, it was natural that many of the designs and symbolic motifs chosen to decorate clothing and household articles would feature images from the surrounding world. Animal and plant motifs were especially popular, not only because they were familiar, but also because of their association with the gods and creatures of mythology. Several motifs have a dual personality, symbolizing both the animal or plant and the deity to which it is linked, while others show combinations of various creatures belonging to a lexicon of mythical beasts that inhabited the heavens and in some cases, the underworld. Many motifs are common to both Central and South America, only differing in the type of animal, bird or plant depicted, depending on climate and geographical location. Some of the Peruvian symbolic patterns have been recorded by Gertrud Solari and these were illustrated for the first time in *The Weavers of Ancient Peru* by Mo Fini, 1984. They are worth studying.

Wild Animals

The Jaguar, which was regarded as one of the most important animals both north and south of the equator, is often referred to as the American Tiger. The original habitat of this large cat ranged from northern Mexico to southern Patagonia in Argentina. Although the jaguar prefers wooded areas it became adapted to other terrain, including the deserts. Few of these animals remain in the north; most of those who survived have retreated to the Amazon rainforest in Brazil. The animal resembles a leopard except for the pattern of black rosette spots that form a stripe along the back of his spine.

The jaguar motif was one of the mystical symbols found on the Chavin and Paracas textiles of Peru, dating to about 700BC. Even earlier examples from about 900BC come from the Cara culture in Ecuador where there is a legend that tells of the union between a woman and a jaguar, from which the people are all said to be descended. The jaguar cult played an important part in the initiation rites of Chichén Itzá. According to Rivera, 'the jaguar represents the beast within; unbridled animal passions. He who sat on a jaguar throne had control of his lower, animal self, both mentally and physically'. This explains why jaguar skin was

Little dogs, or coyotes, worked in wrapped, inlay-thread technique on a single-faced woven huipil *from Solola, Guatemala, 1980s.*

held in such high esteem and used as a cover for the precious Mayan codices containing the religious and genealogical records.

The jaguar motif has many interpretations, but is distinguished by the spots that fill the body outline. Embroidered versions have rounded spots, but in weaving they tend to be diamond shaped. In a woven band from Mexico, the spot pattern is created by a lattice-like surface of inlay weave within the jaguar shape. The elongated body is surmounted by a long, curved tail, a squat head, and four legs ending in claws. As the jaguar motif is very similar to that of the puma, it is important for identification purposes to take into consideration the area from which the textile comes. The jaguar is common to both Central and South America, but the puma only comes from south of the equator. Jaguars are included in the feather decorations of the tribes in Guiana, while a hybrid jaguar–anaconda–caterpillar is shown on an ant shield used in initiation ceremonies, where stinging ants or wasps were inserted into the shield, which was placed against the initiate's skin. He must bear the pain silently, to prove his manhood.

The Kuna women from the San Blas Islands show great skill in depicting animals in reverse appliqué technique for their *mola* blouses. In a comparatively modern work it is impossible to tell if a design represents a lion as a motif imported from Europe, or shows a personal rendering of the indigenous jaguar. Whatever the influence, the animal is embroidered with a definite sense of humour, with whiskers and teeth outlined in chain stitch. On another *mola* the lion's head is shown in the centre of a five-pointed star.

This is more likely to be a version of the sun symbol, surrounded by arcs depicting the heavens. All motifs are open to different interpretations.

The puma, originally so named by the Incas, is slightly smaller than the jaguar. This animal from the cat family is also called a cougar or a panther, or referred to as the South American Lion. The puma, with terrain ranging from Columbia to Patagonia, was found in the mountains of the high Andes as well as in deserts and jungles. Sadly, it is now an endangered species. The Inca people regarded the puma as a god of the Altiplano that lived on the high mountain plains and looked down on the people below. According to Solari, his image was placed on the roofs of houses to guard against evil and bring good fortune. His symbol shows him with cat-like ears, an upright tail and feet with claws. In a weaving context, both the jaguar and the puma are shown with diamond-shaped spots within the design outline.

Coyotes are indigenous to both North and Central America. The coyote dog, which is highly intelligent, bears a slight resemblance to a wolf, but with small ears and a narrower body. According to the manuscript of the *Popol Vuh*, the coyote was responsible for bringing corn to man. It is thus regarded as a symbol of plenty. The coyote was adopted by the Toltec people of Central Mexico as a cult emblem, which among other cults was introduced to southern cities, including Chichén Itzá. These dogs are generally represented as a side view animal motif with four legs, or two legs symbolizing four as in a cartoon figure, with a definite curved tail and perky, upright ears. Rows of little dogs are a favourite design element used for the inlay weave patterns on the Guatemalan *huipil* blouses. As a modern idiom they decorate bags and purses made for the tourist industry. Small dogs are combined with other creatures on Bolivian woven bags, made to contain a day's supply of cocoa leaves.

Domesticated Animals

In South America the alpaca, llama and the vicuna were important animals that provided wool, milk and meat in a harsh mountain environment. Belonging to the camel family, the llama and alpaca are domestic animals bred from the wild guanacos. Within the Inca mythology the llamas were credited with accompanying the dead on their journey into the underworld and were also regarded as the protector of the mountain flocks. The llama symbol depicts an animal in silhouette with an upright head surmounted by short, upright ears and a curled, upright tail. The pattern is particularly popular in Bolivian weaving and is shown on cloths, belts and bands, sometimes in rows, but more often as an individual motif on bags and on modern knitwear.

Although deer are native to both North and South America, in the early twentieth century red deer were imported to South America from the Carpathian Mountains in Eastern Europe, fallow deer from England and axis deer from India. These animals were introduced for hunting. The indigenous deer were held in high respect by the Maya of Mexico and the festival of the Dance of the Deer is still performed today. In Peru the mountain deer was associated with offerings to the gods of the holy Mount Auquis and the animal was credited with bringing treasures from the mountain gods, possibly in the form of good fortune. Some of the deer motifs are easily recognizable, featuring antlers and four legs, but others are more stylized. Some motifs show a tail that curves over resembling a bird, but the deer is identified by little antlers and there are always four legs.

The horse, introduced by the Conquistadors, played an important part in the progress of the Conquest. The horse is not indigenous to the Americas and was regarded by the frightened natives as a combination of monster and Spanish rider in the form of a single element. As soon as the horse became accepted it was included as a symbol suitable for woven patterns. In Bolivian cloths, the horse is depicted with a curly mane, tail and little hooves that are often shown with a voided centre. This makes a delightful repeat pattern, alternated with rows of horses bearing a rider. In most instances the horse and rider are still seen as one design element contained by the pattern outline. In a more sombre context, the execution by the Conquistadors of Tupac Amaro, ruler of the Incas, is shown with the unfortunate man's limbs tied to four horses which all pull in opposite directions.

ABOVE: *The llama is a popular motif on the alpaca wool jumpers sold in Pisac Sunday market – Peru, 1986.*

RIGHT: *Tapestry-weave tourist bookmark, featuring little rabbits together with Gaucho-type men brandishing slings or bolas – Zunil, Quiche area, Guatemala.*

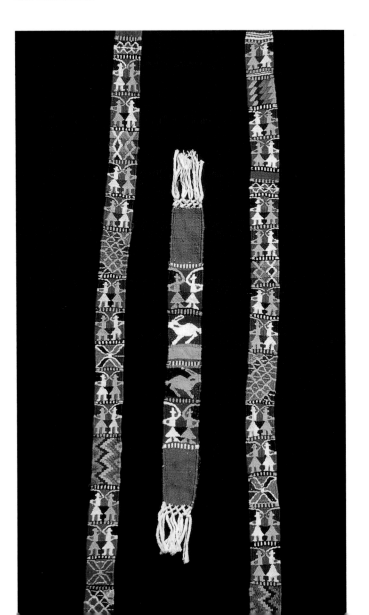

Small Mammals and Rodents

The association of a rabbit with the Moon goddess in Mayan religion has already been mentioned, but this small animal is sometimes included in Peruvian and Bolivian woven textiles, mainly to fill in between larger animals, such as opossums, or with bird motifs. The rabbit can be identified in side view by its long ears and definite, upturned tail. The hare, shown with longer ears and sturdier hind legs, is embroidered onto the hem bands of the underskirt worn by the women of the Yucatan peninsula in Mexico and is included in tapestry-weave bands from Guatemala. A woven band of indeterminate age from Mexico shows various animals including rabbits and monkeys, which fill in the spaces between a large, spotted jaguar.

In the San Blas Islands of Panama, the women show their love of animals in various ways. In one *mola* blouse a pattern of squirrels decorates the front. These creatures are shown from a side view as a repeat with expressive tails in zigzag pattern curving over their backs. The *mola* back has a similar pattern, but here the squirrels are enclosed in cages and their sad bodies are curved and the flattened tail is reduced to a straight line. Small rodents in South America include chinchillas and guinea pigs. The latter are still bred within the warmth of the kitchen area in Peruvian homes, forming a necessary addition to supplement a poor protein diet.

Monkeys were always popular, featuring in many of the ritual dances where they added a mischievous but welcome element to the proceedings. In Mayan mythology, they are connected with the Hero Twins who turned their half-brothers into monkeys, while in the *Popol Vuh* they are identified as scribes, shown together with their writing tools. Woven designs often depict the monkey standing on its hind legs with the forelegs raised, balanced by a high, curving tail, while the monkey motif is adapted to fill a circle on the round spindle-whorls. Here the monkey's body is formed by the central hole, with a raised arm either side of the head, walking legs placed at the base and a curled tail balanced to one side. The Kuna women preferred to show the monkey as a sideways silhouette with from two to three legs and a very curly tail. Although simplified in form, it is still recognizable as a monkey.

Birds of Prey

Bird patterns and symbols feature in every culture throughout the world. Possibly the sight of a winged creature soaring freely in the heavens gave the impression that any association, however tenuous, would be beneficial to the wearer of a bird motif.

In South America it is the condor, with an amazing 3-metre (10ft) wingspan, that naturally takes pride of place. This bird, which is found in both the Pacific coastal areas and the Andes mountains, is slightly larger than the Californian condor, which is now an endangered species. The condors belong to the vulture family and use their hooked beaks and talon-like claws to deal with their prey. In Bolivia, condors are often shown on woven bands in pairs as reversed mirror images with feet facing, their outstretched wings forming a diamond pattern. Bird symbols on woven cloths are not easily identifiable and at times it is difficult to distinguish a condor from an eagle. However, both species are depicted with finger-like divisions beneath the outstretched wings and the claws are well defined. An eagle perched on a prickly pear, with a serpent in its beak is Mexico's national emblem, while on the Mayan spindle-whorls the eagle is shown with a curved beak and pronounced talons, with the wings and tail adapted to fill the circular

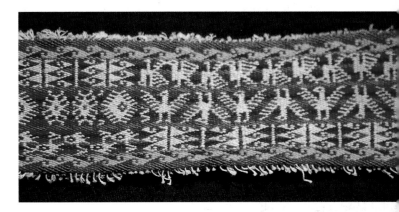

ABOVE: *A* wincha *or headband, in warp-faced double weave from the La Paz area of Bolivia, showing an inverted repeat pattern of eagles and smaller birds – possibly peacocks, fish and Venus Star symbols – early twentieth century.*

BELOW: *A man's sash from the Charazani region of Bolivia, also in warp-faced double weave, with a design of eagles or condors, together with ducks – early twentieth century.*

ABOVE: *Fish and birds are featured on this contemporary, machine-embroidered belt from the Cuzco area of Peru.*
(Lent by Betty Ballard)

LEFT: *Tapestry woven 'duck' panels, worked in separate sections that can be cut to make table mats – Ecuador, late twentieth century.*
(Gift, Timothy Thompson)

area. The buzzard is identified by a shorter beak, smaller wings and a squat tail.

The double-headed bird is an ancient symbol used by the Maya to represent the duality of the gods, commonly found on their seals, stone carvings and pottery. It is not known whether the double-headed bird shown on so many examples of weaving is related to this symbol from a distant past, or whether it is taken from the double-headed eagle of European tradition, introduced when the Spanish Crown allowed the Quiche tribe to use it as their totem symbol. Whatever the original source, the double-headed eagle remains a very popular motif and can be found in textiles both north and south of the equator. Sometimes the design is translated into geometric diamond and triangle shapes, with elongated wing and tail feathers. These double-headed birds can be found on Guatemalan textiles from the Nahuala and Chichicastenango areas. Nowadays they form a distinctive design in brocaded technique on a vertically striped fabric, often used as a sash or head covering, but in the past, double-headed birds were included on the ceremonial garments worn by the *Cofradias*. In Bolivia and Peru this motif is translated into knitting with the bird used as a repeat pattern on the men's caps, or shown singly on a knitted bag.

Water Birds

In the Mayan cosmology the 'Water-Bird' was an important symbol associated with both the sun and with the planet Venus. In a natural context, the inhabitants of lowland swamps and those living by the banks of rivers and irrigation canals would be familiar with the water birds that frequented these habitats. As in many similar aquatic regions of the world, cormorants were used to help catch fish and the 'Water-Bird' is sometimes depicted in this way with a fish held in its beak, thus symbolizing plenty and the continuing availability of a good food supply.

These birds are often depicted in groups, as in ducks swimming or walking in a line. In a narrative context their placing is important – little ducklings shown behind the mother foretold hunger, but when placed in front, a good harvest was predicted. Ducks in disorder or birds in flight show a close observation of nature and different meanings are read into the various ways the pattern is depicted. Ducks and water birds are familiar motifs on flat-weave rugs from Bolivia, Chile, Ecuador and Peru. Modern weavers make small mats, woven as a continuous band with spaced warp intersections. Each section shows a lively duck or bird and can be cut apart and sold to the tourists. There is a definite sense of humour shown in these little birds, either through an inherited design tradition, or more likely through a love of local wildlife.

The flamingo is a long-legged bird belonging to the stork family, found in Central America and in areas of South America. Breeding colonies in the Gulf of Mexico have the distinctive pink colouring, but the Chilean flamingo has grey legs with pink joints. The Andean flamingo breeds on the shores of Lake Titicaca, which shares borders with both Peru and Bolivia. The flamingo is included in many of the woven textiles, easily recognizable by the long legs, wide wings and short tail.

The pelican with its large bill is still a common bird in freshwater lakes and rivers in eastern Mexico. It must also have favoured the arid coastal area of northern Peru, for images of the pelican are carved in half-relief on the adobe walls of Chan Chan, the ruined Chimú city that was once capital of the Moche empire that was at its height before the Incas took over. Their settlements were situated on the limited number of river valleys in the area and these waterways probably provided a haven for the pelican birds, which rely on fish for their diet. Fishponds, served by aqueducts, were built in Chan Chan to help feed the huge population, so the pelican symbol would be one signifying plenty. This bird is represented on the feathered tunics worn by the rulers and the elite. On one tunic, large-scale pelicans are shown borne on litters by a series of lesser pelicans, but the true significance of this combination is not known.

Exotic Birds

The Quetzal bird was once common from southern Mexico to Bolivia. It was prized and revered by the Mayas and the Aztecs as a sacred bird, although the Mayans traded their bright tail feathers for money. Nowadays only a few survive in the Guatemalan highlands, due to over-hunting in the past and the destruction of their habitat in more recent times. The cutting down of dense tropical cloud forests has

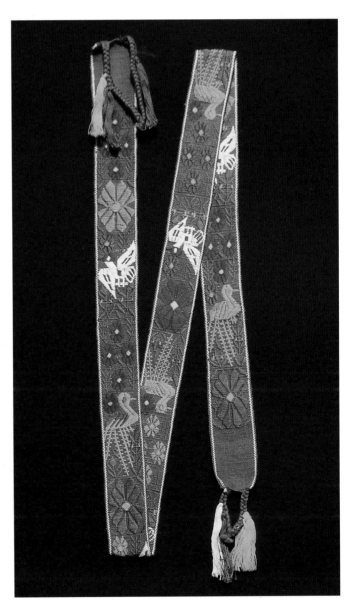

ABOVE: *Long-tailed Quetzal birds alternate with flying ducks and floral motifs on a double-sided, brocade-weave belt – Todos Santos Cuchumatan, Guatemala, 1994.*

LEFT: *A repeat pattern of Quetzal birds forms the design on a little back-strap loom, set up for tourist sale – Guatemala.*

Peacocks and peahens, interspersed with small bird motifs, form the design on a two-faced, inlay-woven head cloth from Nahuala in the Guatemalan Highlands – early 1990s.

reduced the areas needed for nesting sites and the foliage and fruits on which it feeds. Even so, the Quetzal bird is the national emblem of Guatemala as well as being the name given to their monetary unit. The bird emblem is shown on modern silver jewellery and other craft items produced for the tourist trade. In the past the symbol had pride of place on many of the textiles, always showing the rounded crest and the long, blue-green tail plumes that hung downwards before curling upwards at the tips. Quetzal birds are worked on modern *mola* designs, with each outward-facing bird perched on a branch and the two decorative tails hanging down together.

The parrot is another favourite motif. This exotic bird is shown among tropical flowers and foliage, worked in vibrant colours to enhance the *huipil* blouses in Guatemala, including the tapestry woven ones of San Antonio Aquas Calientes. Embroidered panels in wool on cotton fabric are a more recent addition to the textile repertoire, depicting flower and tree-forms together with parrots and other birds. The parrot thrives in warm climates and the 'Amazona' species inhabits the rainforests of Central America including Mexico as well as northern South America. These birds are short with a squared tail, mainly green with bright colouring. The blue-fronted Amazon, which is found in an area stretching from Mexico to Ecuador and Brazil, boasts many colours, including yellow and red. The green parakeet is native to South America but, having escaped from aviaries, is common in other areas. It is not surprising that these brightly coloured birds have found favour with both embroiderers and other textile artists.

Peacocks and Domestic Birds

The peacock, which was introduced by the Spaniards, can be identified by its long tail and by the comb on top of the head, sometimes shown as a triangle. On an inlay weave cloth from Nahuala in the Highlands of Guatemala, the peacocks are shown in three sizes. The larger peacock has a long tail that is an important feature of the design. The smaller birds, possibly peahens, have a truncated tail without the added embellishments sported by the peacocks. Smaller versions of the peacock are shown on the upper part of the cloth. They may represent offspring, or depict peacocks at a distance, as scale is an element that can be changed at the whim of the individual weaver.

Another introduction from Europe was the chicken, but the local turkey motif is more common, including one known as the 'dead-turkey' showing the bird with a neck bent down at right angles. It is thought that this motif, originally found on ceremonial garments, may represent a sacrificial bird.

Aquatic Creatures

The Mayans believed that the world was held on the back of a sea monster, sometimes in the form of a giant cayman, the corrugated back of the floating reptile giving the impression of mountain ridges and valleys, together with caves and inlets. In other versions a giant turtle held the world on his back.

The lakes, rivers and coastal areas provided the inhabitants with seafood as an addition to their diet, at times the only protein choice available. As a general rule the fish motif is simplified to a basic curved outline with the addition of fins and tail, but occasionally fish are depicted in a more naturalistic manner with open mouths and elaborate tail fins. In Peru the fish were said to predict the weather patterns, so were included as symbols that acted as a talisman. In the Amano Museum, Lima, a design of little fish in a pattern of half-drop squares is shown on an open-net fabric from Chancay, about AD1200–1400. This simple design is so effective, it could be used on any modern fabric. Occasionally the fish symbol may be transposed into a mythical aquatic creature, part human, part fish – a cross between a seal and a mermaid. The origin is not known, but these zoomorphic figures are not uncommon.

The Kuna women take a practical attitude to design and are happy to show fish being cooked in pans on a stove, but more often the fish is displayed as a decorative element.

The Kuna women's love of sea creatures is represented in this lively design of a turtle, made up into a cushion cover for tourist sale – late twentieth century.

This motif lends itself to the reverse appliqué methods of construction where additional pieces of coloured cloth can be inserted between the main fabric layers, giving the fish a jewel-like appearance. Turtles, octopuses and sea urchins, together with brain coral, conch shells, boats and canoes are all representations of a life lived by the sea. As well as appearing on the *mola* blouses, fish, frogs and tortoises are made by the Kuna women into three-dimensional toys for the tourist trade. In a similar way, the Huichol bead workers from Mexico feature them as padded motifs for key rings.

In other areas of South and Central America, the frog symbol shows the creature viewed from above, with the four legs upturned at the joints and definite, fingered feet. In small-scale symbols the two diamond eye shapes may be reduced to a single diamond within a diamond-shaped head. Whatever the size, this is a distinctive motif. The Incas believed that their god-king lived in the under-world and would be reborn each year from the frogs' eggs that floated on the lake edge, while the giant toads found in Lake Titicaca were especially revered, as they never came out onto the land, choosing to spend the whole of their lives in the water. Many symbols are connected with the weather. The people of the Chiapas Highlands of Central America believed that the toad sang for rain, the Earth lord of the under-world created the clouds and the scorpion attracted lightning.

The double-headed snake motif is found in both Central and South America. Here it forms the front panel of a Kuna mola *blouse – late twentieth century.*

Serpents, Monsters and Dragons

In Mayan belief the Vision Serpent symbolized contact with the gods and the ancestors and was associated with sacrifice and bloodletting. Serpents often have two heads, placed on the opposite ends of a long and sinuous body. The motif takes a variety of shapes; sometimes the two heads rear upwards at right angles to the body, at other times the snake is horizontal or takes the form of a mystical beast with the heads interwoven between the coils. The body can be smooth or have scales like a dragon, while a beard is sometimes shown on one of the heads. Many of the symbolic creatures that resemble a hybrid of snakes, lizards, mythical monsters and dragons are difficult to interpret without a background knowledge of the culture and an understanding of the stone carvings and any surviving picture writings.

In Mexico the serpents are connected with the Toltec people, whose name originally meant 'reed' people. The Toltecs came from an area north of Tenochtitlán (later to become Mexico City), which they conquered and burned about AD900. They formed an empire of the surrounding states and by the tenth century their leader had founded the cult of the feathered serpent, named *Quetzalcoátl*. This cult, together with the cults of the jaguar and the eagle, was to become an important part of the religious practices in the Mayan cities, including Chichén Itzá. The feathered serpent was the symbol of the Mayan god *Kukulcan*, and is still featured on Guatemalan *huipils* as an 'S' shape, with one head, a tail and spiked feathers along the body. At times the feathers are so exaggerated that they grow into flowers and the serpent is transformed into a cornfield. It was thus associated with the Venus legend, the gathering of crops and the planting of corn.

Snakes are carved into the temple walls of many of the Mayan monuments in Mexico. At times these serpents are indistinguishable from the zigzag patterns that are a feature of this type of architecture. Those that form the wall friezes on the Mixtec temple at Mitla are a spectacular example of step-fret patterns in brickwork that give the impression of serpents in motion, partly the result of deep shadows cast in strong sunlight. This is echoed by the twice-yearly phenomena at Chichén Itzá, with the apparent movement of the serpents down the temple steps.

In ancient Peru the snake with two heads was called *amaru* after a god who originally lived in a clear lake. It is possible that snakes carved in stone were used in cult ceremonies, as it was believed that the serpent was turned into stone after defeat in battle with another god. The motif shows two similar heads at either end of the snake. The statue on the Gateway to the Sun at Tiahuanaco at the temple complex above La Paz, dating from 700–400BC, has sun flames that end in serpents' heads surrounding his face and he wears snakes as part of his regalia. The snake symbol was an important part of the culture and as early as 2000BC a serrated double-headed snake motif was found on a cotton fabric woven by the Huaca Prieta people and is still popular as a design motif in the Andes today.

Sea snakes and serpents are well adapted to Kuna *mola* designs, convoluting across the fabric surface with a definite head at either end of a body filled in with colourful lines or spots. On other *molas* a snake takes the form of a boat with the two heads forming the prows, or zigzags across the sky with one head and a pointed tail.

Flowers and Trees

The sacred tree of the Mayan universe stood with its roots in the under-world, its trunk in the world and its branches in the over-world, thus linking all layers together. The green tree was also associated with the four other trees that indicated the points of the compass and their corresponding colours. East was symbolized by red, the colour of the rising sun, north by white and the colour of the dead, south was yellow and the black west stood for the under-world – all connected with the square of the Earth symbol. The combination of four trees was often shown in carvings and inscriptions as a cross-like Tree of Life. Familiarity with this ancient symbol was one of the reasons for the acceptance of the Christian cross.

The sacred *ceiba* tree, the pine tree and flowers are all depicted as tree-like motifs with little regard for scale, although some flowers are shown in pots. The corn plant is a definite motif with upright leaves or corn husks placed either side of a central stem, although at times even this motif is transmuted into something more complicated. Possibly the context in which it is placed would tell the viewer its origin and purpose.

Few of the countless flower motifs found throughout the areas are easily identifiable and some flower motifs became synonymous with those of the star of Venus. Real flowers were regarded as gifts of nature, so were gathered and placed as offerings to the various gods. It was believed that this would promote healing and the purification of sins. Many sayings were attributed to combinations of plants or flowers and the order in which they grew, indicating good and bad weather, while a bird sitting on a flower looking downwards predicted a bad harvest.

Tropical flowers are a favourite on the tapestry weave *huipils* worked in San Antonio Aquas Calientes, while in Chichicastenango flowers are embroidered in coloured silks round the necks of the woven *huipils*, covering the front and back seam-joins. Spanish influence is reflected in coloured

embroidery in parts of Mexico and designs show fantasy flowers, animals and birds, all worked with close stitches. Machine embroidery has taken over from handwork in many areas and is included on the Mayan *huipils* from the Yucatan peninsula. Elaborate flowers, butterflies and other patterns are worked onto the tunic yoke, replacing the more time-consuming hand stitching.

Kuna *molas* show naturalistic patterns of seedpods together with flower and fruit, many designs having a culinary or practical base. Cane is shown as a plaited construction for house walls and gourds indicate their use as pots or carrying utensils. Leaf designs are popular, shown as repeated or intersecting pattern motifs.

Figures – Anthropomorphic and Symbolic

The figures that decorate the Paracas textiles dated to about 600BC are still an enigma. Those shown on an embroidered mantle in the Museum of Anthropology and Archaeology, Lima, have been likened to flying angels but as each one is carrying a spear in one hand and a fan in the other, this seems unlikely. On alternating rows the horizontal figures are turned upside-down. This may be because the weaver wished the textile to be viewed from both ways, or that they fitted in better that way. Others suggest that they are tumbling, possibly within the heavens, each having hair that streaks out behind. Whatever the answer to the riddle, these figures hold our attention, leaving a permanent impression on the mind. This motif continued to be used on Tiahuanaco textiles and for many hundreds of years later in several South American countries. In a similar way, flying animals tumble across the early Bolivian textiles, said to represent the creatures that lived before the beginning of time, possibly part of a creation myth.

Many of the early Andean textiles showed figures, similar to the designs on pottery, stone carvings and metalwork. Little tapestry woven doll faces are part of the Chancay Valley culture, but pride of place must be given to a model house with eight beautifully made woven dolls, now in the Amano Museum, Lima. These padded dolls are dressed in patterned tunics and several have additional gauze shawls, thus echoing the life of the Valley about AD1200–1400. A full-size tunic from the Chancay Valley features little woven faces placed at intervals with red tassels filling in the intervening spaces – the significance of these faces is not known. A superb example of one of these dolls is in the Ethnographic collection of the Birmingham Museum and Art Gallery. An expressive tapestry woven face has round eyes, a toothed mouth and a high nose. Five-fingered pink hands protrude

A Chancay culture textile Doll from the central coastal region of Peru, AD1000–1400.
(Accession No. 1960 A46. Birmingham Museums and Art Gallery.
Dimensions 34 × 22 × 6cm (13 × 8½ × 2in))

from the striped tunic, while little pink feet peep from below.

Figures with raised arms are striking motifs used in Nasca textiles, found on the southern coast of Peru from 800–500BC. The representation is geometric with the elbows and knees bent at right angles with the feet turned outwards, but hands may be upright, with three finger divisions. An article by James W Reid in the twenty-fifth anniversary edition of *Hali*, deals with the 'Iconographic Mysteries of a Tapestry from Pre-Columbian Peru' and illustrates several of these figures, either in a woven tapestry technique or with the addition of feathers. Reid praises the 'intuitive aesthetic vision' of the weavers, primarily women, who created these amazing textiles. Similar anthropomorphic figures in pottery and precious metals are common to the Andean areas and are still reproduced in contemporary design.

Little doll-like people would appear to be favourite motifs in many countries. Sometimes they are like cut-paper dolls folded out to hold hands in a row. At other times they are shown as a single motif in simple outline with raised hands – in Central America said to represent the Mayan Sky-bearers. More realistic motifs have a shaped body, the women distinguished by a triangular skirt, the men with Spanish-style trousers. They are nearly always shown wearing a hat. Little people, men and women, decorate the woven bands used in Guatemala to bind the hair or to act as belts, while in Peru, little figures of indeterminate sex are included in designs woven into a poncho or carrying cloth.

Many of the narrative embroideries worked in the twentieth century contain people placed within an outdoor scene or within a house or building. The Peruvian women who sit on the shores of Lake Titicaca worked embroidered pictures on woollen cloth using a fine crochet hook to form the stitches that outline the design motifs. The pictures have a variety of themes based on agriculture and fishing. Men and women are depicted wearing local costume, together with ploughs, reed boats, birds and other animals.

People are an important element in the *mola* patterns of the Kuna. The women create scenes relating to political and historical events, they copy pages from magazines, include people from advertisements and portray scenes connected with the picture writing. Although the women had no part in the chanting, or in the memory pictures that accompanied the chants, certain elements became part of the common consciousness and filtered through to daily life. They make reproductions of the spirit strongholds, called Spirit House *molas*, with the Shamans inside, looking out through the windows. Recent versions show church *molas*, an expression of the duality of their spiritual life where they combine fiestas for Roman Catholic patron saints with their own fertility and right-of-passage celebrations.

In South America the *arpilleras* were first worked by the women of Chile as a definite political statement. These decorative fabric pictures are in the form of a padded appliqué worked onto burlap or sackcloth with the little figures made individually and dressed in scraps of fabric. This outlet for expression was taken up by the women of Lima in Peru and eventually spread to Columbia. These pictures are now produced as a source of income.

Geometric and Abstract Designs

The weaving technique lends itself to geometric shapes. A complicated motif that has been worked by generations of weavers will be reduced by a gradual process to a more simplified form – a type of natural selection in reverse. Some of the indigenous weavers have no knowledge of the origin of the motifs handed down to them, but include them in the pattern repertoire through familiarity and inherited tradition. Although many of the patterns might once have had a definite origin, their geometric forms lend themselves to new adaptations, restricted only by the limitations imposed by the grid-like intersections of the weave structure.

Geometric designs and patterns, worked as an embroidery technique onto the woven cloth, follow the lines of the warp and weft. Many of the weaving patterns were copied in cross-stitch embroidery, introduced by the Spanish. Satin-stitch and other counted thread stitches, together with pulled thread stitches, were used to cover areas of fabric in a formal context. Abstract designs on the appliqué *molas* can take the form of intricate patterns, or show symbols such as the key pattern, or an overall repeat of swastikas (formerly a good-luck sign).

Geometric patterns were always used by the Forest and Canoe tribes of the Amazon Basin. It was part of their belief that any naturalistic depiction of a person, animal

The swastika symbol, defining good luck, is encased within inverted pattern shapes on this mid twentieth-century mola *from the San Blas Islands.*

or even a plant, would bring the spirit of that depiction to life and thus haunt or influence the perpetrator, not necessarily for the better. The geometric patterns were painted onto pottery, bark and cloth by the Canoe people and woven as intricate patterns into the basketry of the Forest tribes, as well as forming body painting and scarification. To them, a blank surface was not acceptable and all artefacts needed a similarly structured decoration taken from nature, to become an object imbued with its own spirit or soul. Thus a basket might echo leaf patterns, or the scales on an armadillo's back.

Zigzags and Diamonds

Zigzag lines are particularly popular, together with diamonds, lozenges and squares. The zigzag symbolized lightning, as well as a simplified version of the snake or serpent. They are worked closely together in rows on the Guatemalan *huipils*, making patterns within bands of inlay and forming part of the interlaced diamonds in Peruvian weaving. They can be included as step patterns in Bolivian knitwear or

Zigzag pattern on a basket, woven from naturally dyed fibres, Wounaan Tribe, Panama and Darien Jungle, 1970s. A modern Peruvian pot echoes the geometric designs and the little duck is still a popular motif.

used as a cross-stitch border to outline a Mexican shirt. A combination of intricate diamond and zigzag motifs are worked in the centre of the long *sarapes* from Mexico, while meandering zigzag lines are said to represent rivers, similar to designs found on some of the ancient textiles from Peru. Square and lozenge shapes, abstracted from other motifs and symbols, form repeat patterns and no two pieces of weaving appear to be the same. Within the limitations of the design, the weaver has constructed something unique, an expression of self that transcends any factory-produced item.

Pattern and Design

Motifs can vary in size, often with large and small versions contained in the same textile. While this adds to the liveliness of the design, it can make identification difficult. In woven fabrics, curved pattern shapes are inevitably reduced to a series of steps, the scale of which will depend on the fineness of the weaving and thread count. There are equal problems when translating the motifs to knitting patterns, but far less with free-stitch surface embroidery where a fluid technique will overcome the limitations imposed by the counted thread.

Although many designs are handed down through the generations, it is often the weaver or embroiderer who decides on the particular pattern combinations. The choice of motifs used by any one group of textile workers may be limited, but the permutations of how these patterns are used would appear to be endless. This takes into consideration the fact that there are only seventeen ways of presenting a pattern element as a repeat of itself, a mathematical formula reflected in crystalline structure. The primary pattern methods begin with a simple repeat, then a mirrored or flipped repeat – the first of what are called the 'twelve symmetries'. Within this natural order of patterning, the worker takes a relaxed attitude to fitting the pattern motifs into a given shape, is not worried if some cannot be completed for lack of space – he or she will substitute a different design if necessary, or leave some out altogether.

Textile design has no rigidly defined boundaries and the peoples of certain areas have incorporated pattern methods used by their geographical neighbours. Horizontally striped patterns are still woven by the inhabitants of northern Mexico who were influenced by the designs on the tribal blankets of the indigenous North Americans. Much of Guatemalan weaving is patterned with stripes, including the *jaspe* weave where threads are tied and dyed beforehand. In the areas around Lake Atitlán, the striped fabric is enhanced with surface embroidery stitches superimposed on top of the stripes. No regard is given to the exact placing of the embroidery; the patterns are worked on top as they happen to come. Vertical stripes in *jaspe* weave are an important element in the *Cofradia* costume worn in Solola and are used as pattern weave for the shawls, *tzute* headdresses and skirt panels in other parts of the country.

European Influence

It was natural that the Spanish would bring their own patterning methods after the Conquest. In an alien landscape, reminders of home must have been comforting, especially to the women who came from over the seas to accompany their menfolk. This is quite apart from the imposition of Spanish designs on the weavers who were forced to produce goods to be exported back to Europe. Imports to the New World of printed and woven textiles had a definite influence on native design. Some Guatemalan *huipils* echo the brocade patterning of early Spanish fabrics, with pairs of opposing birds and geometric tree forms. These designs would be adapted to include familiar motifs, sometimes arranged in a different manner.

This two-faced, brocade-woven huipil *from Chichicastenango, Guatemala, shows patterning based on diamond and zigzag shapes. The decorative, chain-stitched area around the neck opens out to form a circle of sunrays – late 1980s.*

Another area of influence was provided by the convent nuns who came to support the priests in the setting up of religious schools and institutions. The European cross symbol soon found acceptance as there were already several versions in the form of the Earth symbol and the Tree of Life. When the constellation of the Southern Cross became visible during early May, a religious festival known as the *Fiesta del Cruz* echoed a much earlier South American celebration.

The convent nuns brought with them various stitching methods, including whitework, drawn thread work and surface stitching. In the convent schools, the nuns taught the indigenous tribal women to embroider in the European manner, either to produce items for church regalia or for sale to raise funds. Eventually these local women found it easier to decorate their *huipil* blouses and other items of dress with surface embroidery than to continue the time-consuming work of woven tapestry, or complicated types of inlay designs. This divorced patterning as an integral part of the weaving structure and allowed the women to add embroidery stitches to an already woven piece of plain cloth, whether made within the home or purchased separately. Although this led to greater mechanization in textile production, especially after the introduction of the European floor-loom, the original versions of patterning within the weave structure continue in many places up to the present day. It would appear that these methods are still held in high esteem, partly because of the time and skill needed to produce them, but also because an inherited textile tradition demonstrates the continuing individuality of any particular ethnographic group.

It is not possible to judge the extent to which the Slave Trade influenced the use of African symbols and patterning. In countries both north and south of the equator, including the islands of the Caribbean, the importation of vast numbers of African slaves to work in the mines and on the plantations continued until the 1840s. The slave masters did everything possible to eradicate the personal identity of their slave workers, changing their names, dress, customs and religious allegiance. However, they were unable to alter the basic way of thought, which expressed itself in various ways including funerary rites and the Mexican festivals for the 'Day of the Dead'. Eventually, the descendants of the original slaves took part in elaborate carnival celebrations. The inhabitants of Portuguese areas of South America, including Brazil and Argentina, have a love of fantasy costumes in the context of fiestas and processions. African dance tradition combined with the Roman Catholic festivals resulted in the Lenten carnivals, particularly popular in the plantation areas on the Atlantic coast of Brazil. This was an opportunity for display and competition between rival groups, which at the present time has escalated to become an annual extravaganza.

Over a period of time the Kuna women have been eager to embrace contemporary design objects and incorporate them into their work. Ships, planes, helicopters, tanks, cars, trucks and any other form of transport including spaceships and rockets are all included. Military emblems, television logos, political posters, Christmas trees, angels and nativity scenes – the list is endless. Modern *molas* may have a greater proportion of embroidered decoration than in the past, but the designs retain their liveliness, evidence of a highly motivated art form. The *arpilleras* of South America have also undergone a similar change. The themes are no longer political, but show adverts for Coca Cola and feature football matches and scenes from everyday life.

In spite of the diversity of the continents, the overall acceptance of European attitudes to design by the peoples of Central and South America was to play an important part in the unification of the countries that formed the vast overseas empires established by the Spanish and the Portuguese.

3

Yarns and Fibres

The stone carvings, pottery painting and the drawings in the codices illustrate many of the types of costume worn by the inhabitants of the different areas. While they cannot show the kind of fibre from which the costume has been made, there is evidence, both in the burial cloths in the ancient graves and in written texts, that the weavers made use of whatever materials happened to be readily available.

Wild cotton was found growing on the coastal levels of both South and Central America, but people living higher up needed something to give greater warmth in a colder climate. In the highland areas of Bolivia, cotton is seldom used on its own, but is combined with wool and other fibres, including the hair of the cameloid animals. Sheep's wool was not used until after the Conquest, as the ancestors of the North American native sheep, which were more like goats, did not penetrate that far south – probably deterred in their migrations by the hot desert areas in northern Mexico.

Imported woven fabrics, both silk and linen, were highly prized by the new settlers after the Conquest, but were very expensive. The sea crossings were fraught with danger as the ships were harried by pirate raids and the merchants paid dearly for any naval protection. Apart from the native cotton, the indigenous population had long made use of various vegetable fibres, including the agave or century plant from which sisal is obtained. Cotton continued to be cultivated by the settlers in all of the established cotton growing areas and it was one of the most successful crops.

Seed Fibres – Cotton

The word 'cotton' comes from the old Arabic *qutun*. For many thousands of years this indispensable plant has provided fibres for the production of woven and other types of

OPPOSITE PAGE:
A weft-faced cloth from Chile with brocaded stripes, woven from naturally dyed woollen yarn – mid twentieth century.
(Gift, Timothy Thompson)

textiles and both the Ancient Egyptians and early Chinese peoples used cotton fibres as early as 1200BC. In the New World there is archaeological evidence that cotton grew in the Tehanan Valley in Mexico more than 7,000 years ago and cotton fabrics dating to around 2500BC have been found in areas of coastal Peru. There is a wealth of textile examples in museum collections from pre-Inca times and evidence of cotton use in Colombia and Ecuador, but with slightly less in Bolivia. Large quantities of cotton are still produced in north-eastern Brazil and in the Chaco province of Argentina, where wild cotton grew in pre-Columbian times. During the twentieth century, the Chaco area was developed for cotton cultivation with the help of irrigation and this led to commercial cotton growing in other areas of Argentina and into neighbouring Paraguay.

The cotton plant is found in most subtropical countries. It is one of the plants belonging to the genus *Gossypium*, the Latin name chosen as a description of the mass of gossamer-like fibres that are revealed when the seed-boll bursts open. This seed-hair plant belongs to the Malvaceae family, which includes the mallows – ground-mallow and marsh-mallow – having a small but similar fluffy seed head. The bushy cotton shrub, an annual that varies between 1–2m (3–6ft), prefers humid conditions and grows well in regions between the latitudes 35 degrees north and south of the equator. The exception is the Brazilian cotton plant, a perennial that grows from 2.5–3.5m (8–12ft) high.

The seeds are planted in the springtime. In the past this was time-consuming work as the hairy seeds had to be sown a few at a time, by hand. In the 1870s a lady identifying herself only by the initials 'S W ' wrote a small-sized but detailed book called *Cotton*. Although the text is interspersed with religious comments, it is a mine of information, evidently the result of lengthy research into the workings of the cotton industry.

She tells us that the winter task of the plantation worker was first to plough the land into deep furrows, with a small trench made on the top of each ridge. The cotton seeds were sewn into this ridge, by a group of three people – normally a man, woman and child. The man would make a hole with a dibble, the woman drops five or six seeds into the hole,

A dried twig with the cotton bolls still attached.

which is then covered up by the child. It was not possible to use any kind of drilling machine because of the furry lint that covered the seeds. As the plants began to grow, the weaker ones were hoed, leaving two or three healthy ones together.

This description is probably true of cotton-seed sowing in any of the areas of past cultivation. When the shrub reaches maturity, the masses of creamy white flowers turn a deep pink before falling off to reveal small green seedpods, called bolls. These bolls, which contain the tightly packed seeds, burst open to reveal the wad of soft cotton fibres. Cotton fibre is generally white, but some species produce brown cotton. Our lady writer goes on to say: 'The plantation presents a most beautiful appearance at mid-summer. Rich foliage, something like that of the vine, covers the ground entirely, studded with blossoms of three different hues. When the flower opens it is of a pure bright yellow, and it keeps that colour through the day; at night it changes to a deep crimson, and on the third day it darkens to a rich brown before it falls off and leaves the precious seed-pod, already of good size'.

She continues in an even more poetic vein: 'This glory and beauty last for three or four weeks, and then a stranger sight succeeds. Under the eye of a noonday sun blazing from out the deep blue sky lies a shrubbery laden with pure white snow which does not dissolve under these scorching beams, but lingers till it is carried off by the touch of busy fingers'.

There are three main groups of cotton classification, based on the average length of the fibre, which is called the 'staple'. The top quality are called 'long-staple cottons' and measure about 2.5–6.5cm (1–2.5in) in length. These long, lustrous fibres are the finest and strongest, the best coming from the Sea Islands and the next quality from Egypt. They are costly and difficult to grow. The Sea Islands, which lie off the coast of South Carolina and Florida, now part of the USA, were claimed by the Spanish in 1568. The English included them as part of the Carolina colony during the seventeenth century. They changed hands several times, as the Sea Island cotton plantations were of prime importance. The term 'Sea Island Cotton' is also given to the long-staple cotton produced on the mainland of the USA, in the states of Florida, Georgia and South Carolina.

The next quality is the 'medium-cottons'. This is the largest group formed mainly of the American types, which are the standard cottons. The fibres are 2.5cm (1in) long, not as strong or fine and soft as the long-staple cottons. The native cotton, *Gossypium hirsutum*, is indigenous to Central America and was used by the early civilizations for over 5,000 years before the Conquest. White cotton is grown today on the lowland areas of Mexico and the Pacific lowlands of Guatemala. In both countries the people of the highlands trade with the lowland producers, as well as finding seasonal work at harvesting time.

The lowest quality, which includes the Indian and Asiatic types, is the 'short-staple cotton' 2.5cm (1in) in length and much coarser and harsher, used for carpets and coarse fabrics. *Gossypium mexicanum*, indigenous to Mexico and Guatemala, is another short-staple cotton somewhat finer than the Asiatic types. Although this native brown cotton is grown in the same areas as the white cotton, it is not a commercial crop and, with a limited supply, was considered more valuable. The hand-spun thread is reserved mainly for the weaving of special cloth for ceremonial occasions.

Christopher Columbus saw cotton growing for the first time on Watlings Island in the eastern Bahamas in 1492, and the start of the Spanish cotton industry on the mainland of Central America followed during the early years of the

Conquest. The discovery of a new cotton-growing area was important during the fifteenth century, as the overland trade routes from Europe to the East were closed, due to the Turkish conquest of Syria and Egypt. Of equal significance is that the final expulsion of the Moors from Spain did not take place until the end of the fifteenth century in 1492. The Spanish were so determined to drive away all those of Muslim faith, that they also drove away many textile producers and workers, including the cotton weavers. They found a substitute in Mexico where the indigenous inhabitants were skilled in the art of weaving one of the few fibres at that time available to them.

At first the cotton plantations were not able to export a sufficient quantity of cotton back to Europe to make the enterprise worthwhile. This was because the cotton preparation was so labour intensive that the workers who removed the hairy seeds from the cotton by hand could not keep up with the supply. It was not until the invention of the 'Cotton Gin' by Eli Whitney in 1793 that the tables were turned and the new problem was finding enough labour to pick the cotton. The market in England for American cotton had grown since the invention of the 'Spinning Jenny' by James Hargreaves in the 1760s and imports of cotton from the New World were needed to supply the growing output of the new machines. This, together with the Cotton Gin, a device for pulling the cotton fibres through the teeth of a revolving cylinder that removed the seeds, was instrumental in promoting the slave industry as an international institution.

'S W' – the lady author of the book on '*Cotton*' – was more than aware of these problems, going into great detail: 'The pods which succeeded these glorious blossoms have ripened and burst, and the cotton pickers come out in parties, a bag fastened round every waist, to load themselves with their spoil. From morning till evening they are hard at work; a good hand will pick two hundred pounds of cotton a day in the height of the season – in spite of the heat of the sun, which at that time of year is almost insufferable'. She goes on to say that past labour was provided by African slaves, without whom the plantation owners considered that neither sugar nor cotton could be cultivated.

In 1481 the Portuguese were the first to import slaves from Africa and sell them to other European nations, but it was not until 1518 that the slave trade proper began with the landing of black slaves in the West Indies. The Spaniards, who had worked most of the native population to death in the silver mines of the New World, were short of labour and glad to replace their workers with African slaves. The Genoese, the Portuguese, the French and then the English carried on the slave trade, providing a seemingly unending supply of these unfortunate victims. The Portuguese considered the whole African continent to be part of their colonies, as confirmed by the Papal Bulls of 1493 which gave them sovereignty over lands to the east of the Cape Verde Islands. They considered that the entire population of the Guinea coast of Africa belonged to them, to do with as they wished.

Although the Portuguese were the last to abolish slavery, they were thought to be slightly more liberal towards their slaves, but that could be interpreted as being slightly less brutal. It is said that they baptized entire shiploads of slaves before taking them to Brazil, thus recognizing that they were human beings with souls that needed saving. They even provided the slaves with coarse cotton cloths to lie on in the slave ships – the normal practice having been to herd the slaves into compartments below decks, where in stormy weather the uneven surface of the wooden planks would rub the flesh through to the bone. They may merely have

A modern Maya couple from the Yucatan peninsula still prefer cotton for their festival dance costumes.

been better at conserving their merchandise, for the normal death rate in slave ships during the passage was always very high, thus reducing profits. It was not until 1880s that slavery was finally abolished in Cuba and Brazil.

The Portuguese imported a greater number of slaves from Africa to Brazil than Spanish and British plantation owners imported to Central America. This was due to a difference in policy. According to Hugh Thomas writing in his book on *The Slave Trade,* the cotton growers in the West Indies and Central America considered it was better for female slaves to pick the more 'delicate' cotton bolls than their male counterparts. This resulted in a greater proportion of females to males and a consequent increase through 'breeding' in the number of children born into slavery. Thus the slave population would be maintained, unlike in the states of South America where the 'breeding' of slaves was considered to be counterproductive.

The descendants of the original slaves continued to work in the cotton plantations long after they gained their freedom. In the new countries into which they had been born, there was little opportunity for those whose ancestors had come from the African Continent to obtain alternative employment. However, they kept their love of music and African rhythms, their fascination with bright colours and fantasy clothing. They have also retained many of their original African beliefs, blended into a new but still quite recognizable faith.

Leaf Fibres – Sisal

There are over 700 species of the agave plant, which grows in a variety of tropical, subtropical and temperate areas throughout the world. The leaves are the most important part of the plant, from which the fibres are obtained. Sisal hemp – *Agave sisalana* – is one of the most valuable products, made from the fibres of the cactus-like Henequen plant.

In ancient Mayan the word 'sisal' means 'cold waters' and is derived from the name of the seaport of Sisal on the Yucatan peninsula in eastern Mexico. This possibly referred to the outpourings of the underground rivers that provided the ancient Mayans with their water supply. The porous limestone soil areas of the peninsula are ideal for the cultivation of the sisal crop, which is made into coarse fibre products such as hammocks, rope and twine, while the raw fibres are transported as material for the carpet weaving industry. Because of its inaccessibility this area was largely ignored by the Spaniards, but during the nineteenth century their later descendants, the Creoles, set up plantations of the Henequen plant – *Agave fourcroydes* – and made their fortunes. This member of the Agavaceae family, sometimes

called Yucatan sisal, is native to Mexico and had been used by the Maya and their ancestors long before the coming of the Spanish. The name of the export destination was stamped onto the bales of Henequen and eventually the seaport name of 'Sisal' was transferred to the actual plant. In modern times, the use of strong synthetic fibres became the norm and although local production still continues, most of the plantations were abandoned. Today, the dilapidated ruins of the old plantation *haciendas* can still be seen, gradually sinking into the scrub-like jungle vegetation that covers the area. Sisal is also grown in Brazil as well as other parts of the world.

It is the sisal fibres that shape and strengthen the fleshy, elongated leaves, which grow from ground level. The flower stalk, which only appears after several years, can reach a height of up to 6m (over 20ft). When flowering is over, little buds fall off and take root as new plants, growing up as the old plant dies. In fibre production the skin of the leaves is first removed, in the old days by hand, but today by machines which scrape off the material. After sun drying and bleaching, a hard lustrous fibre remains, well over 1m (39in) in length. The resulting sisal is strong, with the separate fibres held together by gums. For this reason it was much used for ships' ropes as it has a natural resistance to salt water.

The lance-like leaves of Agave sisalana, *the sisal hemp plant, growing near Teotihuacán, Central Mexico.*

The Century Plant

The century plant, *Agave americana*, is cultivated in many areas of south-western North America, including Mexico and Guatemala. Other names for the agave include *ixtle*, *pita* and *henequen*. This plant has lance-shaped spiny leaves, from 1.5m (58in) in length. After fifteen years, it produces a yellow flower spike up to 12m (39ft) in height with large flower clusters. It is a wonderful sight to see these tall, improbable spikes reaching to the sky. After flowering the plant dies, but leaves small plantlets around the base. The century plant grows in the Cuchumatan mountain and other areas of Guatemala, flourishing at over 2,000m (7,000ft) and specimens thrive in the desert areas of Mexico. The century plants are used to produce a sap that is turned into soap and in other instances, fermented into an intoxicating drink. Near the ancient Mexican site of Teotihuacán, a local guide removed one of the spiky thorns that grow on the leaf edges, deftly pulling it off so that a long fibre of the plant was still attached. This could be used as a combined needle and thread for sewing coarse fabrics together.

A man from Nahuala in the Guatemalan Highlands, wearing the traditional wool 'blanket-skirt' and carrying a bag made from netted fibre.

The Yucca

This is another plant belonging to the Agavaceae family (genus *Yucca*), native to southern North America. Although they are often grown today as ornamental plants because of their sword-shaped spiny leaves and clusters of waxy white flowers, in northern areas of Mexico fibres were obtained from several of the species, one of which was known as *palma ixtle*, often used in the production of netted fabrics.

Maguey

Manila-maguey fibre is obtained from *Agave cantala*, while *Agave lurida*, being shorter and stiffer than *henequin* is used for rope and cordage. In Mexico there are over 200 species of maguey, although in South America the name maguey is used to cover a variety of plants and fibres. At times the weavers used a mixture of cotton and bast fibres, or cotton and maguey, probably benefiting from the combined properties of both fibre types. *Furcraea occidentalis* is another type of cactus plant similar to the agave. Threads spun from the fibres, up to 50cm (20in) long, form the basis of some of the very early Andean textiles, while a type of milkweed belonging to the *Asclepias* species also provided bast fibres (*see* below).

The Panama-Hat Palm

The eleven genera of the Cyclanthaceae family are mainly stemless palmlike herbs found in Central America and tropical South America. The leaves are fan shaped, deeply forked with parallel veins. Fibres are obtained from the textile screw pine, or *pandanus* palm (*Pandanus tectorius*) as well as from aerial roots. According to Britannica: 'In Ecuador and perhaps elsewhere in Latin America, the young leaves of *Carludovica palmata* are collected, cut into narrow strips, and bleached, to be woven into Panama hats'. In Western Mexico, the Oaxaca regions were noted for palm hat making, with several different tribes producing local variations.

Bark and Bast Fibres

The inhabitants of any particular geographical area used whatever fibres were readily available to them. These included the inner bark of trees and filaments from fibrous plants similar to flax and the stinging nettle, well known to the Aztecs and later described by the Conquistadors. Tree bark was used in paper making, while fig-tree bark has already been mentioned as the material used for the codices books. The beaten inner bark was used in strips, woven to form blankets, or to make sandals and was considered to be an important element in religious ceremonies because of its association with the Mayan gods.

Animal Fibres – Silk

Silk worms are not indigenous to the Americas, but Cortes introduced the essential mulberry trees on which they are fed and the imported silk worms thrived in the western regions of central Mexico. This enterprise threatened the home industry back in Spain and by 1697 a Spanish decree was passed ordering the mulberry trees to be uprooted and the silk looms destroyed. Hemp and flax, introduced from Europe and cultivated in Mexico, were well established by the 1530s but suffered a similar fate and both were banned. Although an attempt was made to re-introduce flax in the late eighteenth century, it was not successful, unlike the production of silk which continued in a quiet way until the twentieth century. Many of the mulberry trees had survived the initial uprooting and the localized silk industry was preserved.

A modern tapestry wall-hanging, woven in a mixture of natural-coloured wool and cameloid yarn.
(Lent by Betty Ballard)

Wool and Hair

The cameloids or camel family originated and developed in North America over forty million years ago. Some of the species migrated south and found their way across the isthmus of Panama, became established in South America and evolved into the llama and the vicuña. Other species migrated north and crossed the Bering Straits into Asia, gradually moving to the west and then southwards into northern Africa and the Sahara.

It was once thought that these domestic lamoids (the collective name for the Camelidae), the llama and the alpaca, were descended from the wild guanaco and the vicuña. Later studies of fossil remains and wool characteristics suggest that both were descendants of the wild guanaco, or even from some extinct wild species. However, all agree that the vicuña, which has never been domesticated, should be classified as a separate genus. The lamoids, unlike their camel ancestors, do not have humps. They have slender bodies with long legs. Their tails are short and they all have small heads with long necks and pointed ears.

The guanaco (*Lama guanaco*) is found in southern Peru and Bolivia, also from Patagonia to Tierra del Fuego, inhabiting areas that range from the sea coast to the mountain snow line. This wild lamoid is territorial, with dominant males in charge of groups of females. The hair is coarser than the vicuña but finer than the alpaca, while the rare, downy fleece of the young guanaco is prized as a speciality hair. The pelts of the young guanaco, reddish brown in colour, were used in the fur industry. The adults have light brown hair with white underparts and a black face.

The llama (*Lama glam*), originally bred from the wild guanaco, is the largest of the lamoids, found in the Andes Mountains of Bolivia, Peru, Ecuador, Chile and Argentina. They were used as a pack animal in pre-Inca times long before the wheel was invented, being well adapted to a mountainous terrain. They can carry heavy loads and are normally good tempered – unless they are overloaded, when they will sit down and refuse to go any further! The llama feeds on a variety of vegetation and, like its camel cousins in other desert regions, can go for a long time without water. As well as being a beast of burden, the llama provided meat, tallow for candles, hides and abundant wool for woven and other textiles. These animals normally have light-coloured hair with black or brown markings, sometimes they are brown with white markings, but occasionally black llama are found. The early weavers exploited this

ABOVE: *A herd of llamas graze on the thin grasses of the high mountains above Ollantaytambo in the Cuzco area of Peru.*

BELOW: *Two local women from the high pastures above Cuzco, Peru, pose with (left) a llama and (right) an alpaca with a furry bib.*

choice of colours, together with the use of natural dyes, to produce a comprehensive colour palette.

Llama hair is coarser than that of the alpaca and is often used for outerwear, rugs and rope making. The fibres are hair-like in structure, with fewer scales on the outer layer than normally found in true wool from the various breeds of sheep. The under hair is finer, lighter and slightly crimped, the hairs being smaller in diameter than the outer guard hairs which vary from 8–25cm (3–10in) in length. Shearing takes place every alternate year with a high yield of hair fibres from each animal.

The alpaca (*Lama pacos*) is a slender-bodied, long-limbed cameloid, smaller than the llama with a squat and somewhat rounder body. Unlike the llama, which has an upright tail, the alpaca's tail is often held downwards, close to the body. Although it had a wider distribution, the alpaca is now limited to areas of western Bolivia and central and southern Peru, preferring to live on the high plateaus between 4,000–4,800m (13,000–15,700ft). The domesticated alpaca, which was originally bred in pre-Columbian times from the guanaco, has always been valued for its long and silky hair. The fine hair was reserved by the Inca for royal garments and, to a lesser extent, for the nobility. Two breeds of alpaca were bred by the Incas, the *suri*, which had especially fine long hair and the *huacaya*, which was slightly coarser. Alpacas are generally black or brown in colour, but there are instances of white hair and varied coloration in these animals

Like the llama, the alpaca is sheared every other year with the long-haired *suris* producing the most fleece. Unshorn hair can reach to the ground, but normally the hair grows to about 60cm (24in) between shearings. Alpaca fibres have always been in demand, both for their warmth and their lustrous beauty. It is used in modern knitwear as well as for woven pile fabrics, sometimes combined with other types of fibre. The main alpaca breeding areas are centred in Peru, under supervision from the Government, who monitor the quality and production.

The vicuña (*Lama*, or *vicugna*), another member of the camel family, closely related to the other lamoids, has been classified more recently as a separate genus. This animal has never been domesticated, is smaller than the other lamoids, far swifter and very difficult to catch. The vicuña is a territorial animal with groups of females defended by a dominant male. They are temperamental and spit frequently, especially when disturbed, as well as using a high-pitched whistle as a danger signal.

Their hair is even finer, more lustrous and longer than that of the alpaca, ranging from pale cinnamon to shades of white in colour. For many hundreds of years the vicuña has been hunted for the superb hair, leading to an eventual decline in numbers. The Spanish killed the animals for their pelts, occasionally eating the meat, but the Incas had a policy of rounding up the animals into corrals where they were sheared and then let loose into the wild again. They were intent on preserving the stock of these valuable animals as the Inca nobility regarded the hair even more highly than that of the alpaca.

Today the vicuña is listed as a protected animal and production is supervised. The majority are found in Peru, with a few still in Bolivia, Chile, and Argentina and they inhabit the sparse grasslands found at high altitudes. It is no wonder that this fibre was held in such high esteem by the Incas,

The light-coloured alpaca is held in such high regard that it is depicted on the appliqué pictures sold in Peru.

The Merinos

This fine-wool sheep breed was developed in Spain from native stock before the Christian era. It is possible that the original sheep were of the Italian Terpentine breed whose ancestors had gradually spread westwards from Asia to the coastal areas of Syria and thence traded by ship to Cyprus and Italy. The original Asiatic Mouflons were small sheep, reddish brown with white underparts and the males had large horns which curved upwards and outwards. Sub-species are found in mountainous areas of Asia Minor and Iran and it is told that the Roman Emperor Claudius imported the Terpentine sheep to Spain in AD41. They flourished to the extent that the Saracens, who arrived in Spain during the eighth century, were impressed by a land overflowing with flocks of sheep. They set up workshops with many looms and the imperial weavers produced woollen goods of superior quality.

The original Spanish sheep breeds are divided into two types. The stationary sheep, which spent their entire existence in one location such as a fixed pasture or farm, and the migratory sheep, which have longer and coarser wool and wandered over vast areas in search of new pastures. Although sheep had first been imported into the New World during 1526, the eventual introduction of the merino breed was an excellent choice. Belonging to the stationary breed, they had long curved horns, excellent wool and did not wander.

William Youcett, writing in his book *Sheep, their Breeds, Management and Diseases* in 1862, tells us that wool of the true merinos was prized for its fineness and felting properties. 'The excellence of the merinos consists in the closeness of the wool, luxuriance of the yolk which enables them to support extremes of cold or wet ... the easiness with which they adapt themselves to every change of climate, thrive and retain, with common care, all the fineness of wool under burning tropical sun and in the frozen region of the north, a quietness and patience into whatever pasture they are driven, and a gentleness and tractability not excelled in any other breed'.

for it is still in use today as a luxury fabric – soft, warm, light and silky. Some vicuña have been domesticated and there is an average yield of from 85–550g (3–20oz) of fine hair from each animal. In the wild the dense fleece helps to insulate the vicuña from the variations in temperature found in the high altitude pastures. This same property is transferred to the garment, a definite advantage, whether worn by an Inca king or as a modern fashion product.

Sheep and Goats

The true ancestor of all domestic sheep is the Asiatic mouflon (*Ovis orientalis*), including both the European and the wild sheep of North America and Siberia. The ancestors of the Bighorn, or Rocky Mountain sheep, originally crossed from Asia via the landmass that once joined the Bering Straits to Northern America. These animals prefer to inhabit mountainous areas and formerly ranged from Canada to northern Mexico and the peninsula of Lower California, but hunting and reduction of habitat has curtailed their numbers. Although they are primarily grass feeders, they will eat shrubs and, in the desert areas, even cactus plants. They were never domesticated and probably used for their pelts rather than as a source of wool. They have no relationship with the merino sheep imported by the Spanish conquerors.

A sample of merino wool, showing the high degree of crimp.

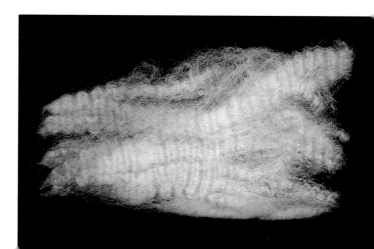

Goats

Goats are not indigenous to the Americas. As inhabitants of the high mountain ridges of Europe, Asia and Ethiopia, they shunned low pastures, so did not follow the sheep in their migrations across the Bering Straits where the land was flat and uninviting for high-altitude browsing animals. Goats were later introduced to the Americas by the Spaniards, not always with the best of consequences.

It is interesting to follow the migrations of both people and animals across the land that once joined together the continents of Asia and North America. If it were possible to record these in a fast time-lapse sequence, the land would be busy at various times with humans and sheep coming from Asia, with the cameloids crossing the other way, as well as many other species of birds and mammals crossing and intermingling. No one at that time, would set out with the intention of discovering a new land but rather, would be lured, millennia by millennia by the sight of better pastures or hunting grounds. All animal hair, including fleece and wool, was to play an important part in the rise of the early civilizations. As the animals became domesticated, this raw material gradually increased in availability and as time passed, the herding of animals became part of a way of life that continues to the present day.

The Woollen Industry

The European woollen industry was established in Flanders by AD960 and by the thirteenth century a new state of prosperity was reached in Spain, when the Spanish King Ferdinand ll finally drove the Moors out of Seville. It is said that here he found 16,000 looms, with the Moors weaving woollen cloth of the finest quality. However, the Spanish continued to import wool from the Flemish, for although they had tried to preserve a monopoly on the merino, the sheep gradually spread to the rest of Europe. The Spanish sheep breed, used to improve the old short-wool breed, was highly valued and eventually was to spread throughout the world.

When the rest of the Moors were finally driven from Spain at the end of the fifteenth century, most of the Moorish workers were expelled, including the weavers and other craftsmen. This turned out to be a great mistake, as the woollen industry went into a decline. As this coincided with the conquest of the New World and the discovery of an indigenous population skilled in the art of weaving, the Spanish soon transferred their industry to the Americas, importing foot looms and dictating the patterns and form that the weaving should take.

Those merino sheep that survived the crossing of the Atlantic Ocean, thrived in their new habitats, but needed constant supervision to keep the status of the breed. By 1811 a report on *South American wool from Spanish Sheep*, by Walton, on *Peruvian Sheep* stated that: 'Both sheep and fleece have considerably degenerated, and too many hairs having begun to mingle with the wool and to over top it. It is very little valued and is used chiefly for broadcloths, carpets and a few other coarse articles'. In South America this inferior wool was used in the manufacture of mattresses and coarse cloths. Although thousands of pounds of wool was exported to England from South America during the 1830s, far more wool was exported back to South America in the form of woollen goods.

A report made to the French Agricultural Society regarding the deteriorating state of sheep in Brazil states : 'that if any flock is kept ten years on the same pasturage, disease breaks out among them and great numbers die, but if they are transported to another soil, although at a very considerable distance, they recover and flourish anew.'

Hair and Feathers

'S W ' – our lady writer, when recording the history of Central America states: 'They used to mix their cotton with the finest hair of rabbits and hares, so as to form a very soft and beautiful material, and dyeing their thread of different colours, they were skilful enough to weave figures of animals and flowers.' The practice of mixing animal hair, feathers and even human hair in with the woven cotton was an ancient one, common to both Central and South America and was employed in many of the pre-Inca textiles. Human hair was included and mixed with other fibres in the early Paracas textiles, while feathers provided a decorative element when coloured feathers were worn as headdresses, or used as ornamentation on tunic borders, belts and waist aprons. Feather headdresses, decorations, breastplates and shields formed an important part of the ritual costume worn by the forest people of the Amazon Basin.

Feathers featured prominently in the early Mexican civilizations, used as distinctive plumes for headdresses and for the embellishment of garment hems. Feathers were incorporated with embroidery to embellish garments and bright colours would lend importance to both priests and royal rulers. Feather capes were worn by both the Aztec and Maya warriors, with the feathers mounted onto a stiffened base. The *Jaina* warriors from Campeche in Mexico, during the late classic period AD600–900, wore knee-length armour in the form of a tunic which was made from tightly pressed cotton fabric into which overlapping layers of feathers were inserted. In battle this combination helped to deflect the arrows and would be comparatively comfortable to wear. Whatever the method of construction used for their armour, these feathered warriors would pose an intimidating sight to their lesser-clad enemies.

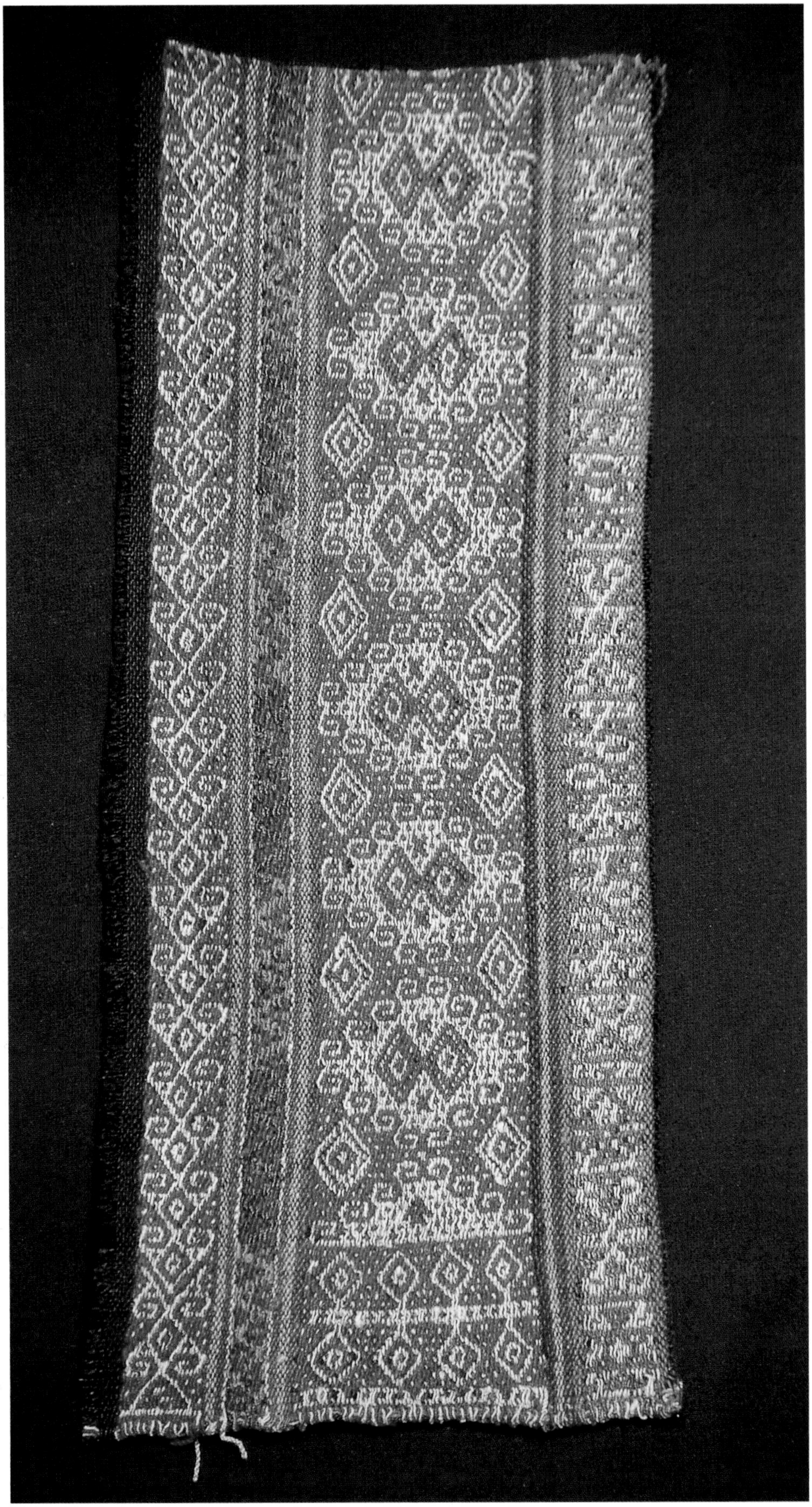

4

Spinning and Dyeing

Preparation of Fibres

Before the spinning process can begin, the fibres of the different plant types and the wool and hair of the various animal breeds need careful preparation. The ultimate development of these skills would probably result from a system of trial and error over many thousands of years. It is interesting that in isolated countries separated by the major oceans, these processes are very similar. It is possible that there is only one basic method that results in a viable end product for any textile process, reached by a kind of 'natural selection' where those methods that fail are ignored by succeeding generations. Natural fibres – including cotton, flax, wool and hair – are referred to as 'staples'. This is the name given to the discontinuous lengths that make up the fibres, which themselves can vary in length. The methods used to prepare and eventually spin the fibres will be those best suited for the fibre type and for the end product chosen.

Wool and Hair

Wool and hair differ to some extent in structure, the smoother hair fibres having fewer scales along the fibre length. The structure of a wool fibre could be likened to a series of scaled cusps sitting one within the other, formed round a hollow, central tube. Stroke the fibre one way and it is smooth, stroke it the other way against the cusp edges and it is slightly rough. These little indentations trap the air, which gives wool its great insulating properties, whether against heat or against cold. The outer layer is formed of a thin membrane, which allows moisture from inside to evaporate, while repelling rain or moisture droplets from the outside. These qualities were always a

OPPOSITE PAGE:
A hand-spun, hand-woven, warp-faced cloth from the Bolivian Highlands. The woollen threads are dyed with natural plant dyes and with cochineal for the red colour – mid twentieth century.

favourite with shepherds – in any part of the world – who shared the same climate as that of their sheep. Wool also has a property called 'crimp'. This refers to the degree of waviness within the fibres, which can vary from breed to breed. A high crimp level will give soft and fluffy wool, but is difficult to prepare for spinning as the scales cling together whenever they meet. The crimp gives elasticity to the wool fibres and unless the wool is treated on purpose to remove the crimp, it will retain its shape after being stretched. This ability of the scales to cling together also gives wool its felting qualities. This is the disastrous consequence of incorrectly washing a woollen garment, for the process is irreversible. However, the felting process is used to make a stable but pliable fabric for coverings, rugs, hat making, bags, saddlecloths and other serviceable items. The felt keeps its shape and has the same insulating and water-repellent qualities as the un-felted wool.

The preparation of wool and hair before the spinning process can start, is a time-consuming one, whether by hand or sophisticated machine. Only the bulk processing of woollen fibres makes the industrial process viable. Wool is obtained from sheep in three ways. In certain breeds of sheep and of cameloids it is better to pluck the fleece, as some animals do not lend themselves to being sheared. Wild sheep moult naturally in the spring or early summer. Plucking allows the finer under-belly wool to be gathered, as the outer guard hair, or kemp, does not fall out until later in the year.

Shearing, the second method, can take place every year, or in alternate years. If the sheep is sheared on a regular basis, it tends to lose its ability to moult. The sheared fleece guarantees a given quantity of wool that is true to the breed type. In South America the alpacas were sheared between December and March. The third method is to process the wool from the hide of the dead carcass. This is more likely if the sheep has been reared for meat, in which case the fleece is not of prime importance and thus of lower quality. In the high altitude areas of Cuzco in Peru, spinners prefer to use the longer wool from the pelts of slaughtered animals, rather than subject the sheep to the risk of shearing in cold conditions.

'Bat' carders and unspun wool on display at a weaving workshop near Oaxaca, Mexico.

Whichever the method of obtaining the fleece, it is bound to be dirty and full of unwanted vegetable matter. The larger pieces of debris are first removed and the fleece then washed several times in order to get rid of most of the dirt. The natural oil or lanolin in the fleece aids the spinning process if this is done by hand, so a certain residue is left. In some instances an initially clean fleece is spun unwashed – referred to as 'spinning in the grease'. The wool or hair on the animal grows in different degrees from coarse to fine, depending on the position on the body. The outer guard hair that repels the rain is longer and coarser, while the under-belly hair and that from around the neck can be very soft and fine. A certain amount of sorting into different types is therefore necessary, with the end product of the wool in mind. The job of cleansing and preparing the fleece was often given to the children. This would give them an early 'feel' for the fibres and eventually introduce them to the art of spinning. In many areas wool is still spun directly from the fleece, the worker first removing any debris, then teasing out the wool fibres while at the same time pulling out an extended length of yarn to form a 'roving'. It is possible that most of the cameloid hair was spun in this way. Goat's hair was whipped up with a stick or a flail, then the fluffed hair was drawn out and lightly twisted to form a roving. This was wound round the wrist, ready for drop-spindle spinning.

After the introduction of sheep by the Spaniards, European methods of fibre preparation are more likely to have been used: after sorting, the wool is straightened by carding. This is a process that helps the individual wool or hair fibres to lie together in a parallel formation before dividing into rovings or making into 'rolags'. Hand carders are still used by crafts people today and in many ethnic societies. Modern hand carders are like a rectangular bat in shape, with one surface covered with rows of little hooked wires. The two carders are scraped together to divide the wool, which is layered across the wires, with the process repeated until the wool is straightened. The 'bat' of straightened wool is then rolled up to form a cylindrical rolag of wool, ready for spinning. In industry the wool is passed through massive carding drums that produce narrow roving strips ready for the spinning process. In Europe and the British Isles, carders were formed in the traditional way with rows of dried teasel heads fastened to the wooden surfaces. Similar spiny plants were used in the preparation of fibres prior to spinning in some areas of Central and South America, but eventually the wire-type carders became available.

Cotton

Until the invention of the Cotton Gin by Eli Whitney in 1793, the preparation of the cotton fibres produced by the plantations was very labour intensive. The tiny seeds have hooked hairs on them that cling to the cotton fibres and originally they had to be removed by hand. The Cotton Gin speeded up the process, but in modern industry the seeds are treated by carbonization. There are many thousands of tiny fibres of about 2–4cm (0.75–1.5in) adhering to the

ABOVE: Fibre preparation – fluffing up cotton, spinning and weaving, depicted on an appliqué panel from Peru.

RIGHT: A woman spinning cotton with a support spindle – at the village of Santiago Atitlán, Guatemala.

rolag. This was bound up with a cord and kept ready for spinning, when it would be lodged into a forked stick. An alternative method was to fan out the fluffed fibres with the hand and arrange onto a forked stick or distaff before drawing off into a roving for the spinning process. In industry, these processes soon became mechanized to achieve a cost-effective product. Cotton was hand-spun initially on the supported spindle and a strong but fine thread was produced by the early spinners of the pre-Columbian era.

Sisal and Leaf Fibres

At one time cotton was reserved for the ruling and priestly classes, the ordinary people had to be content with the agave and maguey fibres. Luckily these were in plentiful supply and preparation was not difficult. The simplest method of removing the fibres was first to cut the spear-like leaf near to the plant base with a machete. The cut leaf was placed onto a flat rock or hard surface and beaten with a stick until slightly flattened. Further beating split the leaf lengthways, revealing the pulpy interior that surrounded the fibres.

seeds. The yellowish-white fibre is tubular in structure, up to 90 per cent pure cellulose with the inner part of the fibre made up of ribbon-like fibrils, arranged in convoluting layers. The outer cell wall is formed of a protective layer containing wax and protein. The wax repels water, but is removed in the washing process, which makes the fibres very absorbent. The fibres gain strength when wet, but lose some of their elasticity.

The native cotton *Gosypium mexicanum* was easier to prepare by hand as the seeds were less hairy. After cleaning, there were various methods used for fluffing up the cotton fibres as a preparation for spinning. The Chinantec women from the Oaxaca region of Mexico first supported a wad of cotton fibre onto a fabric bundle or a filled sack. A group of three canes, tied together at the holding end and splayed out like a fan, is held in each hand and beaten alternately to produce a fluffy mass. In other regions the cotton was whipped up with two forked sticks, while in Guatemala, the fluffed cotton was formed into layers to make an oblong shape that was gradually beaten out to form a rough roving which would be wound up ready for spinning. In Peru layers of beaten cotton fibre were formed into a flat disc that was folded up and then rolled into a cylinder like a woollen

Next, the leaf was opened out and some of the pulp scraped off with a flat wooden blade. This allowed the long fibres to be lifted out and further scraping reduced the surplus pulp. Once freed from the leaf, the fibres were hung on a bush to dry in the sun. This basic method of stripping the fibres from leaf plants is common to many parts of the world. Crushing machines were set up by the plantation owners, but in several rural areas today, the leaves are laid out on the roads so that passing cars and trucks will do the initial crushing. Soaking in water for a period helped to soften the fibres of the leaves and many of the bast fibres were subjected to this retting process. Flat leaves that were cut into strips could only be plaited or woven in one way or another and were used to make baskets, mats or even wall-panels and roofing for simple buildings.

Silk

Silk is an animal filament – one long thread that is unwound from the cocoon of the silkworm larvae. Silk is reeled, not spun. The worm is the larval stage of the silk moth, which changes its skin several times during rest intervals between voracious feeding periods. The fourth moulting is the final one, when it is said to eat twenty times its own weight in mulberry leaves. The worm extrudes a pair of threads, which are slightly gummy, from glands called spinnerets on either side of its lower lip. The head is waved from side to side in a figure of eight motion, gradually covering the body with silk, with finer filaments laid near to its body and slightly coarser ones to the outside. In two or three days this encasement hardens to become the cocoon, which in a natural situation is punctured when the adult moth is ready to emerge. In the silk-rearing industry, it is essential to kill the chrysalis before this happens, as broken filaments cannot be reeled. The worms are stifled immediately with hot steam, or immersed into boiling water, which helps to dissolve the sticky sericin gum, a gelatinous protein formed as part of the silk thread. In some countries the worms are eaten in the same way that shrimps and prawns are consumed in other societies.

To start reeling, the workers place several cocoons into a bowl of hot water, stir with a stick or a bristle-brush until a number of filaments, between six and ten, adhere to the stick. Finally, this group of filaments is transferred to a reeling wheel. As the winding handle revolves, the silk cocoons unwind and the filaments cling together to form a continuous thread. Next, the silk filament groups are twisted lightly together – a process called 'throwing'. Later the hanks of twisted filament-threads are de-gummed by washing in hot soapy water. Alternatively, the washing process may be delayed until after the cloth is woven. The coarse outer layers of the silkworm cocoon are used as wadding or gathered into shorter cut lengths, thus becoming 'staples' which are spun in the traditional manner. The colour of natural silk varies from light brown to a pale yellow – it is the introduced *Bombyx mori* silk moth that produced the white cocoon. In the silk producing area of Oaxaca in Mexico, the white silk is sometimes dyed brown to imitate the native product.

Spinning

No one knows how the art of spinning began. It may have evolved from the simple twisting of coarse bast and leaf fibres by rolling across the thigh or leg, or when twisting fibres on the end of a weighted stone to form into a rope. This twisting was one of the antecedents of actual spinning. The prepared sisal fibres were twisted together to make a string by rolling against the thigh with the flat of the hand while gradually adding in more fibres – the worker making sure to keep the twine of an even thickness. The resulting sisal string was tough, flexible and unlike its modern plastic counterpart, completely biodegradable. Its strength and elasticity made it a popular fibre in hammock making, where reliability was absolutely essential. Eventually, when spinning wheels were introduced, the Mexicans used a rough wooden wheel called a *carreta* to produce a coarse string suitable for making mats or bags, or the indispensable support strings for the back-strap looms. The *Agave sisalana* gave strong fibres that could be twisted into a rope by two men, one holding the fibres while the other walked away, at the same time twisting the fibres by rotating them with a hand-held stick. This method is similar to that used in rope making in Europe when 'rope-walks' were established in most towns and villages.

Softer fibres could be rolled across the hand and for convenience wound around a stick, which eventually might take up the twist and become a rudimentary spindle. The next development was the hooked stick, cut from the natural divide of a forked twig. The fibre is held onto the angled hook and once secure, the twig is rotated with the fingers while drawing out the yarn. This is a time-consuming but viable method of producing an evenly spun thread. It is the forerunner of both the drop-spindle and the hip spindle and even today, spinners in Ecuador still use this method.

Spindles take many shapes in different countries, but they all have one purpose – to allow the fibres to be drawn out from the source in an even manner while at the same time applying a degree of twist. To make a viable spun yarn or thread, the individual fibres need to be added in such a way that they become incorporated gradually while the spinning is in progress. The resulting thread should be strong and even, not varying in thickness – unless decorative slubs are used as a fashion statement.

Spindles and Spindle-Whorls

The shape and size of the spindle depends on the kind of yarn or fibre that is to be spun, the fineness or coarseness of the thread and to some extent, the lifestyle of the spinner. There are three distinct types of spindle: the drop-spindle, the hip spindle and the support spindle. The majority of spindles are weighted with a spindle-whorl. This takes the form of a circular disc that can be flat, spherical or a half-round with a flattened top. In areas of Peru and the Andes, the tiny cotton-spinning whorls may be cone-shaped, cylindrical or indented like a *diabalo*. There is always a central hole in the disc through which the spindle stick is passed. Sometimes this stick is slightly tapered so that the spindle-whorl will only go so far down the stick and be held in place. Occasionally the spindle-whorl is integral with the stick, but this can only be if it is carved from wood or similar material. The flat, circular shaped disc will rotate more slowly, but for a longer period than the smaller spherical whorl, which rotates faster for a shorter time. This enables the spinner to choose the correct type of spindle and whorl to impart more or less twist, as the type of fibre requires.

A spindle left outside a church on the shores of Lake Titicaca, Peru, while the spinner attends morning service.

The Suspended or Drop-Spindle

The drop-spindle can have the whorl situated either at the top, or near to the bottom of the stick. If at the top, the flat surface of the whorl will face downwards so that the yarn can be wound onto the lower half of the stick. If the whorl is placed near the bottom, the reverse will show the flat of the whorl facing upwards. There is no evidence that any but the low-whorl drop-spindles were used in Central and South America. Sometimes there is a notch cut into the top of the stick, which can hold the already spun yarn with a half-hitch loop. The top of the stick is twirled between the fingers of one hand while the other hand draws out a length of fibre from the rolag or roving. When the spindle is released, the twist is imparted to the fibres while they are being drafted. When the spindle arrives at the bottom of the 'reach', the spun thread is wound back onto the hand in a figure of eight motion, which brings the spindle back up to the starting position. The wound thread is then transferred to the spindle and the process repeated again.

In Cuzco, Peru and other areas, the rolag is wound around the wrist to keep it out of the way. If it gets caught up with the spun thread, it can become incorporated at the wrong moment and get into a mess that is impossible to untangle. The long hanks of the agave and sisal fibres can be held over the shoulder with tension gained as they adhere to the clothing. Many societies place the prepared fibre onto a stick, twig or board called a distaff, which can take many forms, depending on the area in which they are used. This type of spinning has the advantage that it can be carried out wherever the spinner happens to be, indoors or when out herding the flocks. Bowler-hatted women on the shores of Lake Titicaca climb the steps of a monument to gain extra

A bowler-hatted woman using a drop-spindle while sitting on the steps of a monument, Lake Titicaca, Peru.

The Thigh, or Hip, Spindle

The high-whorl spindle, or the low-whorl spindle turned upside down, is used for this method where the twist is imparted by rolling the spindle shaft across the hip or the thigh. In some instances the yarn is held in place at the top with a hook placed centrally on top of the whorl, or a slit may be cut within the whorl if it is made of wood. This method, which is generally suited to medium weight yarns, can also be used with the lightweight support spindles for finer threads. As even a short twirl gives immediate twist to the yarn, it is better to draw out a length of controlled fibre and let the twist ride up as required.

The Support Spindle

The support spindle is generally used to spin the finer threads like cotton and alpaca or vicuña. However light, the weight of the spindle would cause a delicate yarn to break if it were suspended, so the lower end of the spindle is placed

A cotton spinner from Santiago Atitlán has an assortment of spindles in her basket.

height when spinning coarse wool with the drop-spindle. Others might lean out of a window or spin when seated astride a donkey.

Throughout several highland areas of Bolivia and Peru, a slightly different spinning method is used. Instead of imparting the twist in one go, the fibre is drafted in two separate stages. A portion of clean fleece is spread out with the fingers, after which the fibre is drawn out to form a roving with a minimum amount of twist. This is achieved by controlling the spindle, which at this stage is not dropped. Next, the length of roving is wound onto the fingers in a figure of eight formation, then gradually released as the final twist from the dropped spindle is imparted to the roving which is drawn out to produce a fine, even thread. This is an approved spinning method as it is found in several other parts of the world.

*A Peruvian woman from the highland area above Cuzco using a heavy support spindle
while sitting beside her horizontal loom.*

into a container such as a small bowl or a half-gourd. The spindle is twirled around by friction between the fingers and thumb, rather like twisting a spinning top. In the Aztec and Mayan areas, the spindle-whorl is situated at the lower end of the support stick, but in Peru and Ecuador, a distinctive round bead-like whorl is placed in the middle of a long stick that is pointed at both ends. Quantities of these spindle-whorls, sometimes together with their pointed sticks, were found in the graves of the Paracas culture along the coastal areas of Peru. Many examples, with their yarn still in place, show that the spun yarn was wound both above and below the central whorl. It is thought that when full this would make a convenient shuttle to be passed between the warp threads in weaving. It would appear that this placement of the spun yarn, both above and below the whorl, did not impede the twisting properties of the spindle.

To use any type of support spindle, the worker needs to be sitting on the ground, or on a low seat. Therefore it was not possible to use the spindle when standing up, walking or travelling, unless one hand was free to hold the bowl. Experiments by modern spinners suggest that a good light is needed to gauge the spinning of the fine thread, so this would be a daytime occupation, possibly the work of pro-fessional spinners. Coarser threads can be spun with this method, in which case the spindle and corresponding whorl are heavier and the spindle point may be held directly onto the ground, within a forked stick or occasionally between the toes. A woman in the high Altiplano area above

Cuzco was spinning wool while seated alongside her hori-zontal loom, possibly having run out of thread. In north-east Colombia, goat herders spin while reclining in their hammocks with the spindle supported in a half-gourd set into the earth below.

Once again there are three stages in the spinning process. First the fibre is drafted out without inserting the twist. The amount of twist is added after the drafting takes place according to whether a hard or soft type of thread is required. Lastly the spun yarn is wound around the spindle stick. Support spinning is also called 'point' spinning, a name common to *charka* spinning wheels and the 'great' wheel as all have a pointed end to the spindle from which the twisted thread revolves. It was the 'point' spindle on which the fairy-tale Sleeping Beauty is said to have pricked her finger. This may have been a hazard of point spinning, a prick could easily be infected from an unclean fleece and induce some form of poisoning.

Plying

The drop-spindle is the one most often used for the ply-ing of threads. Plying refers to the twisting together of two already spun threads. A thread can be spun in one of two directions, to the right or to the left. A right-hand or clock-wise twist is referred to as a 'Z' twist and a left-hand or anti-clockwise twist as the 'S' twists. The spin direction of the initial thread is dictated by the tradition of the society to which the spinner belongs and is helpful in identifying the geographical location of a particular textile. If a mother spins in one direction first, so will the daughter. A right-handed spinner may well prefer to make the initial 'twirl' to the right. It will make no difference to the finished 'single' yarn, except that in plying two threads together, a twist in the opposite direction is used to make a stable doubled yarn that will not untwist when the tension is released. So 'Z' twist yarns are plied with an 'S' twist, and vice versa. Sometimes extra whorls are added to a lightweight spindle when plying, in the same way that a weight lifter adds weights to the lifting bar. The yarn from two separate, fully wound spindles is removed from the spindle sticks as balls of thread. Sometimes these are placed in a vessel, or separate vessels so that they can rotate easily as the threads unwind. A heavier spindle onto which the plied thread is eventually wound, is used to give the required amount of twist to the doubled thread.

Workbasket with spindles and spindle-whorls. Probably coastal grave area, Peru, AD700–1200.
(Accession No. 1952A36. Birmingham Museums & Art Gallery)

There are certain instances where threads may be plied in the same direction to give special effects when weaving. A highly twisted yarn, used for both the warp and the weft of a plain weave, will be cancelled out with one twist facing one way and the other yarn at right angles to it, giving a very springy fabric. There were many varieties of ply combinations used by the pre-Columbian weavers. Their use in specialized weaving techniques was proof of the high regard in which this art was held. Occasionally, two different ply methods were found in an individual fabric, giving both a patterned and a textural effect. Cotton threads were often plied together with the cameloid fibres, incorporated with feathers or used to give strength to softer fibres such as rabbit hair.

Spindle-Whorls

There is a direct relationship between the size and weight of a spindle-whorl and the type of yarn that is to be spun. A coarser fibre like maguey will require a heavier whorl and a fine cotton a lighter one, but this does not mean that a fine yarn cannot be spun on a heavier whorl, providing it is a support spindle. The reverse is not so practical with a finer thread. Archaeologists have found great quantities of spindle-whorls

of varied types and sizes in the different areas of both Central and South America. As the whorls are made from hard substances like rock, bone or clay, they have survived to a far greater extent than the textiles for which they provided the threads. In his article 'Spindle-Whorls, some Comments and Speculations', Robert K Liu tells us how this treasure trove has enabled the archaeologists to conduct all kinds of research projects, working backwards from the spindle-whorls to determine what kind of thread was used in any given area and subsequently, the form of cloth woven.

A selection of disc-shaped spindle-whorls from Mexico, together with one round one and two spindles from Bolivia or Peru.

The specific type and measurements of the whorls found in a single location seldom vary, but occasionally they take the form of a large whorl size and a smaller one, with no gradations of size in between. This suggests that the small whorl is used for fine spinning and that the large whorl may be used for coarse fibres, but more probably for the plying together of the finer threads. Many of the early textiles from the Paracas culture are woven with a plied thread that is highly twisted.

Some of the most intriguing finds from the Chancay Valley graves in coastal Peru are in the form of plaited workbaskets full of spindles together with their spindle-whorls and wound threads. These spindles are of the spherical 'bead' type, set towards the middle of the double-pointed sticks. Some are full of the spun thread, both above and below the whorl, as described before. Other spindle sticks are empty, together with many spare whorls at the bottom of the baskets as well as the little bowls used to support the spindle. These emotive finds remind one of the importance given to the art of spinning, as the deceased is ready equipped to carry on this function in the afterlife. As many as seventy spindle-whorls have been counted in one basket. This has led to further research by the archaeologists in trying to determine how many spinners there may have been in a culture during a given period of time. If they took the amount of whorls found

in the whole of the South American continent, they would have to preclude many areas, such as high altitude ones where furs and skins were used for clothing, or the steamy Amazon jungles where leaf fibres and feathers provided decoration rather than warmth. Taking fifty to seventy spindle-whorls as the average owned by one spinner, or possibly a spinning family, it still gave a picture of a culture led by the art of spinning and weaving and shows their importance as an indication of national wealth. Many spindle-whorls were found in the graves of Ecuadorian, Maya and Inca nobles, possibly indicating their association with textiles rather than their individual expertise in spinning.

Spindle-Whorl Materials

The earliest whorls may have taken the form of a round seed or small vegetable pierced with a stick. Carved wood, rounded shells, chipped stone or pot shards would follow. As it was necessary to drill a hole in the middle of the whorl, the labour-intensive stone whorls would be more highly regarded. A spindle known as a *malacate*, probably made from a malachite rock, was used to spin relatively fine yarn from hard leaf fibres such as the maguey. The holes might be drilled from one side only, changing in diameter to prevent the spindle stick from falling through. Others, like some of the small spherical ones, were drilled from both ends with the central area fractionally smaller to give greater stability to the whorl.

Fired clay was used for many of the Aztec and Mayan spindle-whorls. These tended to be larger and dome-shaped with one side flattened. The clay might be moulded round a stick which, when fired would burn away and leave a hole of the correct size. The relation of the hole-to-whorl size depended on the type of spindle stick that was required. A heavy whorl seldom had a fine stick, but light whorls might have a disproportionately larger hole. The decoration of the whorl is an important factor in identifying the place of origin. Many of the clay whorls from Central America have impressed patterns made by pressing the clay into a carved mould. Others have clay decoration added before the firing. The designs feature many of the symbols and patterns used on the stone carvings, codice paintings and of greater importance, those found on woven fabrics. Animals, birds and strange beasts are cleverly adapted to the circle shape. The carved, spherical spindles often had incised or ground decoration of lines and geometric shapes, sometimes filled in with a lighter coloured mineral or clay. In areas of Ecuador, there was little decoration on the whorls, but the spindle shafts might themselves be embellished. In pre-Columbian Peru, very special whorls were made of gold, but it is not known if they were actually used.

The majority of the whorls become separated from their spindle sticks, which can make identification difficult as many of these tiny whorls are mistaken for beads and sold as such in the antique trade. One key to recognizing the difference is to examine the central hole. A bead hole is more likely to be small in diameter, whatever the size of the bead, as a fine bead thread is normally used. Drilling is a difficult and time-consuming process, no worker makes the hole bigger than necessary. A bead may be asymmetric or have protrusions – only a well-balanced whorl will spin true. The difference in the internal dimensions of the whorl hole is another give-away as bead holes are constant in diameter and always as smooth as possible. Only a familiarity with the different whorl types will enable a collector to determine whether a bead is a whorl or not, as many whorls are still used as beads because of their decorative qualities.

Imported Spinning Wheels

The introduction of the merino sheep to the New World by the Spanish and the Portuguese was soon followed by the importation of spinning wheels. The availability of a good supply of wool and the abundance of the indigenous cotton crop meant that traditional spindle spinning methods were unable to keep up with the increased demand. This did not mean that spinners ceased to use their hand spindles. In fact, many continued to use the old methods with which they were more familiar and which in many instances, gave superior results. In rural areas of Central and South America, this is still the preferred method. The hand spindle gives the user mobility and a choice of spinning venue, whereas the wheel is normally located in one place.

Spindle Wheels

By the fourteenth century the 'great wheel' – a simple mechanization of the familiar spindle shaft – was in use in many European countries. This improvement was achieved by aligning the spindle in a horizontal plane onto a supported bearing that is rotated by a driving band that encircles the indented rim of the hand-turned wheel. The large circumference of the wheel enabled the spinner to achieve a higher amount of 'spinning time' with fewer rotations than of a smaller wheel. This is sometimes called the 'walking wheel' as the worker had first to turn the wheel, then walk away to draw out the yarn as the twist was imparted, then walk back again to wind the spun yarn back around the spindle shaft. The tension could be altered by adjusting the distance between the spindle and the wheel hub. There are many versions of the spindle wheel that vary in wheel size and

method of rotating the wheel, but all require that the worker divides the spinning into separate drafting and winding processes.

Flyer Wheels

A further development was the introduction of the 'flyer' mechanism. This was a 'U'-shaped device, made first of wood and later of metal, attached to the horizontal spindle together with two grooved whorls. One formed part of the spindle, the other grooved whorl – which had a smaller circumference – was attached to the bobbin. A figure-of-eight double-band is passed around the wheel circumference and then divided to go around the individual whorls. The resulting differential allows the spun yarn to be wound onto the bobbin while, at the same time, the actual spinning is in progress. This saved a great deal of time and allowed the spinner to sit down and use both hands while rotating the wheel with a foot treadle.

The flyer wheels, being more complicated in construction, would initially be imported from Europe, but the local workers were soon able to make their own versions of the simpler spindle wheel. Although spindle spinning and wheel spinning still take place throughout the areas of South and Central America, factory-spun yarn is easily available and saves on personal production time. Brilliantly dyed acrylic fibres are very popular, often used for additional decorations such as pom-pom making. While the purist might decry the introduction of modern dyes and fibres, the textile workers are still using traditional patterns and obviously enjoy the freedom of the extra choices available to them.

Dyeing

Natural Dyes

Many of the pre-Columbian textiles found in the dry desert areas of coastal Peru – some dating from as early as 3000BC – have retained a surprising degree of their original colouring. This is testament to the expertise of the dyers who used the natural and mineral materials that surrounded them. No one knows how any early society first discovered the use of these materials as substances that could colour their cloth. Initially it may have happened as a series of accidents where threads came into contact with dyestuff when wet, or

Natural dyestuffs – plant material, bark and roots – on display at the weaving workshop – Oaxaca region, Mexico.

were inadvertently stained when cooking vegetables. It could have been a follow-on from primitive painting where coloured minerals were ground up and applied to pottery or used to decorate the body in cult ceremonies. In the same way that the thread spinning methods appear in different parts of the world, so the art of dyeing became an expression of widely separated cultures, often with the dye-colour obtained from similar types of plants.

Some colour sources could be found only in certain areas, or limited to climatic and geographical locations. Apart from local plants that were used to produce the general range of colours like yellows, browns and fawns, specialized sources were needed for the deeper or more vibrant colours such as red, purple and black. These would include the insect and the shellfish dyes, cochineal red and murex purple. Of even greater importance were the gradations of indigo blues from light to deepest blue-black and the ability to produce a viable green when mixed with other colours. In Peru today it is generally the women who do the dyeing but in the past, according to the anthropologist Bernard Mishkin, it was the men of Quispicanchis who were the expert dyers: 'some known for their rich reds, others for their beautiful purples'.

Mordants

Most natural dyestuffs, apart from indigo-blue and murex-purple, need to be 'fixed' with a mordant so that the fabric does not fade or lose its colour when washed. The word 'mordant' comes from the French *mordre* which means 'to bite'. Alum is used worldwide as a binding agent to fix the dyes on cotton, wool and other fabrics, so that the dyestuff becomes part of the fibre structure and is thus insoluble. Alum, which does not alter the dye-colour, occurs naturally in various minerals, which can be treated with acid to obtain alum crystals. Other mordants used as fixatives included salt, ash, lime and lemon juice, fermented corn beer and human urine. Alum is used with both natural dyes and with the aniline dyes that were invented in Europe during the 1860s and which play such a major part in commercial dyeing. Iron mordant gives darker colours, while chrome mordant sharpens yellows and brightens other colours.

A variety of shades can be produced by treating similar fibres with different mordants prior to dyeing. Even though these fibres are all placed in the same dye bath, each mordant will react to produce individual colours. This subtle shading is one of the skills of dyeing, but only a master dyer will be able to repeat the colours to any degree of exactitude. For that reason, dyers like to dye a sufficient quantity of yarn to enable them to complete the project. Fibres can be dyed before or after spinning. The yarn is first soaked in the mordant solution, then boiled in the dye bath according to the depth of colour required, the deeper shades needing several hours. In order to eliminate air pockets and get an even take-up of colour, wool in Bolivia was soaked first in hot and then cold water and dried before dyeing. The mixing of colours and overseeing of the dye baths was a skilled art, with the master dyers held in high esteem.

An example of weaving from the Mexico workshop, demonstrating the use of natural dyes and showing the Venus Star motif.

Natural Dyes

It was not only the leaves of plants that were used as dye materials. The stems, roots, fruits, seed-pods, berries, nuts, skins and the bark of trees – all provided dyestuff. Lichens and many leaf plants gave yellow variations while in Peru, purple-skinned potatoes were used to make mauves and violet. Walnut bark and roots gave a dark brown dye that could be enhanced with indigo or cochineal; while brazil wood provided a deep, reddish brown. In *The Weavers of Ancient Peru*, Mo Fini, who has studied the names given to dyestuffs in the Quecha language, gives a comprehensive table of the commonly used natural dyes, together with botanical names and the colours obtained.

Minerals from rocks and soil, carbon from burnt wood or soot – all helped to increase the dye palette. Some grave goods from ancient Peru have been found with mineral dyes painted onto the fabric. A Nasca cotton textile dated to 200BC, which is in the collection of the Cleveland Museum of Art, features mythological figures painted in a series of warm earth colours – yellow ochre, reds, browns and black. Some Paracas-painted textiles show simple line designs, also drawn onto cotton cloth, while the Peruvian tribes of the Amazon Basin use river mud to dye both their pottery and their textiles, with geometric patterns drawn onto the cotton cloth that remain even when the fabric is washed.

Natural dyes are used in certain areas today as a commercial project. The Oaxaca area of western Mexico has always been famous for its weavers and dyers. Several weaving workshops have been set up to make rugs and other small woven items to be sold for the tourist trade. Visitors are shown the various dyestuffs that are used to colour the wool used by the weavers. Attractive bowls and fibre baskets are filled with dried plants, cochineal, tree bark and the lumps of indigo paste. The woven pieces have a luminous quality that becomes even more intense when certain colours are placed next to one another.

Cochineal Red

Although a red dye could be obtained from various berries and seeds, none could compete with the vibrant colours – ranging through red to purples and black – made from the ground-up bodies of the female cochineal insect, *Dactylopius coccus*, a parasitic cactus-eating scale insect belonging to the Coccidae family. It is native to tropical and subtropical America, which includes areas both north and south of the isthmus of Panama. The dye was used by Mayan weavers from Mexico and Guatemala and by the pre-Inca civilizations of South America. The use of these dyes spread to areas of northern Argentina, while today an important production centre is situated in the high Andes' valleys of Ayacucho in Peru. According to Mo Fini, cochineal is still used here in combination with aniline dyes, as well as in the high sierra of Peru, the Cochabamba area of Bolivia and in a few places around Lake Titicaca. In some Andean villages, cochineal was used to dye fabrics black, while in others, only the red colours were favoured. The use of different mordants would alter the colour to produce the varying shades of red dye – scarlet, crimson, orange and reddish black. The dyes were obtained by boiling the pulverized, dried insect bodies in water. Cochineal proved an excellent substance for dyeing silk and wool. Dyeing generally took place after the yarn was spun, but occasionally the woven cloth itself would be dyed and in some instances, over-dyed to enhance the colour of other dye substances or used in patterning methods such as tie-dye, where the cloth is tied in certain areas to form a resist to the dye.

The cochineal insect is found naturally on its host plant, the *Nopal* cactus or prickly pear, a familiar desert plant that has a series of flat, oval leaves covered with groups of spines. Wild cochineal was gathered throughout the year, but those farmed for dye collecting were harvested from two to four times a year. The cultivation and gathering of the insects was a labour-intensive process. The cactus plantations were 'seeded' with the live female insects, which were reserved from the previous harvest. Great care was taken to keep the insects from harm – the cactuses were covered with woven mats to protect from the rain, or the cactus leaves, together with the insects, were removed from the plant and brought indoors until the weather improved. The male insects, which are a grey-red in colour, measure only 2–3mm (0.09in). The darker, blue-red females are slightly bigger and outnumber the males by 300 to one. These parasitic insects have a short mouth-tube, with which they suck the nutritious sap from the cactus plant.

Nopal cactus or prickly pear, growing in the front of a garden display bed near Teotihuacán, Mexico.

The females are collected when their swollen bodies are laden with eggs. The insects are removed from the cactus either by brushing them into bowls or finely woven baskets, or by carefully detaching them with a pointed implement or the sharpened end of a feather quill. In the past they were killed by spreading out on cloths laid on warm sand in the sunlight. At night the cloths were carried indoors, then put out into the sunshine again, a process repeated for a period of up to two weeks. This method was considered to produce the best results as too drastic an application of heat would ruin the quality of the dyestuff. Another method was to put the insects onto a metal plate held over a fire, which eventually turned the insects a dark brown. Alternatively they can be killed by immersion in hot water, or subjected to steam, after which they are dried in the sun or heated gently in an oven.

The different kinds of treatment resulted in the varied appearance of commercial cochineal, and insects from Guatemala and Honduras were considered superior. Those specially bred and harvested early gave a better and greater quantity of dye, being larger than their wild counterparts. As the insects are so light, it takes 70,000 insects to make 1lb (450g) of cochineal. This led to malpractices when the cochineal was exported to Europe. Unscrupulous farmers or merchants might adulterate the dried insects with other plant material, or even ground earth or coloured chalk.

In pre-Conquest times, cochineal production in all of the cactus-growing areas was limited to the amount needed for domestic use. This changed with the arrival of the Spanish who saw the value of this prestigious dyestuff which had far superior qualities to the dye obtained from Kermes – a scale insect commercially bred in areas of Central and Eastern Europe. Apart from the mining of Mexican silver, the large-scale production of this valuable new dyestuff was to become one of the most important sources of income for the Spaniards. They imported vast quantities back into Europe and even up to the mid-nineteenth century, Guatemala was the world's foremost supplier. Although the Spanish prohibited the export of the live insects, their value led to an inevitable distribution to other areas including Brazil and Indonesian Java. Eventually plantations were set up in the West Indies and in the Canary Islands. The invention of synthetic dyes to replace cochineal did not result in the end of production in Mexico and areas of Guatemala – weavers still preferred to use the original dyestuff, as nothing could improve on the beauty of the colours obtained by this time-honoured method. Cochineal is still used as a natural colouring for various foodstuffs, including the favourite red sweets in a multi-coloured brand.

Murex Purple

Murex purple is the name given to dye obtained from the gland of the *Murex* snail or mollusc, found on warm ocean shorelines. As it was only possible to harvest a minute amount from each snail, it was very costly and thus held in high esteem.

Purple dyes are some of the most difficult to achieve. Although several vegetable sources gave shades from mauve to a light violet, none produced the vivid purple that was obtained from the murex. The murex marine snail is a gastropod mollusc that attaches itself to a rock by its single pod – or flattened muscular foot. They vary in shape but all have a single coiled shell, sometimes elaborately spined or frilled. Varieties are found throughout the world living in rocky shallows, mainly in tropical areas. According to Britannica: 'the animal feeds by drilling a hole in the shell of another mollusc and inserting its long proboscis. Most species exude a yellow fluid that, when exposed to sunlight, becomes a purple dye'. One of the most famous mollusc dyes is Tyrian purple, obtained from *Purpura blata*, found in the Mediterranean area. The Romans valued this dye above all others. It was reserved for Royal garments, but for lesser nobles took the form of dyed purple bands sewn around the toga hems. Less well known, but of equal importance to the people of Central America, was *Purpura patula*. This mollusc was found on the Pacific coasts of Nicaragua and Guatemala, as well as the Oaxaca area of coastal Mexico.

Only a minute quantity of the precious fluid was available from each mollusc. This was secreted by a gland situated inside the creature's rectum and used as a defence mechanism when the snail was attacked. In Roman times, the molluscs were prized from the rocks and the gland removed, resulting in the mollusc's death. As thousands were needed to produce even a small quantity of dye, their shells have been found abandoned on Mediterranean shorelines to the depth of several feet. The Roman official Pliny the Elder wrote down detailed dyeing instructions. After the dye glands were taken from the molluscs, they were immersed in a carefully measured salt solution and heated gently until the dye was released, after which the dyeing process could take place and the fabric was finally placed into the dye solution.

The inhabitants of mollusc-bearing areas of Central America appear to have had a more life-sustaining attitude to gathering the dye. The molluscs were not killed, but milked. Zelia Nuttall, an American scholar, investigated the dye-gathering methods during an expedition to the Tehuantepec area of southern Oaxaca in 1909. In springtime, dyers would gather several molluscs from the rocks at low tide, then blow on them. This would provoke the shellfish to squirt a frothy secretion, which was rubbed onto skeins of ready spun cotton, first wetted in seawater. An alternative method was to take two molluscs from the rock, rub them together and draw a skein of thread past the glands, while a less common method was to partially remove the snail from its shell and squeeze out the secretion. The molluscs would be returned to the rock, or thrown into a rock pool. In another month the fishermen would return to prise the same molluscs from the rocks and milk them again, even though the second milking provides less fluid. Most of the molluscs survived this treatment, thus preserving the valuable dye source. At first the secretion was a pale yellow, but as the dyed yarn was exposed to the air, it turned green and

Spun cotton threads tied in groups to form a resist before dyeing, Salacaja, Guatemala.

then deepened to a dark purple. This dye is permanent and only fades to a lighter shade after repeated washes, but is said to still retain a slightly fishy smell, which is not unpleasant. These methods are still practised in areas along the Mexican coast of Oaxaca today, but sadly the remaining molluscs are falling prey to pollution in the seawater and one day this dye-producing method may become only a memory.

The difficult-to-produce purple dye was held in high esteem in Central America long before the arrival of the Conquistadors, who reverted to the killing method in order to produce more dye. Traditionally, the murex purple was reserved to dye cotton for the weaving of special garments. According to Zelia Nuttall, even as late as 1909 when the industry was in decline, the Zapotec women of Tehuantepec wore *pupura* dyed skirts, but they were very costly and only affordable by the well-off. Zelia Nuttall praised the dye for its 'beautiful and intense violet' and the different shades were combined with other dyes such as cochineal and indigo, for the weaving of striped fabrics for the wrap-around skirts and the *rebozos* or rectangular shawls. Although the Central Americans were able to add silk and wool to their dyeing repertoire in the post-Conquest period, they continued to use their native cotton when dying with murex purple. Silk was expensive, but small amounts of thread, dyed a lilac shade, were included in the striped fabrics.

Indigo

Indigo is a dye-substance found in a variety of plants, in constant use from ancient to modern times, although a synthesized version is used today by the fashion industry to colour all of our 'blue jeans'. Indigo dyes are unique in producing a stable colour that can vary from light blue to a very dark blue that is almost black. It can be used on its own, combined as an over-dye to produce other colours, or to enhance or deepen the colour of an already dyed fabric, whether natural or synthetic. The indigo-producing plants are found in many areas of the world, most species preferring warm climates. The plants, which may take the form of a shrub or a herb, belong to the genus *Indigofera* within the pea family (Fabaceae). The flower clusters, in white, rose-red or purple, eventually turn into fruiting pods containing the seeds. These shrubs – sometimes referred to as 'butterfly plants' – were found in China, India, Indonesia, Central America and the northern parts of South America. As there are so many different species of this indigo-bearing plant, botanists are not clear about the order of its spreading

The thread groups after being dipped into the indigo dye vat, but before the tied resist threads are removed.

across the world. Native species may have been supplanted by commercially introduced dye-crops and eventually the plants spread down the Pacific coast of South America and to parts of Brazil.

According to Britannica, indigo belongs to a large class of water-insoluble dyes and is known as a vat dye, as fermentation vats are used in the reduction of the indigo plants. The dye is applied in a soluble, reduced form to impregnate the fibre and then oxidized in the fibre back to its original insoluble form. Vat dyes are especially fast to light and washing. Brilliant colours can be obtained in most shades. The naturally occurring precursor of indigo is indican, a colourless, water-soluble substance that is ... easily converted to indigo by mild oxidation, such as exposure to air'.

Once again, it is not known how dyers in such widely separated areas of the world came to discover the properties of the various indigo plants, or worked out the complicated methods of preparing the dyestuff which required a high degree of dyeing skill. In many countries the traditional methods are still in use today, although commercially made synthetic indigo is readily available. Indigo is the one dye that does not fade with time and examples of its use have been found in the pre-Inca textiles from Paracas, Nasca and the Chancay valleys. The Spanish were amazed at the skill of the indigo dyers in Guatemala and Mexico and soon harnessed their expertise for their own needs. Indigo-dyed fabrics have featured in the costume and household fabrics of the peoples of Central and South America for several thousand years. The indigo dyeing tradition is one that links us to the skills of the ancient dyers, from the grave goods of the Peruvian elite to the modern inhabitants of America and the world. Where would we be without denim fabric and the ubiquitous blue jeans?

Although the first indigo dyes would come from plants that grew naturally, the importance of the crop eventually resulted in intensive agricultural cultivation. The ground was prepared thoroughly and after the final tilling, women and children were employed to reduce any remaining lumps of earth. The seeds soon germinated and plants would grow to several feet if the climatic conditions were good. The leaves were gathered when at their best, just before flowering took place – if the plants were cut off too high, the yield was reduced, if too low, new shoots would be damaged, endangering the next harvest in a few months' time.

Indigo preparation is divided into several processes. First the indigo has to be extracted from the leaves, next the plant matter is removed after fermentation and the indigotin solution, formed from the blue dyestuff, is whipped up to promote oxidation so that the chemical reaction is reversed for the dye process. Finally the water is drawn off, leaving the blue sludge ready for drying and forming into indigo cakes. The simplest method of extracting the dyestuff, probably dating from antiquity, was to put the leaves in a water pot, together with urine or ash and leave to ferment, thus reducing the oxygen content. Alternatively an alkaline solution made with lime and wood ash was used. The fabric would be left in the solution, together with the leaves. After the water was removed, the remaining leaf dye paste was dried and stored for use in the near future.

Commercially produced indigo required the use of large water-filled cisterns or vats into which the leaf bundles were placed in an upright position and covered to keep them below the water level. As fermentation took place, bubbles of air rose to the surface until, after a number of hours, a surface scum was formed. This scum was tested repeatedly until the correct moment to draw off the dark blue liquid was determined. This liquid, reserved in a lower level tank, had to be oxygenated immediately by beating or whipping with sticks until the surface scum first became blue, then white. After a couple of hours, dark blue patches of the dyestuff appeared, gradually settling onto the bottom. All kinds of substances could be added to hasten the process, including unslaked lime and tanning agents. Finally, the water was removed and the resulting dyestuff heated and filtered to remove impurities. The dye paste was pressed into cakes or blocks, which were dried very slowly in order to prevent them from cracking.

The actual dyeing methods only differed in the type and number of substances that were added to the dye vat. Indigo needs no mordant to fix it and is unique in that the minute dye particles will adhere to both natural and animal fibres – cotton, bast, linen, silk and wool. The particles cling to the fibres making a permanent bond and repeated dipping in the dye bath will increase the dye layers, rather than penetrating any deeper. Once the dyestuff has been dissolved in a warm alkaline solution (which soon turns a greenish colour) the fabric or thread hanks are immersed. When lifted out, they too take on a greenish colour, but this soon turns to blue as the chemical reaction takes place when the fabric is exposed to the air. The oxygen converts the indigo back to its original form and this was regarded by many people as a magic ingredient needing special incantations or ceremonies. The colour is deepened only by repeated immersions of the fabric into the dye bath and repeated exposure to the air. Although the colour is completely dye-fast and will not fade, it is subject to abrasion, any harsh rubbing revealing the lighter dye layers beneath.

Fabric that was already dyed using natural dyes fixed by a mordant would be over-dyed with indigo to produce other

A display basket containing the dried indigo that is used for dyeing, Mexico workshop.

colours or shades of a colour. Yellows were over-dyed to make a green, a colour that is very difficult to obtain in any other way. Many of the ancient textiles have reverted to a blue where the yellow dye has faded away. In the Chiapas region of Mexico a local dye plant, *sacatinta* (*Jacobinia spicigera*), was used with the indigo to produce purple and grey tones. This area was well known as a centre where the indigo-dyed skirts were woven for the Mixtec communities.

In the sixteenth century the Spanish set up plantations, introducing the Asian *Indigofera tinctoria* to Central America where it thrived under their constant supervision. Soon they were exporting vast quantities of the indigo dyestuff back to Spain, where it was sold to the European market. Their only problem was in the production of the indigo dye. Although the huge vats were installed on a factory basis, the dye had to be stirred for several hours in the crucial stage after fermentation. At first they used indigenous labour, forcing the reluctant workers to wade for several hours through the vats while thrashing the indigo solution with sticks. The terrible stench was accompanied by swarms of flies that tormented the workers, who soon succumbed to illnesses and refused to carry on. The Spanish were reluctant to force the native labourers who were of more use to them in other trades and, as a result, they turned to slave labour. It was said that the indigo cakes were so valuable that they could be exchanged in the market, weight for weight, with that of a single slave worker.

Later developments included the installation of hand-turned paddles and finally the mechanization of the stirring processes. Guatemala continued to be the foremost exporter of indigo until recent times. Today, even with readily available synthetic indigo, the natural indigo is still regarded as the best source of the dye as the results are impossible to improve on. This fascinating subject has been fully covered by Jenny Balfour Paul in her book *Indigo* and in *Indigo Textiles, Techniques and History* by Gösta Sandberg. For a selection of actual dyeing methods, consult: *A Dyer's Manual* by Jill Goodwin.

Synthetic Dyes

The chemical or aniline dyes were imported into Central and South America during the later part of the nineteenth century. In the southern continent their use spread from Peru into Bolivia, the bright and easily obtained colours making them popular. Sometimes a teaspoon of powder dye would be added to give colour depth to a natural dye bath. Recent research into dye crafts in areas of the high Andes revealed an abandonment of the use of natural dyes in favour of synthetic. When asked for the dye recipes, the women brought out tin cans full of powder dyestuff, adding that they used 'one spoonful of red, or two

A modern huipil *from Panajachel, Guatemala, with the tabby weave dyed with synthetic red.*

spoonfuls of yellow'. However, certain areas still favour the uses of natural dyes and there is now a desire to return to the use of these lovely colours.

In many areas of Mexico and Guatemala, once famous for their expert use of natural dyes, the synthetic aniline dyes have gained supremacy. They have the advantage of working on all types of fibre, including the bast fibres. The aniline purple dye was discovered by William Henry Perkin in 1853 while working as an assistant for von Hofmann at the Royal College of Chemistry, London. While trying to synthesize quinine as a remedy to combat malaria, he obtained a deep bluish substance instead. In 1856 he was to patent his discovery as a dye, known as aniline purple, Tyrian purple, or mauve. It soon became very popular as a fashionable colour and it was not long before it reached the Americas.

Alizarin is a red dye that came originally from the root of the common madder plant, *Rubia tinctorum*. A method of preparing alizarin from anthraquinone was discovered by German chemists in 1868 and a commercial synthetic dye produced in 1871. It was necessary to use a mordant for dyeing natural fibres and the different shades of red, brown and violet were obtained by varying the mordants. These two dyes, together with synthetic indigo – eventually synthesized in 1897 by a German company – were to revolutionize the dyeing process, whether in a domestic context or as part of worldwide commercial enterprise.

Resist Dyeing

There are various pattern methods used in resist dyeing. Each one reserves an area of the cloth or the spun fibres and keeps it from the dye. Thus the original colour is reserved beneath the resist, which results in a dye-patterned fabric or thread. Additional resists can reserve the colour of the first dyeing, then of any subsequent dye baths, at times building up to a complicated dye-pattern structure. Dyers always work from the lightest colour first, altering or darkening the following colours.

Cloth Resists

A painted or printed resist – whether in the form of a layer of wax or animal fat, as a vegetable starch resist, or in the form of a mineral substance like clay – is one of the simpler forms. In the first instance it could well have occurred accidentally when something was spilled onto a cloth prepared for dyeing. After dyeing, the resist is removed to reveal the colours beneath. Wax can be removed by boiling in water, letting the water cool and removing the layer of wax that floats to the top. Alternatively the wax can be scraped off, or in a modern context, ironed off. Fabric reserved with a vegetable starch resist cannot be put into the dye bath or the resist would disappear. The cloth is painted with the dye and fixed by heating. Afterwards the paste is scraped off, leaving a less defined, but attractive pattern where the dyestuff seeps into the resist areas. A resist-patterned woven cloth was found in one of the graves belonging to the Chancay Valley culture in Peru, dating from about AD1200–1400. Alternating squares show geometric designs in white, brown and black, but the type of resist used in not known.

Tie-Dye

This dye-patterning method appears to have been used more widely than the painted resist type throughout our area. The fabric is bound tightly with threads to form a series of resist areas before immersion into the dye bath. This is generally referred to as 'tie-dye' but there are many other names given to this dye craft. Additional bindings can be added or removed for subsequent dye baths. Pre-dyed bindings can contribute colour to the bound area if the dye bleeds into the resist area. The fabric can be folded in a variety of ways before the initial tying process to produce a series of resist-patterns. When unfolded after dyeing and drying, a series of mirrored patterns is revealed – linear or circular according to the tie method used. Other patterns are

A Guatemalan woman from Salacaja ties threads on a frame ready for resist dyeing known as jaspe.

achieved by over-sewing or gathering areas of the cloth, a stitch resist method called *tritik*. The sewing threads are removed after the first dyeing, or they can be partially removed and re-sewn for subsequent dye baths. We tend to think of tie-dye as a relatively modern resist method, possibly because of its popularity during the 1960s and 1970s, but it is found in most countries of the world and has been around for a very long time. There is a multi-coloured tie-dye mantle that comes from the Huari culture on the south coast of Peru. This dates from AD600–1000 and shows patchwork squares in a typical tie-dye pattern of resist-tied circles. In more recent times, Mexican women decorated their wrap-around skirts with tie-dye patterns, using the *ixtle* fibre to bind the cloth, before it was dipped in the dye bath. At one time, woollen cloth was preferred for the sewn *tritik* method as it absorbed the dye well.

Resist Tied Threads

This is a method of patterning the yarn or fibre threads to be used for woven fabrics. Thread groups are resist-tied in a predetermined sequence onto either the longitudinal warp threads that give support to the weaving, or the weft threads that will interlace within the warp. In only a very few countries are both warp and weft sets tied at the same time to produce a very complicated pattern. Before tying, it is necessary first to wind the threads onto a frame that is equal to the warp length or the weft width. This allows the worker to tie a pattern sequence that after dyeing will produce the correct alignment of the resist areas. Additional ties are added

Threading the dyed jaspe *warp between posts set up in the main street of Salacaja.*

Adjusting the indigo-dyed warp threads so that the pattern will remain true when woven.

or subtracted during the different colour dye baths. If the pattern threads are used for the warp, a finer weft thread will sink within the weave to allow the warp pattern to dominate. Thicker weft threads will allow the weft pattern to take precedence.

Among modern dyers, this type of patterned weave is currently known as *ikat*, a term abbreviated from the Indonesian *mengikat*, meaning 'to tie'. Called *watado* by the Quechua people of the Andes, warp-*ikat* was a speciality in some villages and was used in the making of ponchos and saddlebags. Although examples of pre-Conquest *ikat* patterned textiles have been found in the grave areas of Peru, none has been found in Mexico. The *ikat* method is thought to have been introduced to Mexico by the Spanish and it soon found favour with the native weavers and remained popular well into the nineteenth century. This method is still practised in certain areas of Mexico today, the workers preferring to work with silk or rayon.

In Guatemala this popular technique is known as *jaspe* and is used with both indigo and a selection of natural or synthetic dyes. The people of the township of Salacaja in the Guatemalan highlands are famous for their *jaspe* weave. Workers in the indigo dye workshops specialize in tying the threads ready for the warping process before the warp threads are stretched backwards and forwards along many yards of the main street. The taut threads are carefully aligned so that the pattern areas are constant, before winding up ready for the loom. Even in the outlying villages weaving families share the tasks. The *jaspe* tying frame is set up in the courtyard of the house, sharing space with children and wandering chickens. The mother might take on the job of the time-consuming pattern tying, as well as the initial reeling of the thread with a hand-turned wheel while father oversees the warping and setting up of the treadle loom. The resulting fabric has a quality that cannot be achieved in any other way.

In San Antonio Palopó, one of the villages on the shores of Lake Atitlán, the *jaspe* patterned threads are combined with plain colours to make a striped fabric that is woven to make the *huipil* blouses of the women, the collared shirts of the men and the wide sashes that encircle the waist. The women of Junil, a town situated under the shadow of a volcano, use this striping method to pattern their tubular skirts. Although the initial tying and dyeing methods are the same, the individuality of the patterns allows the weave source of the different areas to be identified. Whatever the origin of this patterned weave, it has been used in many parts of Central and South America to decorate all the main types of woven garments as well as carrying cloths, bags, head coverings and blankets.

5

Weaving

According to the children of Chinchero, a village in the High Andes, they were never taught to weave, saying that they taught themselves. A fascinating article by Christine Franquemont is adapted from the research of her late husband, Ed Franquemont, who spent many months living with the village people. She gives details of the learning process, where the older women said it was a matter of 'watching, watching, counting, counting.' Ed Franquemont's article takes the same title and was first published in *Human Nature*, Vol. 1, in 1979. We are indebted to him for the painstaking and sensitive fieldwork that reveals a very special form of shared endeavour that benefits the entire village community.

In one sense, the children absorb the arts of spinning and weaving from an early age, as the work is going on around them all the time. The order in which the various tasks are performed by the members of the village, depends on both age and status. Even very small girls are given spindle and wool to play with – they learn by watching slightly older girls and by the time they reach the age of eight, are expert spinners. By the age of ten the girls go to the mountain pastures to herd the sheep, where once again, they watch the older girls making narrow woven bands on primitive stick-looms.

They soon become proficient in pattern weaving and in the fullness of time, return home to learn domestic tasks in readiness for marriage and childbearing. Once again, an older woman supervises the weaving of elaborately patterned *chumpi* belts for the marriage. The large-scale backstrap looms are not used until after the first child is born, for fear of straining the back. The young woman enters into a very special weaving relationship with the older woman, or *allwi masi*, who guides her through all the intricate patterns. In later life, the woman herself becomes an *allwi masi*, passing on her own knowledge. In old age, when the eyesight dims, the old woman returns to spinning while herding the sheep for her children. Her grandchildren will watch

her spinning and the whole craft-cycle repeats itself, as it has done through the centuries, over and over again.

Loom Types

In order to make a fabric of interlaced threads it is necessary to hold one set of threads at tension. The longitudinal threads are the ones that form the basic 'warp' through which the cross-ways or 'weft' threads are interlaced. This interlacing can take many forms, depending on the patterning process. In the simplest type of weave, where the weft threads interlace with every alternate warp thread to make a balanced cloth of plain or 'tabby' weave, it is possible on a small-scale piece to darn the weft thread in and out with a long darning needle. This is time consuming and difficult to work unless the cloth is very narrow. The solution was to divide the warp threads into alternate sections, so that one set could be lifted, allowing the weft thread to be passed through this opened 'shed'. The second set would be depressed to form the alternating shed which allowed the weft thread to pass through the opposite way, thus forming the first two rows of tabby weave. The shed was kept open with a wide, pointed wooden 'sword'. This was first threaded through alternate warp threads across the loom width. Shed sticks, which could be removed and re-inserted when necessary, were inserted to make the alternative shed openings.

The next development was to hold up every alternate warp thread with a 'heddle'. In its simplest form this is a loop of string that passes over and under alternate warp threads. If the string is attached to a bar or a rod, the entire set of string heddles can be lifted, which in turn raises every other warp thread, thus making a shed. An alternative was to have a fixed heddle – one that was formed of a piece of wood or metal with a row of alternating upright slots and centred holes. One thread was passed through the hole, the next through the slot along the row. When lifted, the hole threads were raised, thus forming the shed. When depressed, the threads slid down the slots, making the alternating shed.

An example of a back-strap loom from Mexico with brocade weaving in progress.

A small-scale version of the back-strap loom is used to weave braids in the streets of Cuzco, Peru.

The weft threads used for weaving are wound onto a shuttle that can take several forms. The simplest is a flat piece of wood with a 'V'-shaped notch at either end, or a piece of bamboo or stick with similar notches. The thread is wound onto the shuttle between the notches and unwound each time it is passed through the shed.

Back-Strap or Hip-Strap

The back-strap is a simple but most effective loom for weaving anything from a narrow band to a sophisticated length of brocade-pattern cloth. The bar holding the warp end is tied to a post or a tree, while the weaving end is wound round a second bar with the protruding ends attached to a band that passes round the worker's back or hips, thus holding the warp at tension. A row of string heddles are lifted to make the first shed and the weaver can slacken the warp tension by moving backwards or forwards when using the sword to depress the second shed. A popular version of this loom is the foot-held back-strap loom, used for narrow-band weaving. One end of the narrow warp is held by a cord which is looped round the big toe, or attached to a sandal, while the weaving end is tied round the weaver's back or hooked into the waist-belt. String heddles lift one shed, but the sword and several flat shed-sticks are inserted at intervals, each one picking up a different set of warp threads according to the pattern. These are removed after the weft thread is woven and replaced the other side of the string heddles, thus preserving the pattern sequence. Most bands are warp-faced with the warp threads prominent and the plain weft threads hidden between the rows. The warp is set on as a series of vertical coloured stripes and it is the order in which they are lifted that forms the pattern.

Even today the weavers sit in the streets of Cuzco, Peru, leaning against the Inca-period stone walls, weaving belts and camera straps for the tourists. Sometimes they are wearing felted bowler-type hats, at others they look even more distinctive in the traditional round hat with a concave flat top and decorated sides – always happy to be photographed as long as they make a sale. It is no surprise to find them seated on woven rugs on the high slopes of the Altiplano, bare-footed in spite of the cold, their bands making a bright splash of colour against the dark of the rugs.

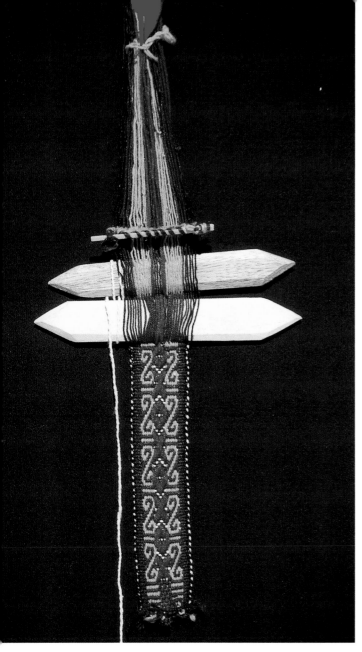

ABOVE: *The actual loom and braid purchased from a weaver in Cuzco, 1986.*

RIGHT: *Mountain braid weaver with braids laid out on display.*

BELOW: *Two women, sitting at the roadside in the high mountain area above Cuzco, weave braids for the tourists.*

These modern bands are woven with acrylic threads in the bright colours of synthetic dyes. They are attractively cheerful and have a place in their modern society. It is not until these bands are compared with the traditional ones made from finely spun and naturally dyed wool, that the contrast is brought home. One antique band purchased in Cuzco has seven pattern sections across the row, a wonderful example of weaving expertise.

Woven bands from Bolivia show intricate patterning techniques, featuring many of the symbols already described. Not only are they used as belts and carrying straps, they also act as headbands, or *winchas*. Descriptive bands are woven on the reed islands of Lake Titicaca where the bands tell a story, rather like a comic strip that can be read by anyone familiar with the cultural history. Very brightly patterned bands are woven in Todos Santos Cuchumatan in the Guatemalan mountains. They are worked in an inlay technique where the pattern threads are added as a supplement

Maria ties one end of her back-strap loom to the house post on the veranda.

to the weft. Narrow bands serve as hair ties, wide ones as belts or sashes. Stripes combining the *ikat* technique with plain sections are found on the many bands in the areas around Lake Atitlán and the highlands. Simpler bands, patterned with a series of coloured vertical stripes, are made in Panama, Mexico and Guatemala and are used in many ways.

In the hands of an expert weaver the back-strap loom takes on altogether different dimension. Maria Lopez, who in 1994 was the head of a weaving family in San Antonio Aquas Calientes, near to Antigua, Guatemala, is in such a category. Working in the courtyard of her simple house, she used the inlay technique to make intricate brocade woven patterns, with the warp end of the loom tied to one of the posts that held up the veranda roof. Other family dwellings, occupied by weaving daughters and relations, surrounded the courtyard where a separate kitchen was reserved for cooking the staple diet of corn tortillas. Maria sat kneeling on the floor on a mat, a position she was able to hold as long as necessary. She used a pick-up stick to select the pattern threads for the smaller inlay motifs. The sword-stick is then inserted into the shed opening formed by the interlaced warp and weft threads. This operation is quite independent from the pattern threads, and together with the use of the string heddles to lift the alternate shed, allows the normal tabby weave where the weft thread is used to secure the pattern threads in place. Apart from keeping the shed open, the sword-stick is used to batten the weft thread down into position. The resulting inlay patterned cloth was used to make *huipil* blouses for the family as well as for sale to the tourists.

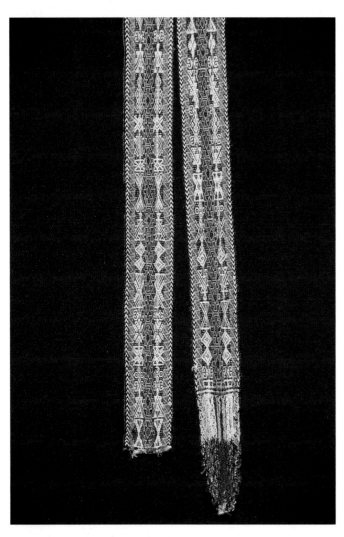

A warp-faced braid from earlier than the one on page 81 shows superior workmanship with seven different vertical pattern variations – Cuzco area c. 1950.

Horizontal Ground Loom

When weavers are on the move or herding their animals in the high altitude areas around Lake Titicaca, there are few trees available to act as uprights for securing their warp ends. The Aymara people have solved this problem by developing a portable horizontal loom supported by four wooden pegs driven into the ground. The circular warp is threaded around a pair of parallel bars which are tensioned between the wooden pegs. Rocks or stones lift the loom above the ground and act as stoppers to keep the pegs in position. Once again, a row of string heddles lifts the alternate threads and shed-sticks are inserted for the pattern formation. The weaving can be removed and rolled up for transportation. These looms were often used to weave the heavier yarns as the warp could be tensioned by a pair of ropes, held by yet more stones. The modern Maya people of Sonora in Mexico use a similar loom supported by strong pegs to weave their woollen blankets. In northern Mexico pre-Conquest weavers used a loom constructed of four strong wooden logs, the two side ones notched to hold the end ones. The end bars of the weaving could be attached to these and removed from the log supports when necessary. A Bolivian variation is the smaller, lashed-beam loom that could be propped against a wall but was only capable of producing a narrow width cloth. These narrow lengths were joined to make larger pieces – a more productive use of the weaving time available.

As with the back-strap loom, the width of the cloth is limited to the distance that the weaver can pass the shuttle with ease, normally about half an arm's length. Anything wider on a simple loom would require the use of both hands, one to put the shuttle in, the other to take it out. Normally the other hand is used to change the shed by lifting or depressing the heddles before passing the shuttle back to the original side.

Upright Loom

The upright loom, although capable of being moved, is often set up and kept in one place as it is of more robust construction, generally used for weaving rugs or heavy-weight cloth. A framework of wood supports the top and bottom bars around which the warp is threaded. Sometimes the bottom bar is not fixed to the frame and the cloth is tensioned with loom weights that can take the form of rocks or stones, occasionally with holes drilled through them. These weights can be removed temporarily, which allows the finished weaving to be wound up and more warp threads

unwound. Once again, the string heddles can be used to form the shed, although at times the heddles are dispensed with when the loom is used for tapestry weaving where the threads are woven in separate sections. At intervals, the woven threads are beaten firmly into place with a sword-stick or a heavy comb-type rug beater. Carpets and rugs are still woven on looms of this type, although the floor loom has taken over in many areas. In Bolivia and Columbia, versions of the vertical frame loom were used for weaving tapestry-woven blankets and saddlecloths. These upright looms were capable of being dismantled to bring indoors when necessary.

Floor Treadle Loom

The European treadle loom was introduced by the Spanish who, once they had discovered the talents of the indigenous peoples of their new colonies, were eager to speed up the weaving process. The basic structure of the treadle loom is a framework that supports the weft threads in a horizontal position, tensioned at either end by a back beam roller and a front roller. These rollers are set into the framework but can be lifted out. The use of separate string heddles with an eye tied in the middle, and later of metal heddles with eyes,

A frame loom set up in the courtyard of a Mexican weave workshop.

ABOVE: *A weaver with a woollen tapestry rug in progress.*

RIGHT: *A young girl, working on her narrow-band loom. A similar woven tape is entwined in her hair – from San Antonio Palopó, Guatemala.*

in front of the shafts to keep the threads separate. The reeds are held inside a firm frame, as wide as the maximum weft and several centimetres (a few inches) deep. If made of wood, the divisions are made from slivers of wood or plant material – thus the name 'reeds'. The divisions of a metal reed can be set finely, or further apart to allow for different thread thicknesses. The heavy reed is also used to batten down the weft threads so that they lie together closely across the warp after each weft throw. The wider shed allows the shuttle to be thrown through the opening, increasing the viable weaving width. Shuttles became more sophisticated and various shapes were invented. One, called the 'boat' shuttle, had a hollow in the middle in which a smaller shuttle or 'pirn' held the thread. This unwound as the shuttle was passed across.

Counter-balance looms were introduced into Mexico by the Spanish and soon found favour with the weavers. One of the great advantages of the treadle loom, to both the Spanish employers and the workers, was that it was possible to weave a broader cloth width, thus speeding up productivity. These looms are used in many areas today with modern weave workshops in Guatemala and especially the Oaxaca regions of Mexico, producing cloth for indigenous use or as part of the tourist industry. Contemporary 'Brazilian' hammocks are still woven on the floor loom to provide

were further developments. A row of heddles is set into a frame called a shaft, with two to four shafts used for normal weaving. Some looms can accommodate eight to sixteen shaft-frames, according to the pattern set-up. The shafts are suspended from a framework set over the top of the loom, called a 'castle'. The shafts are lifted and lowered by a series of pulley cords that are attached to a set of foot treadles placed just above floor level beneath the loom. Some looms can have counter-balanced lifts for the shafts with the treadles tied up so that the heddles lift alternate warps. In a counter-balanced loom, the shafts balance each other to make a central shed. In a counter-march loom, one warp is lifted and the other one depressed, thus providing a wider shed for the shuttle to pass through easily.

Using both feet, the weaver depresses one or more of the treadles to create the various pattern sheds. The weft threads are passed through a wooden or metal 'reed', a device placed

ABOVE: *Winding a series of different colours to make the striped warp.*

LEFT: *A woman from San Antonio Palopó starts winding threads onto a warping board in a figure-of-eight formation.*

a close-worked fabric for cooler use – unlike the Mayan and Nicaraguan hammocks that are made in the openwork 'sprang' technique. Brilliantly striped patterns are tightly woven in cotton threads, with the extended warp threads drawn out to form the support strings at either end of the hammock. A spacer bar is often included at the top and the hammock sides are decorated with ornamental fringing.

A smaller version of the treadle loom is used for making narrow bands in several villages of Guatemala as well as throughout the regions of Central and South America. It is not known whether the use of similar loom types is due entirely to Spanish influence, or whether they spread with commerce, either by land or by sea. In the village of San Antonio Polopó on the shores of Lake Atitlán in Guatemala, a family of weavers specialized in making tape bands. Their simple loom was set up with two shafts threaded with string heddles with the eye tied in the middle, while two foot treadles were linked to the shafts by a set of pulley wheels. The word 'braid' in its true context means one that is plaited, but by common usage has come to mean any narrow woven construction. These long, flat woven tapes – only about 2.5cm (1in) wide – are woven in a plain colour except for the ends, which are decorated by combining multi-coloured stripes. They are used as hair binders with the plain area twisted around two long ponytails of hair, which are then twined over the head. The decorative ends are crossed at the top to show at the front.

Warping Methods

Whatever the type of loom, the warping threads need to be wound on in an ordered manner. Basically, the continuous warp thread is wound round a series of pegs let into a flat board, or set into the ground at intervals.

A more sophisticated method was to use a circular frame called a 'warping mill', and European-type warping frames were introduced into Mexico by the Spanish. In order to maintain the two separate weave sheds it is necessary to make a 'cross' by winding the warp thread in a 'figure-of-eight' formation. The thread-cross is temporarily tied in position before the loops at one end of the wound warp are slotted onto the loom back bar and the surplus is rolled up. Shed sticks or strings are then inserted to keep the cross formation. There are various methods of threading and tying on, according to the loom type. For looms with fixed shafts and a reed, the threads are taken in sequence from the back to the front, threaded in order through the shaft heddles and finally through the reed divisions before tying on in groups onto the front bar. On the simpler loom types, the warp can be kept as a continuous circle of threads with the tension adjusted by the weaver's body on the back-strap loom or with the adjustment of loom ties on the horizontal loom.

The *jaspe* weavers of central Guatemala wind their long warps over stands set up over a distance along the road-

Opening the 'shed' with the wooden sword – a member of the weaving tour group demonstrates back-strap weaving.

Back-strap weaving in progress – lifting the string heddle rod to form the alternative 'shed' opening between the interlaced warp and weft threads.

verge or down the side of the village main street. This allows them to adjust the *ikat*-dyed warp threads so that the pattern will weave true. When the warp maker is satisfied, the whole warp length is wound up by chaining the initial loop-end through itself and the following loops to make a bundle that will unwind easily when it is set onto the loom. The *ikat* threads are further adjusted when set onto the large treadle looms which take up most of the space in the small village workshops.

String Heddles

The back-strap weavers in San Antonio Palopó use the continuous string heddle method where the string is looped over a rod and then under every alternate warp thread as each thread is slotted by a second person onto the warp beam. Thus the string heddle loops are in position as soon as the finished warp is set onto the small, frame loom.

In most areas of Peru, Guatemala and Mexico where the back-strap loom is used, the string heddles are put in place after the warp has been taken off the warping frame and slotted onto the front and back bars. On the back-strap loom, both ends of one bar are tied to a rope and secured to a post. Both ends of the other bar are secured to the back-strap which goes round the weaver's waist. The initial cross of the threads, which was secured temporarily with string, is held in place with shed sticks: a wide, wooden sword is used to open the shed to lift the warp threads so that they make a space of crossed threads, rather like the interlinked fingers of clasped hands.

In order to make the heddles, a differently coloured length of string is inserted into the open shed and held securely at one end. The coloured string is picked up one loop at a time in sequence from between each thread from the lower warp. The continuous loops of the coloured string heddles are held onto the fingers and then transferred to a rod. When all of these are in place across the row, the coloured string is tied across the rod, over the top to secure all of them in place. When this rod full of coloured string heddles is lifted, all of the alternate warp threads will be lifted.

Four-Selvedge Warping

The advantage of this warping method is that there are no warp ends to finish off, either by knotting or making a hem. It is used mainly for garments where the warp is the correct length for the finished garment, or garment sections, or for making bags and mats. Once the string heddles are put in place, the weaver arranges the warp threads into even groups along the bottom bar. Next, a strong, white thread is inserted into the open shed from left to right, just above the bottom bar. A second bar, which is placed over the warp, is tied firmly at the right-hand end. The free thread-end is taken down through to the back of the warp and then brought up through each warp-group in turn and around the extra bar, thus enclosing both the inner thread and the outer bar in place with a spiral of strong thread. This thread is tied off securely at the opposite end when the binding is complete.

The back-strap ties are transferred to the new bar and the old one is discarded. This new bar is pulled firmly into place. The warp threads are now held onto – but not around – the new bar, in groups, by the string binding. This means that weaving can start at the very bottom of the warp and a few rows are worked to set the weft threads. The loom is then turned upside down and the process repeated for the other end. The weaving is worked from both ends, ending in the middle, or sometimes towards one end. The final threads have to be inserted with a long thin needle, as there

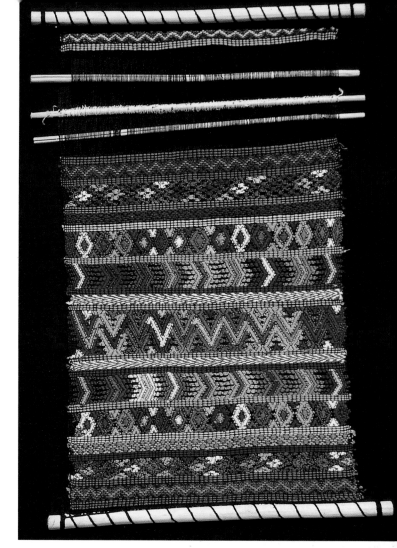

A small back-strap loom from Guatemala shows four-selvedge weaving in progress. The spiral binding threads are seen on the bottom bar and a section of weaving is worked at the top, ready for a join lower down.

is no space left for the shuttle. This can give a distorted area, depending on the skill of the worker and is one of the clues as to whether the fabric is a four selvedge one. This was a favourite method in Bolivia for the little *ch'uspa* bags, woven to contain the day's ration of coca leaves, as well as for other items. The distorted pattern area is generally arranged so that it comes on the lower fold of the bag and this is always covered with a binding or embroidered finish of one kind or another.

Horizontal Scaffold Warps

Janet Willoughby of *Ends of the Earth* has produced an excellent video film showing the women of Pitumarca in the Cuzco area of Peru working on these four-selvedge multi-sectioned warps. The finished construction of the cloth is a series of interlocking linked warp sections that change colours at pre-determined intervals. This is achieved on the four peg horizontal ground warping frame, with the

In Salacaja, Guatemala, a four-shaft frame loom is used to weave the indigo resist-dyed warp threads that form the jaspe *pattern.*

addition of three or more metal rods placed horizontally at intervals across the frame and held upright on the outer sides by 'scaffolding' supports. The loom end bars are tied in place onto their upright pegs and the scaffolding uprights and horizontal bars are lashed together, with the addition of a strong cord passed across each horizontal bar and tied in place.

Two women do the warping, starting with one coloured ball of wool that is passed in a figure of eight formation to each other, from end to end. On the next section, two colours of wool, one from each end, will pass to the first horizontal rod, link and interchange. The next section will interchange colours at the halfway mark and the third intersection at the final rod. When the warping is completed, the horizontal rods are removed, leaving the strong cord in place to hold the sections together. The warp can now be removed and wrapped up, ready to be placed onto a horizontal or a back-strap loom. It is necessary to have a separate set of string heddles for each warp section, as the shed will only open up as far as the linked join. It is possible that this may have been the method used to weave the multi-coloured chequerboard patterns worn by the Inca warriors.

Weaving Types

A balanced weave is one in which the warp and weft threads have equal prominence and requires the same weight of thread for both warp and weft. The warp will be set to interlace equally with the weft, producing a plain or tabby weave. This is the most common type of weave construction and is the basis for many of the decorative effects produced by the addition of supplementary threads. Patterning can be achieved by setting on the warp as a series of coloured stripes, by using stripes in the weft only or by combining both to make a checked fabric. The Paracas textiles dating to the ninth century BC contained all of the techniques subsequently used by the Incas and their descendants and as no complex art appears in its completed form all of a sudden, these techniques must have taken several centuries to develop. Many weaves featured coloured stripes, and the use of *ikat*-dyed threads, either for warp or for weft stripes, is a much favoured pattern element and is found in all of the back-strap weaving areas. Simple, four-shaft treadle looms are used for the *jaspe* weave in the Guatemalan indigo-dye towns of San Cristobal Totonicapan and Salacaja.

Additional patterning can be achieved by altering the number of warp threads that are interlaced by the weft threads. If the weft thread crosses more than one warp thread, this is called a 'float'. Four shafts, lifted in pattern sequence, are needed to make a 'twill' weave where the weft thread float moves one place to the left or to the right on each weft row, giving a diagonal effect. Combinations of these lifts will produce a variety of patterns, but as this is easier to achieve on a treadle loom, was only common after the Spanish Conquest. In Solola and Nahualá in the Guatemalan Highlands where the treadle loom is used, twill weaves give texture to the plaid woollen cloth from which the men's wrap-around 'skirts' are made. On finer fabrics, if

Three warp-faced sashes combining coloured and jaspe-*dyed threads in the stripes* – left: *a belt from Panama;* centre: *a man's sash from San Antonio Palopó;* right: *a sash from the Guatemalan Highlands with anthropomorphic figures in the* jaspe *pattern.*

the weft floats are a prominent feature of the weave and almost cover the surface, this is referred to as a 'satin' weave. The closely packed weft floats reflect the light and give the characteristic glossy appearance to the finished cloth.

Weft-Faced

A weft-faced cloth is one where the crossways weft threads are prominent. This is made possible either by inserting weft threads that are much thicker than the warp threads, or by packing them closely together. This obscures the warp threads so that they are hidden by the weft. A wadding of thick threads will make the weft even more prominent, as in the Peruvian picture weaving from San Pedro de Cajas. Thick rovings of naturally dyed, unspun wool are inserted into the weft, taking precedence over the thin cotton warp threads. This is a comparatively modern innovation as the woven pictures are based on figurative designs and naturalistic scenes, often taken from paintings or photographs. Weft-faced weave methods are used for making horizontally striped fabrics and can be seen in Mexican blankets where plain stripes are emphasized by rows of decorative *ikat* patterning.

Warp-Faced

The complete opposite of the weft-faced method, this weave construction obscures the finer weft threads giving prominence to the heavier or more closely packed warp threads. Warp-faced textiles were discovered among the grave goods in coastal Peru and Columbia. Although the warp was wound on as a continuous length, different colours could be joined in at pre-determined intervals to form the vertical pattern stripes. The weavers of San Antonio Palopó on the shores of Guatemala's Lake Atitlán, use a simple warp-faced method to weave their distinctive striped fabric. The warp threads are tie-dyed in a *jaspe* pattern, combined with plainer stripes which help the *jaspe* pattern to stand out.

Warp-faced patterns have been used for thousands of years to weave bands, belts and even wider fabrics. Colour-threads are selected from the warp by the worker, either by fingers or a pick-up stick made from wood or from llama bone. These selected threads, which are changed for each pattern row, are held up to make a shed while the weft thread is passed behind. If the same thread is selected for several rows, a warp float will appear. Each weft-thread row is beaten down well so that it sinks within the patterning. This is a time-consuming method, but most effective and special pieces rank as high art, rather than everyday craft.

Double Weave

The warp can be set on in a variety of ways to give a plain-weave cloth that is a complete tube, or a tube open on one side that will open out to double width, or two separate pieces of cloth open at both sides layered one above the other. Two colours can alternate, so that one warp layer can be dark and the other can be light. This allows the weaver to make patterns that can interchange by picking up the light threads from below with the pick-up stick, bringing them up to the dark layer. These counter-change patterns, which are such are a distinctive feature of Bolivian weaving, can be shown as both positive and negative elements on the same side of the fabric. They appear on their belts, headbands and coca-leaf carrying bags and show many of the creatures and mythical symbols described in a previous chapter. A Paracas double-cloth weaving from about 600BC shows an anthropomorphic figure worked on brown cotton with geometric style outlines in white cotton, reversing to brown outlines on white. A double-weave cloth showing a repeat pattern of pelicans, is one of the outstanding items in the collection of the Museum of Archaeology and Anthropology, Cambridge University.

After the Conquest and the introduction of the treadle loom, double weave, worked with four heddle-shafts, would provide a counter-change cloth where the pattern is repeated in sequence across the weft, to make an overall design. This is the type of patterning used on the Welsh blankets and the coverlets of Colonial America.

Tapestry

Tapestry weave is a discontinuous weft construction: the weft threads do not pass across the entire width of the cloth, but form woven areas that are built up individually in different colours to form a pattern. These patterned sections can be divided from one another, interlink or alternate to form an integrated area. A series of woven areas are worked individually across the weft, with each section beaten down well with a tool or a rug comb. Gradually these sections will build up to make the whole design, which may cover the entire warp, or form a border within a plain weave. Sections that are not linked with their neighbours form tapestry 'slits' and are often included as part of the design. In some instances, these slits are sewn together after the weaving is finished. Colours that are worked in a series of short rows that interchange to give the appearance of colours seeping into one another are referred to as 'hatching'.

Some of the early twelfth century woven textiles found in the Chancay Valley area of central Peru, are woven in the tapestry technique. One in the Amano Museum, Lima, shows little figures wearing headdresses, seated between

ABOVE: *A duck forms the motif on a tapestry-woven mat from Peru.*

BELOW: *Reverse of the mat, showing the technique of linked-thread sections.*

giant centipedes. Each figure is contained in a rectangular block with the slits visible at the sides where they have come apart. Lengthways rows of these blocks would be woven on a narrow loom and joined together afterwards to make a larger hanging. An almost complete tapestry tunic was

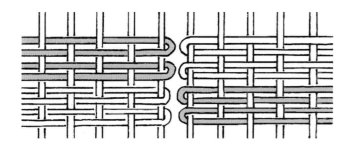

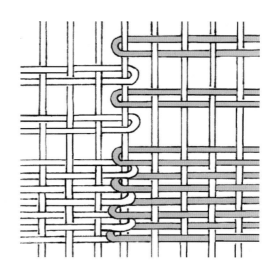

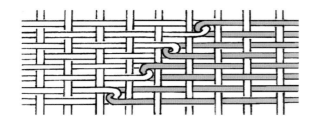

Tapestry-weave techniques – top left: tapestry slit; right: dovetail joins; lower left: linked joins.

found on a mummy figurine from the south-coast Peruvian Huari culture, dating from AD600–800. These tunics usually form one of the outer layers of the bundle containing the mummified corpse. The separate design elements in the tapestry are joined by interlocking – a highland technique. There are several examples of these Huari tunics in the Amano Museum, Lima. The warp would be of cotton and the weft of alpaca. The design elements contain many of the Huari symbols shown on their decorated pottery. Another Huari culture textile shows a version of the tapestry technique combined with darning in a multi-coloured tie-dyed alpaca mantle. This has separate weave sections formed by crenulated pieces that are later joined to plain and tie-dyed squares, with their warps interlocking. The degree of textile expertise needed to make this garment implies that it must have been reserved for a high-ranking person.

Today, tapestry woven rugs are a source of income for the weavers of Santa Anna in Ayacucho, Peru. Many of these contemporary rug designs have a definite link with the past, showing patterns and symbols that would have been familiar to the pre-Conquest weavers. Birds, insects, small animals and flowers are often combined with geometric patterns and zigzag lines. Nowadays these rugs and wall hangings are made on the treadle loom, frequently set up in the weaver's home. Although mainly synthetic dyes are used, the colours chosen are not strident, possibly a reminder of the softer shades once obtained from the natural dyes.

Supplementary Weft Techniques

A supplementary weft is one that is additional to the main weft threads that form part of the fabric construction. The supplementary weft is added during the weaving process. The various kinds of supplementary weft patterns have been used in both Central and South America for many hundreds of years. The technique was one of the splendours of pre-Hispanic weaving, with many examples found in the Paracas, Chancay and Nazca cultures.

A proud mother shows off her baby wearing a distinctive brocade woven hat – from San Antonio Aquas Calientes.

Maria Lopez from San Antonio Aquas Calientes working inlaid brocade techniques on her back-strap loom.

Brocading

Brocading is a technique found in many countries across the globe. There is some confusion in the use of this term as it often employed to describe a fabric enriched with metal thread patterning. It is referred to as 'continuous supplementary weft' patterning and whether the additional threads are of wool, cotton or gold, the technique is the same. Here the supplementary, or extra thread is passed right across the distance of the weft, sandwiched between one of the open sheds. This thread can be let in singly or worked in and out of a series of weft threads to form a pattern. If the weft thread crosses over more than one warp thread it is called a 'weft-float'. These weft threads can be laid within the upper warp layer only, called 'single-faced' or 'open-shed' brocading. The pattern threads show more prominently on the weave surface as the brocade threads do not pass through to the underneath surface of the weaving. If they are worked in and out of both warp

layers simultaneously, they form a 'two-faced' or 'closed-shed' brocade. Here the inverse of the pattern will appear on the back of the fabric. In a 'double-faced' brocade, the pattern will be the same on both sides of the fabric. Here the pattern thread is inserted between corresponding threads from an upper and a lower warp, using a pick-up stick to select the warp threads.

After each pattern-thread row, the normal tabby weaving process is continued, thus binding the pattern-thread securely in place. The shed is changed and the pattern threads continue back the other way. The pattern sequence is achieved by working the thread in an out of the counted warps with the pick-up stick or a long needle. On a four-shaft loom, the patterning is determined by the threading sequence of the shafts and the lifting order of the pedals.

In a 'discontinuous supplementary weft' technique the extra weft threads do not extend right across the weft width, rather they are worked in blocks of patterning that can be linked together or remain as isolated motifs. When the

thread is worked back across the pattern block the loop at the end is called a 'turn', which can be on the front or the reverse of the work. Once again, this technique can be worked on the open-shed or around the closed-shed warp-threads. If the weft thread is laid into an open shed without forming any weft floats it is called 'inlay'. Small pattern areas can be worked at intervals with the turning threads showing on the front or on the back. Whichever pattern method is chosen, the finished row is always held in place with a normal tabby weft-pass. A combination of these techniques can produce the most intricate pattern sequences, many of which resemble surface-stitched embroidery.

Maria Lopez, the weaver from Aquas Calientes in the Antigua Guatemala area, was a master of this art. Kneeling in front of her back-strap loom, she inserted numerous coloured threads across the weft row, deftly selecting the pattern warps with her pointed stick before manipulating the sequence of coloured threads. The surplus of each colour thread hung down onto the front weave surface, ready to be used again on the following row. She kept them in order and they did not tangle. New threads were added when the old ones ran out by inserting the thread end between the weft a short distance from the pattern area. This would be enclosed by the tabby weave after the next binding row.

LEFT: *Selecting the pattern warp threads with the pick-up stick.*

BELOW: *Measuring out threads for the continuous brocade stripes.*

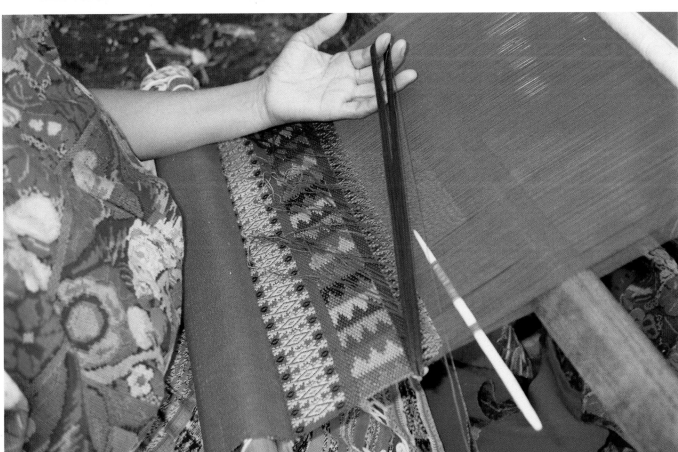

A huipil from San Antonio Aquas Calientes, woven in a combination of single-faced brocading and a double-faced brocade technique – made by Erica Lilian Lopez, 1994.

The weavers of the Chiapas Highlands of Mexico use a supplementary weft technique where the threads go in and out of the entire warp, thus producing a positive and negative image. The fingers manipulate the inlay threads that hang down behind the work, without the use of a pick-up stick. One plain weft thread is worked in tabby weave between each pattern row and when completed, a curved bone needle is used to raise up the pattern stitches so that they stand above the plain weave on the front. It is said that the brocade weaving techniques used by the Mexican Huave people were brought from Nicaragua by the Zapotecs.

Modern weavers from San Antonio, Aquas Calientes in Guatemala are equally proficient at double-faced brocading where the woven pattern appears the same on both sides of the fabric. This time-consuming technique entails the use of a pick-up stick to select the warp threads for the pattern area.

*A detail of the double-faced brocaded shoulder area showing
a pair of Quetzal birds in a jungle setting.*

The coloured threads, which hang down behind the work, are inserted one at a time into the picked-up area by hand, gradually working across the row. The double-faced pattern weaving is reserved for the shoulder area of the *huipil* blouse while the rest of the garment is of single-faced brocade. Although contemporary colours are very vibrant, they suit the subject matter of tropical vegetation, exotic flowers and Quetzal birds with long tails.

Wrapping

When the pattern thread is bound completely round a group of warp threads it is known as 'wrapping'. The wrapping can take several directions. A series of diagonal stitches can be worked up the cloth, similar to stem stitches in embroidery. These can reverse direction on subsequent rows giving a zigzag effect. Horizontal wrapped threads, also

known as *soumak*, lie parallel to the cloth weft. This for-
wards-and-backwards wrapping technique is especially
popular in Guatemala and is used to work their favourite little animals and birds, giving an almost padded appearance.

In vertical wrapping, the horizontal pattern threads are
worked up the cloth resulting in a two-faced design that
resembles satin stitch. Vertical wrapping on an open shed
will produce a pattern that looks similar on the surface to
the previous one, but without the floats showing on the
back. The Trique peoples of southern Mexico use this technique to decorate their *huipils*.

The collars and cuffs worn by the men of Todos Santos in
the Cuchumatan mountain area of Guatemala, are woven
by the women on the back-strap loom. This close patterning formation is achieved by finger wrapping the colour
thread around a single warp thread at a time, into the top
shed of the work. Two plain weft rows secure the patterning,
which barely shows on the back.

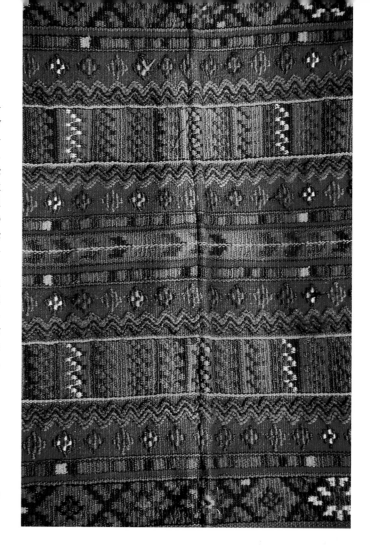

*RIGHT: A man's shirt collar from Todos Santos Cuchumatan woven in a
single-faced, wrapped-brocade technique. Shown as woven, but worn
folded in half.*

*BELOW: Huipil from Panajachel, Guatemala. The wrapped brocading is
woven into the front shed only, leaving the reverse fabric plain.
This gives the little animals and birds a padded appearance.*

Each area of Guatemala has its own patterning method, so that *huipil* blouses, skirts, shawls and the men's trousers are quite distinctive, making it possible to name the very villages from which the weaving originates. The same holds true for Mexico as well as all the weaving areas of Central and South America. It is to be hoped that this distinction does not fade with outside influences and thus diminish the sense of a community belonging to a particular geographical area.

All of these supplementary weft techniques are dealt with fully by Lena Bjerregaard in *Techniques of Guatemalan Weaving* and by Suzanne Baizerman and Karen Searle in *Latin American Brocades*. Excellent diagrams of 'Simple and Multiple Weft Wrapping' techniques can be found in *Textiles, a Classification of Techniques* by Annemarie Seiler-Baldinger. The video films produced by Janet Willoughby of *Ends of the Earth* are invaluable as a visual reference source for all of the warping, weaving and brocading techniques.

Leno and Gauze Weave

Normally the warp threads do not cross over one another, but are intertwined in various combinations with the weft threads to form the patterns. The exception is found in the 'Leno' weaving technique weave where an open pattern construction is formed by twisting selected warp threads across one another. This forms a hole adjacent to the twisted warp, giving a lacy effect. Separate heddle threads called 'leashes' are threaded round chosen warp threads along the row and lifted to either side to achieve the pattern. After the weft thread is taken across, the leashes lift the warps the opposite way, thus enclosing the weft. An alternative method is for the weaver to lift the adjacent warp threads over one another before inserting the weft thread by hand.

Leno weave is not the same as the spaced or gauze-weave constructions, well known to the weavers of ancient Peru. These openwork fabrics were achieved by omitting sections of both the warp and the weft threads. The warp threads would be spaced out by setting them on in groups at pre-determined intervals. A corresponding space would be left when aligning the weft thread intersections and at times the weavers secured these intersections with a knot to prevent the movement of the thread blocks. In some instances the thread intersections were drawn up to such an extent that they form a bound pattern, totally altering the character of the textile. Another method uses plain tabby-weave rows alternating with tapestry-woven weft blocks to form a similar open construction, while a lozenge pattern was achieved by linking a series of tapestry-woven free warp sections at regular intervals. The permutations afforded by these methods allowed the weavers to create numerous open-weave variations. Several of these methods are illustrated in Raoul d'Harcourt's book, *Textiles of Ancient Peru and Their Techniques*.

Pre-Conquest Weaving Methods

We have already examined several of the pre-Conquest weaving methods. Most of the examples of woven cloth that remain to us are from the dry desert areas of north-western South America. Few examples have survived the humid climate of Central America, but there is no doubt that their weavers were equally proficient in all of the textile arts.

Embroidery on the Loom

It is easy to mistake supplementary weft techniques for embroidery and this is the one subject that is open to discussion. The many examples of decorated textiles found in the Paracas, Nasca and Chancay cultures feature what is generally referred to as 'stem-stitch embroidery'. The term 'embroidery' means a decoration that is applied to the finished cloth, after the woven fabric is removed from the loom. Therefore the embroidery is additional to the weaving construction. Remove the embroidery threads and the ground fabric is not altered in any way. Diagrams of the counted thread stem stitch and satin stitch decorations are frequently shown using embroidery stitches rather than supplementary weft insertions. As the ground fabrics are closely woven with a high count of warps per inch, a very fine metal needle would be necessary to achieve the close stitching that at times covers most of the warp threads. So far, no examples of metal needles have been found in the ancient tombs, although there are examples of cactus thorns with pierced holes, kept in cane cases. Llama bone needles were readily available, but these are not fine enough for detailed embroidery. They are easy to sharpen, but apt to splinter.

These ancient cultures were highly skilled in the art of metallurgy, but the only minerals readily available to them were the soft metals – silver, gold and copper – but with tin, lead, and platinum used less frequently. The working of gold metal does not appear in Peru until over a thousand years after the art of loom embroidery had been perfected. Some of the earliest embossed sheet-metal ornaments from Chongoyape in Peru were made sometime between 1000–500BC and the art did not reach the valley of Oaxaca in Mexico until about AD900. Gold casting did not begin until sometime during the first centuries AD in the Mochica area of northern Peru. It was possibly from here that it spread northwards into Ecuador, Colombia, Panama, Costa Rica, and finally Mexico. Some archaeological finds in western Mexico suggest that knowledge of the craft came by sea, rather than overland from South America. Needles of gold or silver would be very flexible and bend too easily; the only possibility was copper, which becomes hardened by a process of cold hammering and annealing. Even then the needles would soon blunt and need continual sharpening.

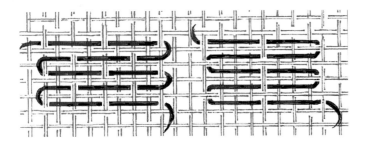
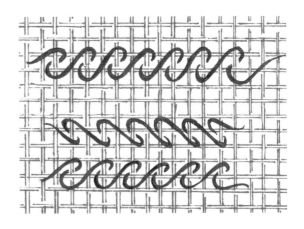
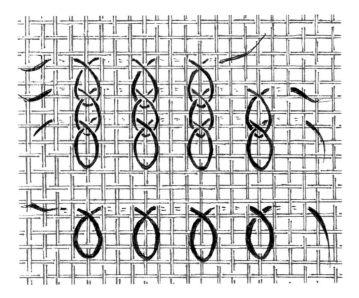
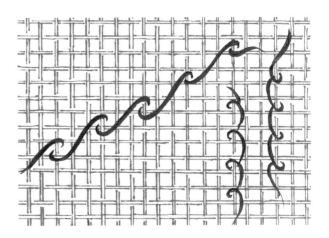

Brocade-weave techniques – top left: inlaid supplementary wefts showing turns on the right side and turns on the wrong side; top right and bottom right: supplementary weft-wrapped warps; bottom left: pile-loop techniques, the lower loops hanging free, the upper rows linked through the loops beneath.

In Europe, apart from the early bronze-age needles, the first iron needles were made by the Romans and they continued to be produced well into the fourteenth century. These needles had no eye but a closed hook to keep the thread. Needles with eyes were eventually manufactured in the Low Countries during the fifteenth century, although steel was considered hard to work and seldom used. As a result they were rare and coveted items. Earlier, the Spanish had discovered the secret of making steel needles from the Moors when Spain was under Arab rule. The Spanish metal workers took their knowledge to other European countries when some of them were evicted from their homeland and it was the Spanish who eventually introduced steel needles into the New World.

Lena Bjerregaard, writing in her book *Techniques of Guatemalan Weaving*, states that it is easier to work single-faced brocade patterns on the loom than it is to embroider them, while Frances Schaill Goodman, referring to what she calls 'finger-weaving or loom embroidery' in her book *The Embroidery of Mexico and Guatemala*, makes an additional point, saying that needle-worked embroidery stitches are more likely to pierce the background threads unevenly, and do not necessarily fit exactly between the weft-thread pairs.

An experienced weaver, who is also an embroiderer, knows that it is much quicker and easier to insert the threads with the fingers and use of the pick-up stick, rather than set to work afterwards with a needle and thread. The warp is not static, but a set of supple, longitudinal threads that can be divided by the fingers, opened out in order to insert or manipulate a decorative thread and then released to close up again. The speed with which Maria inserted her pattern threads across the row indicates that this a preferred and practical method and the video films of the present day back-strap weavers of Guatemala, Mexico and Peru demonstrate this technique to perfection. Examples of patterning on double cloth from Paracas dating to 600BC prove that the ancient weavers were already past masters in the art of thread manipulation and in a contemporary context, there are several weaving societies in areas of the world such as Bhutan and south-western China where equally intricate patterns are worked on the loom as an inlaid woven thread technique.

The only way in which this question can be resolved is to find a piece of Paracas 'embroidery' where the embroidery thread pierces either the warp or the weft threads. If woven, then all of the decorative threads will pass between, or wrap over, or around the basic warp threads. If the stem stitches are worked backwards over more than one weft row below, then they would need to be stitched as embroidery, as in weaving it is possible to insert the thread any number of rows upwards, but not to go back downwards.

At times it is very difficult to distinguish modern 'brocade embroidery' from hand embroidery. A pair of striped trousers, purchased in Solola market, are decorated with what at first appears to be hand-embroidered satin stitch over the striped fabric. Closer inspection reveals that the supplementary threads are introduced during the weaving process, with the various colours worked up the stripes in a horizontal figure-of-eight formation while at the same time linking on each row with the neighbouring colours. One pattern is exactly the same on the reverse, the other has a slight difference. Starting and finishing threads are enclosed within the weave structure, making them almost invisible. The contemporary use of stranded embroidery threads for inlay weaving, makes identification even more difficult.

Embroidery threads would be easy to insert into the gauze and leno type fabrics when removed from the loom as the spaces would allow a bone or wooden needle to be passed through easily. This would necessitate stretching the fabric onto a frame before the embroidery could be started, so it would be much more logical to work the embroidery while still at tension on the loom, rather than frame it a second time. Bone needles are still in use for inserting the central threads in the four-selvedge loom technique and used in some areas as a pick-up stick for choosing the pattern threads.

Pile and Loop-Stitch Weaving

Pile weaving is one of the rug-loom or velvet-weaving techniques where rows of loops are formed by the fingers, or by winding the weft thread round a rod to form each loop. A single plain weft row or a number of weft thread rows are inserted into the warp at pre-determined intervals after each loop row is formed. These loops can be set apart, or worked

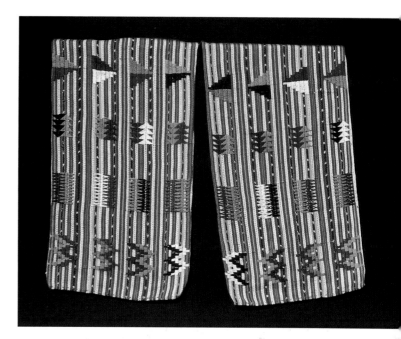

ABOVE: *A man's pair of trousers from Solola, near Lake Atitlán. Double-faced brocade threads decorate the lower legs.*

BELOW: *Detail of the brocade technique showing, at the top, the figure-of-eight formation and at the bottom the two-faced brocading.*

very closely to make an overlapping pile as subsequent rows are added. The rod is removed after each row and the loops can be cut through or left whole. This is similar to, but not the same as, the Asian technique for making knotted-pile rugs where the yarn is cut after each knot has been inserted into the warp by hand.

Supplementary threads that are inserted on the loom during the weaving process can be worked sideways, upwards, diagonally or wrap the warps completely. These loom stitches cannot be worked back downwards, which means that chained stitches that are not embroidered would need to be worked on the loom using pile-weaving methods, where the starting loop is supported and always hangs downwards. Unlike embroidery, where the chain stitches are worked downwards from top to bottom, the pile-weave process requires that the chain stitches are formed from the bottom upwards as the weave progresses.

Several of the early textiles included looped structures where the chained loops are worked upwards in a series of interconnecting vertical lines with the loop threads of the following row linked behind the loops of the first row and then every subsequent row in turn, giving the appearance of cross-knit looping. This method would require the use of a pick-up stick or a bone needle, and in this way quite complicated chained formations can be worked. Each row of loops is secured with at least two weft-thread passes in tabby weave. True embroidered chain stitches are dealt with in Chapter 7 – Embroidery and Appliqué.

Another possibility is the technique described by Birgit Olson Barron as 'Knitting on the Loom' in her booklet of the same title. She describes a method where a 'ladder' of weft thread loops is left as a gap within the tabby weave structure, by twisting the weft thread around a rod or needle in the same vertical ladder position on every subsequent row. When the rod is removed, the first and every following vertical loop is drawn through the one above with a hook, to form a line of chain stitches going up the woven cloth. These chain stitches can be worked as a single vertical line, or as a series of adjacent vertical lines and different patterning methods are obtained by the order in which the loops are intersected. Weft rows can be skipped and a pattern of diagonal chain-stitch lines can be worked upwards on the weft floats of a twill weave. It is easy to jump to conclusions when examining ancient textiles, as there are generally several alternative methods that may have been used.

Feathers in Weaving

Apart from the use of feathers worn to deflect arrows in the context of armour, feathers were also used to decorate entire garments. The peoples of the arid coastal deserts of Peru and the inhabitants of the mountain areas regarded the feathers of tropical birds as items of luxury as they would have to be traded with the tribes from the Amazon jungles. The feathers were attached in a similar manner to that of forming the armour. The quill ends of the feathers are bound to a cotton cord and these cords are usually incorporated within the weaving, but the feathers can be attached to the cotton backing fabric, held with a type of starch-paste or natural glue. Similar techniques were employed for making the feather cloaks worn by the Maya and Aztec chiefs in Central America, where the many species of tropical birds provided a plentiful supply of colourful feathers.

Feathers were inserted within the weaving by first securing each one to a weft thread at intervals. The end of the feather quill might be folded over and tied in with a knot, or the feather end was first wrapped and then secured. A second row of knots was made below the first one, in order to prevent the feathers from slipping sideways. These feather-knotted threads were then inserted into the weaving as a weft thread and subsequently secured with a tabby weave. Various methods of securing feathers are illustrated in Raoul d'Harcourt's *Textiles of Ancient Peru* and in Annemarie Seiler-Baldinger's *Textiles, a Classification of Techniques*. Overlapping rows of these feathers were used to make the wonderful feather capes and tunics of the Peruvian Chimú culture, from AD 1000–400. A Nasca feather tunic in the collection of the Cambridge University Museum of Archaeology and Anthropology shows this construction. On several parallel rows within the woven cloth, the feathers have worn away to leave only the raised protrusion of the tied insertion thread that once held the feathers. From this it is apparent that the feathers were inserted at close intervals, so that the quills at one time were almost touching and the rows are set at approximately 2.5cm (1in) apart, but this would alter in relation to the length of the feather size chosen. The feather workers from Chimú chose the brightest feathers for their creations. A feather-decorated fragment in the Ethnographic collection of Birmingham Museum and Art Gallery shows a selection of colours. Feathers were obtained from the blue-and-yellow macaw, the scarlet macaw and the red-and-green macaw as well as a variety of other birds.

The people of the Peruvian Ica-Chincha culture, dating from AD 1200–400 covered their tunics and ceremonial cloaks with designs and motifs worked in different coloured feathers. A feathered tunic in the Amano Museum, Lima, shows angular figures with upturned arms in a design very similar to an earlier feather *coraza* or ceremonial chest piece from the Nazca culture of southern coastal Peru dated from AD 100–600. As these figures are not depicted on the later woven textiles, it would appear that certain designs which originally were worked in feathers continued to be used, but only in the context of feather decoration – a technique which demanded overlapping rows, thus forming an angular pattern.

A large fragment of feather work – Chimú/Inca AD1200–1530.
(Accession No. 2005.2479. Birmingham Museums & Art Gallery.
Dimensions 37 × 27 × 2cm (14½ × 10½ × ¾in)).

There is a long tradition of working with feathers in the Mexican state of Chiapas. Even during the latter part of the twentieth century, the actual feathers were woven into the cloth to make feather borders, in the same way that tufts of fine fur or strips of leather had been included in the past.

All of the peoples of Central and South America were equally talented in the arts of weaving. Designs would naturally differ from area to area, but as the basic weave constructions are common to all, the finished results have a definite affinity. The main difference would be in the base materials used – cotton and bast fibres in the hot and humid regions; wool, llama hair or a mixture of cotton and hair in the colder districts. It is not surprising that these woven fabrics formed the economic base of all the countries of the pre-Hispanic Americas. Although weavers were still held in high esteem, the appreciation of weaving as an art decreased once a monetary system was introduced and, gradually, a different set of values was accepted.

6

Costume and Accessories

Garment Structure Based on Woven-Cloth

No weaver, who has spent many weeks' perfecting a piece of cloth, takes kindly to having the resulting fabric cut. A special piece of cloth woven for a religious ceremony was in itself regarded as an object with cult significance. To cut it would be an act of desecration. Any piece of hand-woven cloth is imbued with certain mystical properties, evidence of the magical interplay of threads that combine to make a fabric that is both strong and supple, that can be lightweight but at the same time give comforting warmth. Wrapping the woven cloth around a person would transfer some of the properties of the weaving to the wearer. The high priest, clothed in a patterned garment that had taken many months to weave, would have his status increased purely by association.

A length of cloth used as a shawl, cape or covering is common to all areas, both geographically and through time. The same cloth could double as a blanket or a carrying cloth for goods or for the baby. In Mexico a rectangular shawl called a *rebozo* has been worn by the women since the time of the Conquest, a development of earlier costume. A similar length of cloth is worn today in Guatemala as a protection from the sun, in exactly the same way that the women of Bolivia and Peru wear an extra wrap called a *manta* to keep out the cold. Women from Tenejapa in the Chiapas Highlands of Mexico wore a square shawl with the two top corners tied diagonally across one shoulder and then under one arm. Presumably this was less likely to slip off in wear as this method is seen in many other areas and was even used to wrap the baby onto the mother's back with the additional corners tied underneath.

In areas of Guatemala men still wear a rectangular woven blanket over their trousers called a *ponchito* or a *rodillera*. This blanket transmutes into a hip cloth or a skirt. Small *ponchitos* can be folded and hang down in front like an apron or a loin cloth. It would seem that there is no end to the diverse ways in which these rectangular pieces of fabric are used.

OPPOSITE PAGE:
Two women display their embroidered blouses and jaspe *woven skirts –*
the baby is held by a shawl with a striped bag on top –
from Almalonga market, Guatemala.

RIGHT: A woman sits in Chichicastenango market, Guatemala, wearing
the typical striped huipil *and the folded* tzute *headcloth.*

Basic Shapes

After a period of time the single piece of cloth was joined together by seaming or over-sewing. The best-known garment in the Peruvian and Bolivian areas is the poncho. This is made from two oblongs of woven cloth joined together with a central seam, but with an opening for the neck left in the middle. The resulting rectangular shape can be left plain, or finished with fringing on all four sides. Some experts believe that the poncho, which is not joined down the sides, was a pre-cursor of the tunic, others think that it developed after the introduction of Spanish horses, the open sides making it suitable for riding when it was taken up by the Spanish cavalry.

Another version of the South American poncho was made from two rectangles of cloth sewn together across the shoulder seam, leaving a space for the neck. This time the width of the cloth would form the neck to hem measurement and any weft striped patterning would lie vertically. Eventually, the length of fabric would be folded across the shoulders and a horizontal slit made for the neck by finishing off and re-starting a section of the weaving. A further development was to arrange the neck slit vertically into the centre of the cloth where it was folded to make the shoulders. This was achieved by weaving each side section of the neck area independently, then re-joining when the slit was completed. One Mexican construction type was formed of three narrow lengths of cloth, each one having selvedges on all four sides, which were seamed together to form one long oblong. This was folded across at the shoulders with a vertical slit in the central panel for the neck opening. None of these garments was sewn up the sides.

In Columbia an over-wrap is made from two long pieces of woven cloth, which are joined down the centre back, leaving the front pieces open. In a second version, two oblongs of cloth are seamed together at right angles by joining the short end of one piece to the lower, long section of the other piece. Depending on the length of the panels, it can be worn with ends that hang down the front or be thrown across one or both shoulders. The Columbian climate is very varied and it is said that they experience all four seasonal changes every day, making this a versatile garment. Today it is even worn by businessmen over their suits in the capital city of Bogota. The best ones are made from alpaca wool and are worn as a status symbol.

The Mexican *sarape* is formed from an oblong panel of weaving with a slit in the middle for the head. It could be worn as a type of poncho with the head passing through the slit or as a cloak with one end thrown over the shoulder. The *chamarros*, a smaller version found in the Chiapas Highlands, is finished with a fringe at both ends. Complex weave and embroidery patterning techniques made this a prestigious accessory and tapestry woven *sarapes* were produced in the northern town of Saltillo during the nineteenth century. Woven with a woollen weft on a cotton warp, they developed originally from the woven blankets that were traded during the late eighteenth century. The design elements included the serrated diamond shape that is connected with the symbol of the planet Venus, which still appears in modern Mexican weaving. According to Judy Cheyney, writing in the *Journal for Weavers, Spinners and Dyers*, designs changed after Mexican independence in 1821, gradually adapting to the aristocratic tastes prevalent under the reign of Archduke Maximilian during the 1860s. With the introduction of threads from France, colours became brighter and flamboyant floral designs replaced the geometric motifs of the past.

A Mexican version of the poncho, which is called the *quechquémitl*, is joined in different ways and resembles a shoulder cape. In one version, two oblongs of cloth are seamed together in the same way as the Colombian wrap, then both pieces are folded in half and the other ends joined together in a similar manner. This results in a diamond-shaped poncho-type garment with a 'V'- shaped neck. These capes were decorated in many ways, but deep striped borders, following the 'V' shape, were the most effective. A simpler Mexican version is to take two squares of cloth and place together on top of one another so that they form a diamond shape. The two bottom sides of the diamond sides are left open and the top sides are oversewn together, leaving two 'V'-shaped flaps for the neck opening at the top. The corners are worn to the front and back, but married women may choose to wear them hanging at the sides. The *quechquémitl* is a garment unique to the Central American area of Mexico, but excluding the Yucatan peninsula and neighbouring Guatemala. According to Frances Schaill Goodman, writing in *The Embroidery of Mexico and Guatemala*, the tropical areas of the Yucatan and of Guatemala share the background of a Mayan heritage and this may have influenced the way their costume developed.

The word 'blouse' is sometimes used to describe a garment that is straight cut – only if the sleeve pieces are joined on at the sides to make a 'T'-shaped garment, is it considered to be a tunic. As most people tend to think of a blouse as a garment that reaches to about waist level, then a tunic is possibly a more acceptable description. Long cloaks, constructed in a similar manner to the poncho, have been found wrapped around mummies, but as many were also clad in simple tunic-blouses, it is difficult to surmise which came first. The basic tunic is made from two rectangular pieces of woven cloth, half as wide and twice as long as the finished garment. The lengths are folded in half across the width and both are joined together by a central seam, leaving an opening in the middle for the head to pass through. The side seams are sewn upwards from the hem, leaving spaces at the top to act as armholes. The fullness of the garment would be held in by a woven sash or a belt. The side

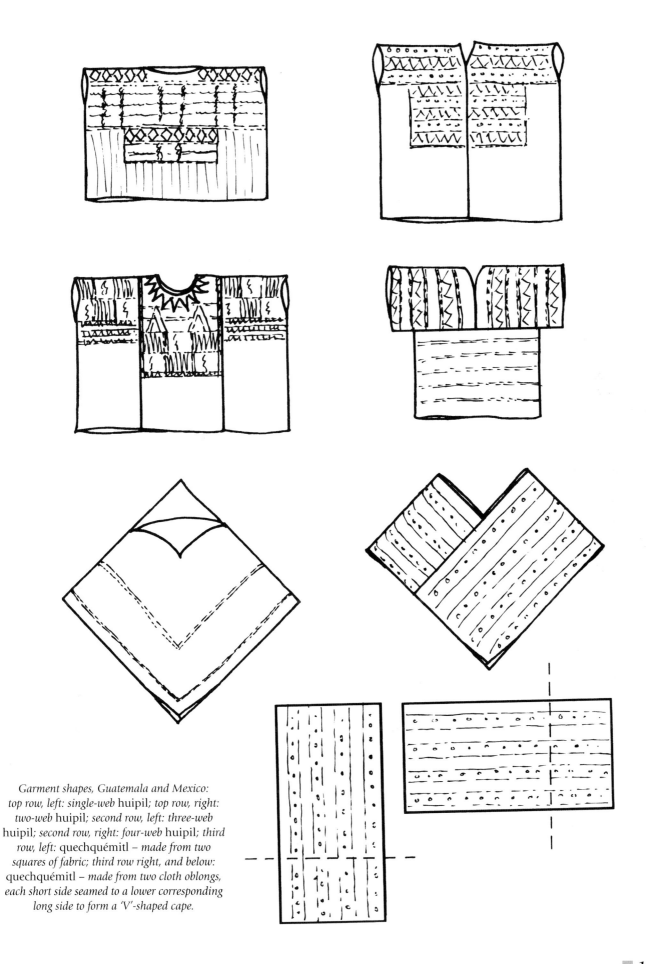

Garment shapes, Guatemala and Mexico: top row, left: single-web *huipil; top row, right: two-web* huipil; *second row, left: three-web* huipil; *second row, right: four-web* huipil; *third row, left:* quechquémitl *– made from two squares of fabric; third row right, and below:* quechquémitl *– made from two cloth oblongs, each short side seamed to a lower corresponding long side to form a 'V'-shaped cape.*

seams could be left open as slits at the base of the tunic to give ease when walking or doing manual work. If the four-selvedge weaving technique was used, there was no need to neaten the hem. Alternatively, warp ends were plaited or left as a secured fringe. For special garments the weavers were expert enough to make rounded corners to the tunic hems as part of the weave construction by substituting warp for weft threads at the weaving base.

South America

Pre-Inca Costume

The earliest garment shapes of about 700BC, which come from the archaeological finds from Paracas in north-western Peru, are formed from predetermined fabric lengths. Many of these finds are fragmental, but careful unwrapping of the mummy bundles revealed a surprising diversity of garments, some still in a condition that revealed their construction and type of decoration. The mantle is a garment frequently found in connection with the early grave goods, often forming one of the outer layers before the final wrapping, so must have been regarded as an article of some importance.

For men, the sleeveless tunic top was very short – coming to just about waist level – a shape that appears to have been universal – but there was a choice of lower garments. A loincloth, or breechcloth, was worn as an outer garment but as there was also a choice of wrap-around skirt, coming to just above the knee, a loincloth was probably worn underneath this as well. The short skirt was held around the waist with ties and at times was decorated with pleats at the hem. Both garment sets would be topped with a small poncho and a band of cloth was tied around the head with the ends hanging down the back, or the cloth was worn in the form of a wrapped turban. The mantle cloak, woven in a mixture of cotton and wool, would be worn over the top of everything, either for warmth or as a status symbol. The different articles of clothing were often ornamented with stripes or symbols within the weave and sets of garments found in the Paracas graves are decorated with design elements common to each set, with border patterns repeated on both the mantle and the tunic hems. Similar pattern sets were found in the graves of the Chimú culture, dating up to 1,000 years later. Apart from the fact that the loincloths were larger, with ties that had increased in size to form a panel in front that resembled a skirt and that the tunics now had sleeves, the garments were still very similar.

Research has shown that many of the funerary garments appear to have been made especially for the internment, some to a smaller scale than normal. Others are obviously original garments, showing stains and signs of wear with areas that have been carefully mended. Although the body was clothed in the very best garments to assure an appropriate position in the afterlife, those that had been worn in life are sometimes ripped, torn or knotted. This was possibly to destroy the garment so that evil spirits did not enter into a 'living' fabric and harm the deceased. This concept did not apply only to the dead for it is said that any clothing no longer worn by Emperor Atahualpa was ritually burned each year to prevent a similar occurrence.

According to depictions on the ceramics of the time, women's costume was similar in concept to that of the men, but they wore a longer tunic covered by a shorter mantle. Versions and adaptations of these garments continued to be worn for many hundreds of years. As the decorative aspect of the weaving was of prime importance, a society whose wealth and status was expressed in the beauty and complexity of the cloth had no need to change the form of their simple garments.

Men's Costume – Inca to Post-Conquest

In Inca times the Bolivian men of the highlands wore a knee-length tunic and loincloth in the same style as their ancestors. In Quechua language the tunic was called the *unku* – a word that now refers to the shoulder cape or *ponchito*, still worn by the men of Tarabuscan. In both Bolivia and Peru, the tunic, which was generally woven in a decorative warp-faced technique, was made from two lengths of cloth joined vertically in the middle with an opening for the head. Longer and more decorative tunics woven with chequerboard and geometric patterns were reserved for the noblemen and for priests or government officials. The tunic would be covered by a mantle, which was worn knotted over the shoulder. This, as in the past, could be removed and used for other purposes such as a bedcover, a sitting cloth or for carrying goods. In the tropical regions of Columbia and Venezuela, the men of the Waayu tribes have long worn a loincloth called a *guayuco* and little else in a hot climate, except for feather headdresses and decorations.

Women's Costume – Inca to Post-Conquest

Women's garments were mainly adaptations following the woven culture of the earlier civilizations. In a society where garment shaping was not considered necessary, it was inevitable that changes would be slow and depend more on the development of patterning methods rather than alteration of cut. The Inca women wore a long tunic called an *aksu*. An oblong of cloth encircled the body, rather like a sarong, with the two ends taken from the back over the shoulders and fastened at the front with silver pins. All was held in place with a sash. On top she would wear a cloak called an *lliclla* in the Quechua dialect. Made from two joined oblongs of cloth to form a larger rectangle, it was held round the shoulders and fastened at the front with a decorative silver pin, or tied together at the front with a knot. At times the top section was folded over to make an extra layer around the shoulders to protect against rain or the cold. This simple, rectangular woven cloak is still in use today, sometimes held together with an ordinary safety pin. Occasionally it is worn over a machine-knitted cardigan worn together with a gathered skirt called a *pollera*.

A bowler-hatted market woman wears a gathered pollera *skirt, a fringed blanket and carries a bundle on her back – La Paz, Bolivia.*

Central America

The Aztecs and the Maya

The lowland areas of Central America differ from the mountainous areas of South America in that the climate is warm and moist, and this was reflected in the earliest costumes. As the climate was not conducive to the preservation of textiles, most of the information regarding dress – apart from some fragments – has come from some of the stone carvings, ceramic figurines or pottery paintings that have survived. Later, the codices or picture manuscripts gave valuable information regarding the current form of costume worn at that time, but as most of the pictures depicted the nobility and priestly classes, this gives little indication of the dress of the ordinary man and women, except where slaves or captives are illustrated. The simplest type of dress would consist of a loincloth and a rectangle of cloth for a cape.

The earliest dress was somewhat minimal. Figurines of women show them clothed mainly in jewelled neck ornaments, earplugs and head cloths, with the occasional waist cloth or an early version of the G-string. Men wore a loincloth, headdress, earplugs and high-backed sandals. A rectangular cloak might be added and the women wore an early version of the shoulder cape. Gradually the costume became more complicated and the women took to wearing a wrap-around skirt, neck ornaments, a *quechquémitl* and a large hat or headdress. The earliest version of the tunic was a simple type with open sides, held together with a waist sash.

The men might wear more than one loincloth with one tied around the middle and the other hanging down in front. Some statuettes show the frontal loincloth tied into a knot about halfway down at knee level. Even later, a triangular hip cloth was added, probably formed from a rectangle of patterned cloth folded on the diagonal. This hip cloth was worn tied around the waist with the point at the back and the folded loincloth would hang down over the front area. A variety of skirt types of different lengths were worn over the loincloth, including fringed and beaded versions, while pleated ones were worn by warriors. By the Classic Maya period the loincloth had turned into the more complicated breechclout or *ex*. This consisted of a band of cloth, which was wound round the waist leaving one decorated end hanging down the front and the other hanging behind. Occasionally an ankle length piece of cloth, heavy with ornaments, was worn over the front like a ceremonial apron.

Some figures are shown with a netted fabric tied round the neck and hanging in front like a scarf to cover a short tunic. Men as well as women are shown wearing a *quechquémitl*, the 'V'-shape reaching down to just below the waist. There are various forms of patterning, but it is not possible to define the method used. Illustrations in the codices show a great elaboration of feathered headdresses and helmet-type caps with high plumes. Sometimes these decorations appear to be incorporated with the hairstyle, while foreheads are shown sloping backwards – the custom of encasing the baby's head in two flattening boards is common to both North and South America and was regarded as a sign of beauty.

In earlier times feet were bare, but occasionally plain ankle rings were worn. Later the leg and armbands have tassels or metallic decorations attached, possibly with little bells to make a tinkling noise. Sandals became a definite fashion item and are shown in a variety of styles, many high backed and some that appear to tie round the ankle. Footwear was generally made from leather, but plaited and woven shoes were made from vegetable fibres and even from strips of bark – a method which has survived in remote areas until the present time.

Forced Adoption of Items of Spanish Clothing and Foreign Influences

The Spanish soon realized that if they were to hold dominion over the vast extent of their new territories, they would need stern laws to keep in check a population that far outnumbered them by many thousands. As their first target was the indigenous ruling classes, they began by prohibiting the wearing of royal garments and regalia by the Inca chiefs in South America and their counterparts in the Aztec and Mayan communities in Central America. By depriving the local leaders of their visible rank and insignia, they were in effect emasculating them, demoting them in the eyes of their followers and rendering them powerless. This policy proved so effective that gradually they forced the indigenous male populations to adopt Spanish-style dress. The fact that this was often combined with elements of the native costume was overlooked, so long as the overall effect was maintained. In most areas the late sixteenth-century Spanish court fashion of a short jacket, together with knee-length breeches adapted from military uniform was to become the current form of dress, which in many cases still continues in certain areas today.

In South America the poncho and the mantle were still worn as over garments and the sash continued as an article of dress in both continents. Certain aspects of Spanish dress were adopted by the women, mainly in the form of the gathered or pleated *pollera* skirt and the felted hat. Many who lived in the remote mountain areas were slow to accept any change, but others had been taken as wives by

the colonists and gradually a mixed blood group of *Mestizos* came into being, where Spanish fashions were more readily accepted.

Dress Imposed by the Religious Orders

When the Spanish friars arrived in the newly conquered areas of Central America, they were shocked to find that many of the native tribes wore very little clothing. Naturally these people, who had adopted a mode of dress that suited their living conditions and the humid climate of these tropical areas, were more intent on bodily decoration than wearing cumbersome items of clothing. The friars proceed to forbid the more severe methods of bodily scarring or head-deformation, considering these to be the practices of the devil. Although the Aztecs were to some extent less scantily clad, even their garments were considered insufficient and the friars disapproved of the extended ear lobes distorted by heavy jewellery. Women were made to cover bare breasts and in areas of Mexico, women still wear bibbed aprons in the same context. The female native custom of wearing the *quechquémitl* with nothing else beneath was soon banned, even though it was long enough to overlap the wrap-around skirt at front and back. One of the reasons for the continuous wearing of the *huipil* over several hundred years is that it was approved as a modest garment by the Church. In South America, the friars objected to the tunics worn by the women of Bolivia and Peru, as the open slits of their tunics were considered immodest and the women were forced to sew up the gaps.

A number of the people, who had converted to Christianity and accepted Spanish-style dress, were slighted by many of their fellow countrymen who refused to comply with the new laws and continued to wear their native costume. The converts were forced into woollen garments – plainer versions of the jackets and breeches worn by the Spanish themselves – and must have suffered greatly from both the indignity to their cultural identity and from the unaccustomed wearing of highly unsuitable clothing. In the tropical areas lighter fabrics came into use, cotton for those who could afford it and bast-fibre cloth for the less fortunate.

Dress of Slaves and Indigenous Slave Workers

At first the slaves were allowed only the minimum of clothing necessary to keep them decently covered in as simple a way as possible using coarse fabrics. Loose, knee-length drawers and a loose over top, with the addition of a coarse cloth that would serve both as a cloak and as a protective back cover when carrying heavy loads, was normally all that was provided. The slaves, unless they were actually married to one of the indigenous people of the country, were prohibited from wearing local costume. Punishment for anyone who offended was severe as a rigid class or caste system was instigated by the Spanish, who wished to differentiate between the various ranks of the colonial immigrants, the original inhabitants and the slave classes. As with all sumptuary laws, this did not always work. The law was further undermined by the later colonists who, wishing to ape their rich European counterparts, dressed their household slaves in fine livery with jackets bedecked with gold and silver lace and all the accoutrements of the Spanish flunkeys found in the aristocratic houses of their home country.

Female slaves were dressed in a wrap-around skirt topped by a blouse or a version of the *huipil*, with the addition of a rectangular cloth that would double as both a shawl and a head covering. In a domestic situation, an apron would be worn, together with a white cap or a head cloth wrapped as a turban. After the abolition of slavery, a certain number of the women became integrated with the new wave of immigrants from Europe. Eventually some of the half-caste *Mestizo* and Creole women married well and sported the latest Spanish fashions together with a wealth of jewellery.

Men – Post-Conquest

In Central America the men soon came to adopt the Spanish fashion, first for knee-length breeches and later for trousers, influenced both by their conquering masters and by the Missionaries. They continued to wear many of their familiar articles of dress, such as the tunic top and the various over garments such as the *quechquémitl*, as well as the *chamarros* which was like an open tunic with a vertical slit for the head, sometimes finished with a fringe at the hem. In some remote areas the original pre-Hispanic costume was still worn, while in others the inhabitants were forced to adapt, or came to accept new ideas. Soon the tunic was exchanged for the tubular shirt as worn in San Antonio Palopó today, where the striped shirt has a front neck slit and a narrow stand-up collar. Other versions followed the open-front shape with an attached collar forming reveres and with the addition of decorated cuffs.

The *capiaxy* is a long, shirt-shaped woollen outer garment worn in the highland areas of Guatemala. The sides are left open and although sleeves are added at the top, they are purely decorative as the wearer ignores them and uses the side slits as armholes. The open sides are generally held together with a waist sash. A version of this garment with vestigial sleeves is worn by the men of San Juan Atilán over a red shirt with a woven collar and white calf-length trousers. Shorter versions of this sleeved garment are sewn

up at the sides but have slits left open for the arms. Similar garments are worn by the *cofrades* of Nahuala together with decorated panels over their loincloths.

Trousers and Jackets

Until fairly recent times the trouser shape worn by men in Guatemala was very simple. Two oblongs of woven cloth are folded in half lengthways, the two upper portions are seamed together to make a crotch seam, while the lower parts are joined to make the two cylindrical trouser legs. Very occasionally, a gusset is inserted. The wide top of the trousers, which has no shaping, is pleated round the waist and held by the sash, or the fullness may be controlled by a drawstring. These trousers vary in length, with shorter ones to mid-calf level worn in the areas around Lake Atitlán. Many of these trousers are made from striped fabric and sometimes have additional decoration, either within the weave structure or as additional embroidery. Very short trousers, more like a fashioned loincloth, are worn under the *ponchito* blanket skirt by the highland men of Nahuala. The men of Solola, in the area of Lake Atitlán, can still be seen wearing this plaid-patterned *ponchito* over their striped trousers.

In Mexico the men continued to wear knee breeches or white cotton trousers, often rolled up to the knee, together

The men of Solola, near Lake Atitlán, wearing the plaid-woven ponchito *skirt over their patterned trousers.*

with a shirt – sometimes with the addition of an over-shirt or the dark jacket of Spanish origin. Embroidered or woven sashes were generally tied outside the shirt, which was worn over the trousers. At one time, shaped over-trousers were worn on top of the white ones beneath and for many years, trousers continued to be a status symbol. The loose cotton drawers or *calzones* worn for work by the slaves or the native classes were not considered suitable garments by the authorities for social wear, and for a brief period at the end of the nineteenth century were banned in the towns. The modern Maya men in the Yucatan peninsula wear a white cotton jacket and trousers, together with a coloured sash or cummerbund and a wide, sombrero hat.

The adoption of Spanish dress was slower in South America, although the Inca nobility who wished to retain their autonomy were more ready to comply with their conquerors. The result was a mixture of both types of dress and at first the tunic and mantle would be worn together with the Spanish-style breeches and hat. A round-necked shirt was made from a warm woollen fabric called *bayeta* and the same fabric was used to make jackets. Normally, the trousers were knee length, at first wide and baggy but later more fitted. Those from the Cuzco area were black, but white trousers were worn in other areas, including parts of Bolivia and Ecuador. The women continued to wear their shawls but, when they were obliged to give up the tunic for the wide Spanish-style skirt and the simple blouse, they still wore their traditional *chumpi* belts. The men were compelled to wear the poncho when the mantle was banned in an endeavour to stamp out their native identity.

The men of Todos Santos Cuchumatan show off their costume of striped trousers, split over-trousers and jackets with woven collars.

RIGHT: *A young boy from Chichicastenango wearing the traditional breeches and embroidered jacket.*

FAR RIGHT: *Back view showing the red fringe on the lower hem.*

A variety of distinguishing headgear, much of it adapted from Spanish Military uniform, became the favourites of the men in certain areas. There are versions of three-cornered Napoleonic type hats, but the most unusual example is worn by the Bolivian men from Tarabuco where a copy of the Spanish metal helmet is translated into a leather 'casque', or helmet, with curved protrusions over the cheeks. The brim line is softened with a border of pleated lace that peeps incongruously from beneath, while feather plumes are added for special occasions. Knee-length trousers and long horizontally striped ponchos complete the outfit.

The Guatemalan costume worn by the men of Todos Santos Cuchumatan is unlike any other, consisting of a striped shirt with an attached inlay-patterned collar made from a folded rectangle. Over this is worn a dark blue jacket with lapels, metal buttons and woven cuffs to match the shirt collar. In warmer weather the shirt is worn on its own, over a modern coloured T-shirt. The trousers, which are quite long – almost lapping the ankles – are always in a red fabric with white stripes. Over these a second pair in black woollen fabric is worn, split up the front of each leg to reveal the red trousers beneath. On either side at the front, vertical rows of little white buttons outline the trouser openings. A woven sash is tied above, round the waist. The outfit is finished with the sombrero hat and decorative headband and the men always carry a woven or crochet shoulder bag. In other areas, versions of these split over-trousers are worn by some members of the *Cofradia* brotherhoods.

Another adaptation of eighteenth-century Spanish dress was the wearing of short knee breeches in black wool. These had pocket flaps protruding on either side, no longer used as such but deemed to be part of the costume. They are decorated with embroidery by the men themselves and are generally worn tucked up into the waistband. The amount of chain-stitch embroidery worked by the men onto their trousers and jackets indicates their position and importance in society. A young boy from Chichicastenango was wearing the traditional breeches from the area, together with the embroidered jacket that reached to waist level at the front. The back was cut longer and a red fringe was added to the lower hem. All was topped with a turban head-cloth in the typical Chichicastenango woven zigzag pattern and finished at the back with more fringing and red pom-pom tassels.

Gauchos

The Gauchos, at one time a nomadic people, are the subject of many folk legends in Argentina and the neighbouring countries of Uruguay and Chile to the south-west. These are countries of the Pampas grass, home in the early days of the Conquest to the feral horses tamed by the war-like Mapuche

people. The Gauchos are mainly descended from the half-caste *Mestizo* whose expert horsemanship suited them to both the role of mercenary guerrilla soldiers and that of cowhand when the cattle herds were imported into the grasslands.

Their costume reflected their occupation and was especially suited to riding on horseback. It has altered little and today they still wear long trousers called *bombachas*. The wide-cut legs, with the fullness controlled by accordion pleating, are held at the ankle above the boot tops. This fullness gives freedom of movement and insulation from heat and cold. On top, a woven poncho provides protection when riding and can act as a wrap when sleeping out in temporary grass-roofed huts on the Pampas.

Women – Post-Conquest

In South America the women adopted certain items of military uniform, such as the fitted jacket with pocket flaps and cuffs, decorated with buttons, braid and embroidery, combined with the full, gathered skirt. The Tarabucan women also wore a plainer version of the leather helmet-hat, together with a wrap-around skirt and a warp-patterned striped shawl. Portuguese influence was felt in Brazil, with a gradual acceptance of European fashions and the eventual wearing of lace and open-work embroidery, especially for shawls and mantillas.

In Central America the simple tunic became the *huipil* blouse. This can vary in length from the shorter Guatemalan

A baby's striped huipil *blouse from Colotenango, Guatemala. The diamond inlay pattern is worked into the upper weave shed and the neck and armholes are outlined with crochet.*

A three-web huipil *from Chichicastenango worked in the double-faced brocade technique.*

brocaded *huipil* to the long cotton *huipil* worn by the Mexican women, including the Maya in the Yucatan peninsula. These simple garments do not have separate sleeves. The Guatemalan *huipil* is similar in construction to the open poncho in that it is made from rectangular pieces of woven cloth, but with the sides seamed up, leaving slits open for the armholes. Sometimes these armholes are bound with velvet fabric, or oversewn with embroidery to match the neck binding. Occasionally, the woven yoke of the *huipil* is made as a separate oblong piece that is folded along the shoulder line and joined to the main front and back sections of the *huipil*. A slit is woven into the centre of the yoke for the neck opening, but in some areas a circular or a square neck hole is now cut out and reinforced with woven braid or embroidery stitches.

Although there are several of ways of joining the narrow widths of back-strap loomed cloth, the basic shape stays the same. The *huipil* is formed from either two, or more usually three, of these fabric widths, sometimes referred to as a two- or a three-web *huipil*. The central join may be a decorative seam incorporating embroidery stitches, or in modern circumstances a seam sewn together by machine. In both Mexico and Guatemala it is quite common to see a vertical pleat on either side of a two-web *huipil*, sewn to imitate those made from joined sections of cloth. In areas of Guatemala the *huipil* can alter in length, but is never much below hip level. Occasionally it is possible to see a *huipil* with two vertical feeding slits made in the front of the garment, to give

easier access for feeding the baby. These slits may be bound with a contrasting fabric, or become incorporated as part of the moon symbol, applied by mothers as a protective element associated with the Moon goddess of childbirth.

The tubular skirt is also common to both Mexico and Guatemala. The skirt is made from a joined piece of woven cloth and varies in length according to the custom of each area. The woman first puts on her *huipil*, steps into the wide tube of the skirt and then arranges the excess fabric in pleats around the waist, enclosing the lower hem of the *huipil*. This pleating may take the form of one large overlap, or a series of smaller pleats. Once arranged to satisfaction, the pleats are held in place around the waist with a woven sash. In Guatemala, the women of San Antonio Palopó wind the sash tightly, but as it also covers the bulk of the heavily woven *huipil*, it provides a decorative element rather than a definition of the waistline. Occasionally the skirt is made from one length of unseamed fabric, in which case the overlap at the front will hang freely to one side. Many skirts are made from two lengths of woven cloth, joined together horizontally in the middle with the decorative *ruanda* seam.

In Mexico, plain indigo-dyed skirts are still worn in the areas of the Chiapas Highlands, bordering with Guatemala. Their longer *huipils* hang outside the skirt, sometimes looking like a tubular over-dress. Normally woven from cotton, they are can be very decorative, incorporating both striped and brocade weaving techniques. The Mazatec

women from the Oaxaca area wear two-tier *huipils* over a long tubular skirt. The fabric is white cotton patterned with horizontal stripes in red and blue, with brilliantly coloured birds and flowers decorating the top blouse section. In the Museum of Anthropology in Mexico City an upper floor is devoted to the costumes of the different areas. All the women's clothes are based on this basic tunic shape. It is the vibrant decoration that distinguishes the costume of one village from another. Embroidery is the chosen embellishment for a lighter cotton fabric, suitable for wear in a humid climate.

In other areas the woven *huipil* is more like the ones found in Guatemala, often following the garment construction of three joined panels, with the square neck made from the lower central one. In certain locations such as Chiapas, the neck areas as well as the shoulders are decorated with brocading or surface stitching, incorporating many of the designs and symbols from the past. In the Trique area of Oaxaca the *huipil* becomes a long garment that reaches down to the ankles with the side seams left completely open to show the skirt beneath. At other times the *huipil* lengthens to become a dress and on ceremonial and festive occasions is worn as an over-garment. The width of these large *huipils*, which are not held in by any sash, is emphasized by the brocaded patterning that stiffens and holds out the fabric. When worn for practical work, the sides can be draped up and held over the shoulders, thus exposing the short skirt.

LEFT: *Today, the Mayan women of the Yucatan peninsula, Mexico, prefer machine-embroidered* huipils *made from cotton fabric.*

BELOW: *Mayan teachers in charge of a school trip, rest in the ball court of Chichén Itzá while wearing their embroidered* huipils.

In several villages of the Yucatan peninsula the Mayan women wear their distinctive costume on an everyday basis. This consists of an embroidered *huipil* made from a piece of commercially woven cotton fabric, double the finished length. A square neck is cut out of the fold across the shoulder line. This neck area is heavily embroidered to give the effect of a square yoke. The garment is wide enough for the excess at the sides to form short sleeves. More embroidery is worked around the hem area, formerly by hand, now often by machine. This below knee-length tunic is worn over a white cotton tubular waist petticoat with a deep hem of lace, crochet or eyelet embroidery, which shows beneath the dress – longer versions of the costume are worn by young women for dance festivals and tourist entertainment. This gala costume can be quite elaborate with three layers of matching embroidered frills, one on the *huipil*, one on the long skirt and a third on the cape-like embroidered collar on the shoulders. The outfit is completed by wearing a long, narrow shawl, which is draped around the shoulders or held behind at waist level. These *rebozo* shawls, once made of artificial silk but now more likely to be made from synthetic threads, are still considered as status symbols.

Full Skirts and Petticoats

It was after native rebellions during the eighteenth century that the women of the Andes were forced to abandon their

An apron from Antigua, Guatemala, with decorative stitching and a gathered frill.

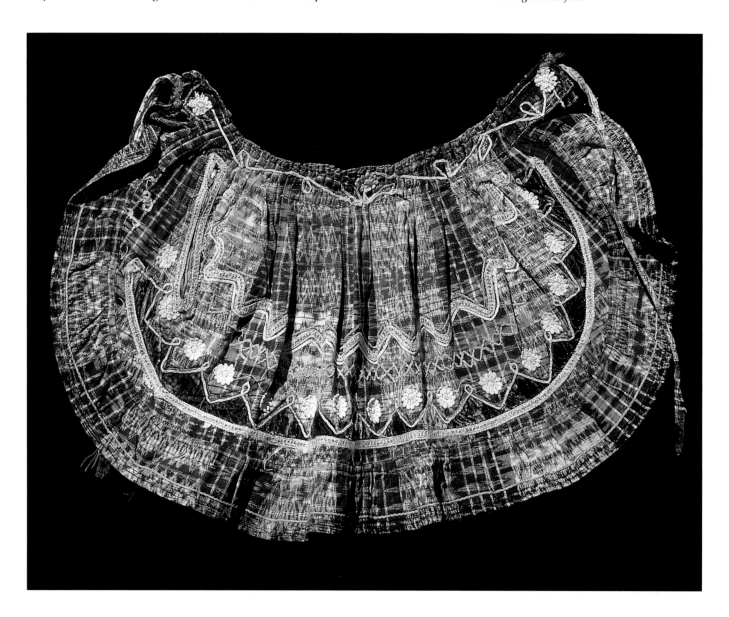

straight-line tunics and adopt the full skirts and petticoats worn by the Spanish colonial women who had eventually followed their menfolk to settle in these areas. The more skirts and petticoat layers the better, especially at times of public and family gatherings or when worn in church or at the market. The women who come to Pisac market in Peru, either to buy or to sell vegetables and other goods, seem to vie in displaying their splendour. A woman, bending over to arrange the vegetables on the floor cloth below, shows a series of calf-length layers reminiscent of a ballet dancer's tutu skirt. This is evidence of her wealth and may well be an effective method of attracting a suitor. A similar costume of full, gathered skirts is worn in Bolivia, the Aymara women wearing layers of skirts together with fringed shawls and felt hats. Petticoats are worn underneath and these help the skirt to swirl outwards at dance festivals. In Central America, Guatemalan and Mexican women also wear several skirts in a series of layers. This has nothing to do with the climate, but once again, is a sign of wealth and the evidence of plenty.

Oaxaca Women's Petticoats and Lace Collars

In the Mexican city of Oaxaca the women wear an extraordinary adaptation of the Spanish collar or ruff, fashionable at the time of the Conquest. A strip of lace, some 35cm (14in) wide, is pleated along one long edge and sewn to the neckline of the *huipil*. The starched neck frill was turned up and tied around the face to form a deep, lace halo. At one time a second, even wider starched lace frill was sewn around the waist. This frill could be turned up around the shoulders to act as a sunshade. At festival times they still wear the wide collar as a surround to the face and a deep lace frill of similar design is attached to the base of a gathered skirt heavily embroidered with naturalistic floral patterns. Occasionally the lace is substituted for embroidered white-work with a scalloped edge.

Festival or dance costume is complemented with a selection of heavy gold jewellery in the form of long pendants threaded with gold coins or discs, reaching as far as the waistline, and equally heavy drop earrings. The central pendant medallions are in the form of the sun symbol, sometimes with the addition of a cross on a separate chain. Filigree gold-work is one of the technical skills of Oaxaca that has been passed down to present-day workers as a tradition from long before the Conquest. Their ancestors had mastered the arts of embossed decoration and chasing, while the Mixtec goldsmiths were renowned for fine hollow-wax castings. Earrings can feature the moon symbol as a pair of double crescents linked by the filigree work with additional decorative wire-work and a series of droplets forming a golden fringe beneath.

Gathered and Embroidered Blouses

In several areas of Mexico the straight-sided *huipil* evolved into one where the plain top became a yoke onto which was attached a separate front and back section that was far wider than the yoke measurement. The top of this section was gathered and sewn onto the base of the yoke. A variety of stitching methods were used to control these gathers, some of them resembling smocking. The top yoke area, which varied in depth, was cut with a square neck and had short square-cut sleeve pieces, which were attached together with a triangular gusset to give underarm ease. Floral embroidery decorated the yoke and the sleeves. In the Chiapas area a circular neck yoke was attached with a frill to the combined sleeve and blouse sections, which are gathered to fit. In many regions the blouse shape of European origin gradually replaced the traditional *huipil* and now can take a variety of forms, each decorated in an individual manner.

Aprons

The apron has found great favour during the twentieth century in many areas of Central America. In Guatemala the apron is worn as a decorative addition to the costume rather than as protection against dirt and grime. These aprons, which have gathers around the waist, reach to about mid-calf length. Decoration in the form of an applied braid is machined to the borders, pocket slits and sometimes the waistband. Additional embroidery, mainly by machine, holds areas of applied velvet onto the *ikat* woven stripes of the ground fabric. Braids can be plain, or include shiny lurex threads and the zigzag-shaped ric-rac braids in various widths, which are applied in rows. The base of the apron is always finished with a gathered frill. These aprons are worn over the tube or wrap-around skirts and above the sash that holds the *huipil* in place. While the women in Aquas Calientes who demonstrated weaving were only too happy to show off their frilly aprons, members of the family engaged in cooking wore a serviceable apron of woven striped fabric that covered the wrap-around skirt.

The women in Almalonga market were each wearing an apron as an addition to their already brilliant costumes, but these aprons were more in the form of a pinafore, of the type popular in Europe and the USA during the 1930s. The bodice front is gathered into the waistband below and to a square yoke above that passes over the shoulders where it is joined to the arm slings and back-waist ties. The gathered skirt of the apron reaches to just below the knee and is decorated in a variety of ways, sometimes with applied braid. Occasionally an oval, frilled waist-apron is worn, thus showing the embroidered top of the *huipil*. Fabrics vary from the traditional *jaspe* woven cloth to commercially

Almalonga women display their pinafores on market day, together with brightly coloured head cloths and woven bands.

made fabric prints, checks and stripes. In spite of the cacophony of patterns and colours formed by the skirts, aprons, *huipils* and pom-pom decorated headdresses, in the bright morning sunshine the costumes merge into and become part of the equally colourful vegetable market.

Women from the Oaxaca region of western Mexico also wear a pinafore in the European style of the late 1930s. At one time they were bare breasted above their decorative skirts, but the Spanish religious community objected to this display on moral grounds and the women were obliged to cover up. The pinafores are made from factory printed cotton cloth and edged with modern bias binding. These women are featured in the *Ends of the Earth* video in 'Backstrap Weaving of Mexico and Guatemala'.

In both South and Central America, men still wear decorative apron panels for fiesta and carnival costume, often in conjunction with trousers. The heavily patterned loincloth of pre-Colonial times was almost indistinguishable from an apron and has echoes today in the European Masonic Apron and a variety of other interpretations in folk costume.

The Amazonian tribes wore little else than an apron or half-skirt made from vegetable fibres, often decorated with feathers and beads. Originally beads were made from natural seeds or coastal shells, but later, trade beads were incorporated when they became available.

Kuna of the San Blas Islands

At one time the tribes of the Kuna people inhabited both the inland area of the isthmus of Darien as well as the rivers and the eastern coastal areas that are now part of the Republic of Panama. Gradually they were driven further and further to the east, either by neighbouring warlike tribes, or by the Conquistadors who had found a convenient land route to Columbia and the other countries of South America. The Kuna withstood all assaults on their way of life and spiritual beliefs with an amazing tenacity, refusing to be converted by the Jesuit Missionaries or subdued by the Spanish. Their final retreat to the San Blas Islands and the coastal strip now called the Kuna Yala, led them to lead a secretive lifestyle, resisting all contacts with the outside world unless they themselves were willing to assent.

Original reports of their habits and clothing have come down to us through the chronicles of the early explorers. A seventeenth-century buccaneer named Lionel Wafer records his life with the natives when he was stranded in the jungle during 1681. He tells of how the men were clothed only in a loincloth made of bark cloth, beaded necklaces and an elaborate feather headdress, while the women wore a simple wrap-around skirt, a nose ring and the beaded necklaces, which only partly covered their breasts. Their main form of decoration was body painting, which in some cases took the form of tattooing. The colours were obtained from natural sources, earth minerals and plant dyes. The favoured colours were red, yellow and blue. It is interesting that these colours are those most frequently used in the decoration of their *mola* blouses today.

Traffic from the silver mines together with the silver fleet that took the booty back to Spain, as well as the British and French pirate ships that frequented these coastal waters, brought the Kuna into contact, however unwillingly, with commerce. Eventually, during the early nineteenth century, they were prepared to trade their goods and produce for imported male clothing, commercially dyed cotton cloth, steel needles and scissors. This led to a change in dress, so that by the mid-nineteenth century the men had adopted flannel shirts and hempen trousers but many still adhered to traditional clothing, wearing the loincloth even as late as the 1870s. According to Captain Jacob Dunham, an American writing in 1850, 'The young men are not allowed to wear their shirt flaps inside of the waistbands of their trowsers (*sic*) until they are about forty years old, when they assume the character of old men'.

At first the women wore a longer skirt of cloth onto which they transferred some of the body-paint patterns in blue indigo across the hem area. Although there is some debate as to whether there was a direct transfer of designs from one

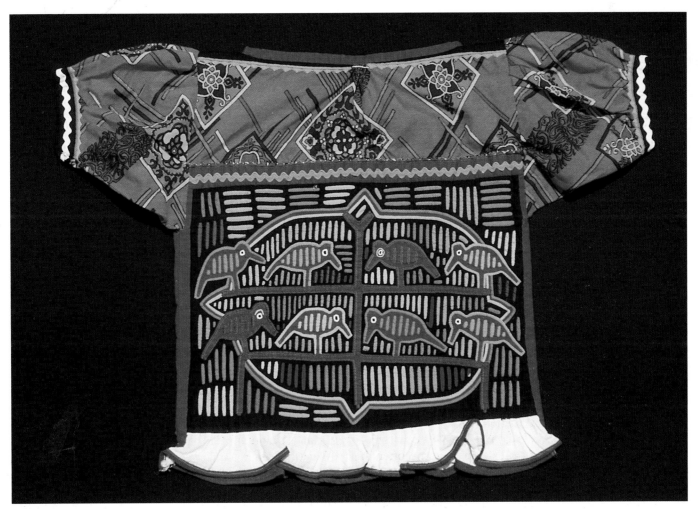

A mola *blouse showing the reverse appliqué front panel, fabric yoke and puffed sleeves.*

media to the other, it is more logical to infer that patterns that are part of a cultural heritage and thus ingrained in the psyche would continue to be used. At some stage during the late nineteenth century the skirt was abandoned in favour of a loose chemise-type garment of simple cut that came to below the knees. The original skirt became a type of under-skirt or petticoat worn under the chemise. At first the painted patterns were transferred to the chemise surface, but remained on the lower edge and were eventually replaced with fabric in bands of red or yellow.

It is not known when the first layered fabric cut-through designs were used. The climate is not conducive to the preservation of textiles, but when an American lady named Eleanor Bell visited the area in 1909, she reported to the Smithsonian Institute that 'Their garments consist of a short skirt and sort of chemise of coloured cotton, composed of various layers of appliqué work neatly sewn together forming very curious designs'.

A stall holder selling religious mementos outside the Cathedral, Mexico City.

By the 1920s the chemises were shorter, decorated with the reverse appliqué patterns apart from the back and front upper yoke area. Gradually the chemise shortened to become what we now call the *mola* blouse – *mola* being the Kuna word for cloth. The rectangular embroidered panels form the front and back areas and are joined to a yoke at the top and to a frill of cloth at the bottom that is normally tucked into the wrap-around skirt. Sleeves are added, which over time have become larger and more puffed in shape. These fabric additions are made in factory-produced cloth, often in bright, floral-printed designs. Although the subject matter of the *mola* designs has changed over the years, the basic shape has altered very little, becoming slightly more shaped to the body.

Religious and Ritual Costume

The wearing of special clothing to celebrate various rituals, whether pagan, Catholic or a mixture of the two, continues right up to present times, sometimes transmuted as dance or festival costume. The Chicicastenango family of the Mask-maker, at the shrine of *Pascual Abaj*, were wearing elaborate costumes, decorated with glitter threads and beadwork, topped with high, plumed headdresses when performing for the visiting tourists.

The religious brotherhoods of the *Cofradias* in Guatemala were responsible for organizing the processions and rites instigated by the Church when the friars substituted their Catholic saints for the pagan gods of the Maya and Aztec civilizations. Each *Cofradia* is connected with an individual saint and was answerable to the Council of the *cofrade*, elected from highly respected members of the community. For the major religious celebrations they wore a distinctive style of dress which incorporated the split over-trousers similar to those worn by the men of Todos Santos Cuchumatan. When worn over their normal striped and patterned trousers, the bottom ends of these over-trousers were tucked up into the waist sash by the *Cofradias* of Sololá. Patterned shirts, a *tzute* head cloth worn under a dark boater-shaped hat and a folded *rodillera* blanket with fringed ends placed over the left shoulder, completed the costume.

Other versions are worn in Chichicastenango based on the short jacket and knee-length trousers with the wide, embroidered side-flaps. An elaborate turban, woven in the zigzag lightning pattern, completes the costume. The wives of the *Cofradias,* together with their families, were held in respect, assuming some of the powers by association. The women also dressed in special costumes, which varied from

RIGHT: *Children of the Mask-maker family, Chichicastenango, show off their festival finery.*

BELOW: *A masked dancer performing in San Antonio Palopó, Guatemala – modern-day fringing takes the place of the original fur costume.*

place to place but were based on the *huipil*. This might take the form of a large over-garment or fine white cotton covering which excluded all but the face. In the town of San Juan Sacatepéques, once again the men wear the dark coloured, split over-trousers, revealing the lace-edged white ones beneath. The jacket is short and wide and the bright colours of the inlay-patterned waist sash are echoed in the decoration on the two wide *tzute* cloths that form the turban and the shoulder cape. On these special occasions the wives, dressed in their best clothes, twist their hair up into elaborate coiffeurs, which they partially cover with a lacy veil.

In Mexico, as in the other countries in our area, special costumes are worn for Easter celebrations and parades. *Los pintos*, the bare-legged painted men of Tarahumara, dress in white *quechquémitl* over patterned shirts together with colourful neck scarves and headbands. During pastoral parades, the Mazahua women may wear flower-decorated hats and fringed *quechquémitl* over their factory-made skirts. At Christmas time, outside the Cathedral in the Zócalo square of Mexico City, women were wearing decorated skirts with four fringed tiers, over which each had suspended an embroidered plaque depicting a saint.

At times it is not easy to differentiate between these religious costumes and the ones worn in connection with pre-

Christian rites. A fine line is drawn between the mask dancers of Guatemala and those taking part in the annual Day of the Dead festivities throughout Mexico. The fiestas of the Central Valley area of Oaxaca feature a pre-Hispanic dance called *La pluma*. This refers to the elaborate headdresses comprising vertical bands of coloured feathers and little decorative mirrors. In the coastal Mixtec area, pre-Columbian dances celebrate the hunting of the jaguar and men wear suitably spotted costumes to represent the jaguar pelt together with jaguar masks that have a long tongue protruding from the sharp-toothed jaws. Other masks show horned 'devils' and the men wear 'fur' trousers to suggest an animal origin.

A Solola market vendor wears her best striped huipil, *embroidered on the yoke with flowers, and a matching* tzute *cloth over her head.*

Accessories

Hats, Head-Decorations and Cloths

The Inca women of Peru wore a long woven cloth or sash wound round the head and, on Lake Titicaca, the women of Taquile Island still wear a draped head cloth that hangs down like a veil at the back. This is generally dark indigo blue in colour, but the women of Amantini Island choose a white fabric head covering made as a hood from two seamed oblongs, sometimes decorated with machine or hand embroidery to match their *huipil* blouses.

In Guatemala, the women of Chichicastenango wrap lengths of woven cloth around the head, letting the decorative fringes or tassel ends hang down on one side of the face. Called *tzutes,* these pieces of cloth can be mistaken for sashes, but they are more likely to have a dual function. In Solola market, the women sat on cloths spread onto the ground, together with their baskets and sacks of vegetables, wearing large, loose turbans of cloth woven in the traditional striped *jaspe* patterns. The fabric was so arranged that several folds of cloth hung down behind, thus protecting the back of the neck from the fierce sunshine.

The women of the San Blas Islands wear a headscarf made from an oblong of cotton cloth formed from two printed squares. These scarves have developed from the commercial printed fabric that has a repeat pattern down its entire length, allowing it to be cut into the relevant sections later. The scarf is worn draped over the head, sometimes with the surplus tucked behind the ears, at others hanging loose to hide one side of the face. It was not until recent times that

An oblong of factory-printed cloth is folded in half to make a head square for the Kuna women of the San Blas Islands.

some of the women took to tying the headscarf at the back of the head. This may have been to keep the loose ends from impeding their work, but as their mothers and grandmothers had managed perfectly well in the past, it may simply be a fashion statement. Headscarves made from brightly coloured factory-printed cloth and tied round the head in a similar manner are worn by the northern Mexican women of Tamahumara in Chichuahua State, who may have been similarly influenced.

Occasionally the Inca cloth was folded up and placed on top of the head. This style of costume continued for many years and Central American *tzute* cloths are still worn in a similar way in modern Guatemala. The folded cloth would have a certain amount of weight, preventing it from being blown away by the wind. Most of these women have excellent deportment, are used to carrying bundles or various articles such as baskets or plastic bowls full of vegetables on their heads and find the folded cloth a serviceable head pad. If the basic cloth is rectangular, it can be taken from the

head and unfolded for any new purpose, such as holding the baby, or for a carry cloth.

Braids and Tapes

Although decorative braids are wound around the hair or are incorporated as part of the headdress in many areas, the women of Santiago Atitlán on the shores of the volcanic lake have a very distinctive headdress, although this is worn less frequently today. The headdress, looking when finished rather like the brim of a hat, is made from a long length of narrow, woven tape which is wound round and round the head to form a layer to stand out from the head like a halo, several inches deep. The greater part of the band, which is covered during the winding, is left plain – only the very outer layer of the circumference is decorated with striped patterning or inlay. Another version of this

A long braid is wound in circles to form a headdress for this woman from Santiago Atitlán.

The disc-shaped headdress is worn less often nowadays.

bound headdress is worn by the women of San Sebastián Huehuetenango, where the woven band is made of plain red wool. The surrounding villages each have their own particular way of winding the tape into a turban-like structure, sometimes adding a folded *tzute* cloth which is placed on top. These narrow bands, which can measure anything up to 15m (49ft) long, are woven by the men on the narrow-braid looms.

Women from other Guatemalan villages bind up their long, thick hair, incorporating the bands in a variety of ways. In Zunil, the women first secure the tape around the head, then twist it around the ponytail of hair before laying it around the top of the head to form a braided coronet. The ends of the tape are finished with deep tubular tassels, which lie parallel with the band on the top and the side of the head. Once again these decorative bands can double up in use as a tasselled belt wound around the *jaspe* woven skirt. In Almolonga market in Central Guatemala, the women look particularly colourful with the zigzag stripes of their *huipils* complementing the equally colourful headgear, which ranged from a single plaited braid tied around the hair, to folded *tzute* cloths with a profusion of tassels hanging down the back of the head.

Shorter versions of these bands are worn around the crown of the men's white straw hats in the mountain village of Todos Santos Cuchumatan. They are wrapped round several times with the fringed end or a tassel left hanging down on one side. It would appear that there is no end to the usefulness of these narrow woven bands, whether as a purely decorative element or for more practical use as bag handles or for securing and tying bundles, or as halters and harness pieces for pack animals.

A street seller peels oranges in Todos Santos Cuchumatan. His typical Panama straw hat is decorated with a woven band.

Printed ribbons are plaited into the long braids of this woman from Almolonga, Guatemala.

Bowler Hats – Bolivia

There is a story that tells of a consignment of bowler hats destined for some city in Bolivia, which inadvertently went astray in the high mountain areas around Lake Titicaca. It was the women, rather than the men who adopted these hats as headgear. Whether there is any truth in this story or not, it is a known fact that the British engineers who came to work on the high altitude railways that eventually linked these areas, wore bowler hats. These probably acted as a type of crash helmet for workers in a dangerous situation. Whatever its origin, the bowler hat became a prime favourite with many of the tribes in this area and is worn by women even farther afield, being taken up by the *chola* women who are racially part-Spanish. The women on the Peruvian side of the lake can be seen sitting in chattering groups by the shore, while busy spinning or working their traditional woollen embroidery. They each wear a bowler hat, perched on the top of the head, sometimes at a rather jaunty angle.

Over on the Bolivian side of the lake, in the area around the capital city of La Paz, the bowler hat is much in evidence and is worn by the women who come to the central market. These hats are generally dark in colour, but occasionally lighter ones are seen. In many instances the bowlers are worn over a woven band called a *wincha*, which is placed across the back of the neck area, brought round and tied on top of the head with the cords. The *wincha*, which measures about 36–40cm (14–16in) long by 6cm (2½in) wide, is woven in a firm double-cloth patterned weave. The tying cords are plaited and often end in a tassel. Little girls are sometimes shown wearing the *wincha* across the forehead instead of at the back, in which case this is the only head covering and they do not wear a hat on top. The *wincha* can be used in this style as extra protection for the forehead when carrying a load on the back, suspended by the head-strap. As before, many of the women in the La Paz market wore their bowler hats tilted at various angles above the *wincha*.

A variety of hat styles worn at the Sunday market place in Pisac, Peru.

Decorative fringes are added to these hats worn by women selling grain in Pisac market.

Felt Hats – South America

Hats made from felted wool are worn by both men and women in the High Andes. These can be simple in shape and not as hard as the traditional bowler hat. In Ecuador they are made from felted llama hair, but in all areas they are equally likely to be made from sheep's wool, or a mixture of the two. The layers of wool are dampened and kneaded, beaten or rolled until they felt together to form a firm fabric. This is pressed onto a wooden mould in the shape of the hat crown together with the brim, or alternatively, the brim can be formed by hand when a simple crown mould is used. The moulded hat is left to dry and the edges are trimmed. In Bolivia these pressed felt hats are called *monteras* and those worn by the women from Challa can be decorated around the brim with colourful hand embroidery, together with a series of woven pattern bands wound around the upright crown. In Peru today, equally colourful felt hats are embellished over the crown and brim with machine embroidery, the product of modern workshops.

The men around Lake Titicaca wear softer felt hats over their knitted *ch'ulla* hats in the winter, probably for extra warmth. Hats of a similar shape, but in different colours, are worn by the men who live on the island of Taquile in the middle of the lake. The conquering Inca divided this small island into two sections with further subsections, forcing the Aymara-speaking people to assume the Quechua language. These divisions still exist and may well be reflected in differences in colours and styles. The hatbands take the form or a cord, or one of the narrow woven bands that show the picture symbols in the distinctive red, green and white colouring.

There are many versions of the felt hat in Peru. The Pisac Sunday market in the Ollantaytambo Valley is a meeting place for the surrounding tribes who walk many miles across the mountains with bundles on their backs to buy and sell their goods. It is here that the diversity of styles and shapes can be seen, defining the identity of the wearer. Some women look distinctive in their white trilby-style hats, often with a woven band encircling the crown. Others wear a similar version, but in brown or black. The crown may be flat, rounded like a pudding basin or indented at the top and brims can be turned up or down. The women from the Ayacucho area wear felt hats with cylindrical crowns, rather like a tall boater hat, while the rounded hat of the women of San Pedro de Cajas has a wide, upturned brim. A modern version of the hard felt hat is produced in a deep red colour, having a rounded crown and an upturned brim, heavily decorated with patterns in machine embroidery.

Some of the women who frequent Pisac market wear another distinguishing hat which looks rather like a fringed lampshade. This takes the form of an under-hat over which is superimposed a square of woollen fabric with a contrasting fringed edge sewn on all the way round. The darker square of cloth drapes unevenly around the hat, allowing the four corners to hang down in a decorative manner. Two heavily braided plaits of dark hair protrude from behind the wearer's hat and the surrounding fringe both frames and enhances the face.

Panama hats are still made in the country of origin and worn as headgear in many other parts of the world.

The *Montera*, a distinctive type of round hat, is worn by both men and women in the Cuzco area of Peru. A flat type of hat is formed from a large upturned brim with a shallow crown that sits on top of the head. The angle of the brim can be almost horizontal, or slope up steeply to the wide disc of the shallow crown. This hat is usually black with some decoration, often in the form of purchased braids, while the exposed underside of the brim is coloured a deep red. These hats are worn by the men on their own, or over the knitted *ch'ulla* hat and together can form part of the processional costume adopted on religious feast days. The women's hats are flatter and lower than those of the men – evidently the taller the hat, the more important the wearer.

Hats – Central America

The felt Sombrero hat, worn in areas of Mexico and the south-western USA, is a large high-crowned hat with a wide brim rolled up at the edges on both sides. Beaver felt, which repels the rain, was once used in making the traditional ten-gallon cowboy hats. Decorative variants of these practical hats are worn for dances and fiestas and tourist versions are on sale in Mexican cities today. Dancers in the Los Rayes area of Central Mexico wear sombreros with embroidery and applied braid around the crown, along the brim edge and even on the entire under-brim surface. Plain felt hats can be worn by both men and women on an everyday basis, but in a hot country, the woven straw Panama sombrero is more practical.

Panama Straw Hats and Sombreros

The straw hat originated in Ecuador, coming from the coastal town of Jipipapa, which also gives its name to the hat. The art soon spread to Columbia and Venezuela in the north and these hats were exported to other countries. They were very popular in the Panama area when the canal was in the process of construction during the early twentieth century. The enterprising merchants sold the hats to the construction workers and later they became part of the tourist trade and have been known as Panama hats ever since.

Both straw hats and straw mats are made in Nariño in southern Columbia where plantations of the *iraca* palm provide the raw material, although Cuenca is now an important hat-making centre. The mature palm leaves are cut and sliced into strips before drying in the sun. They can be boiled to whiten them or dyed with natural or with chemical dyes. The weaving of these fibres is an accomplished art and the finest hats are supple, can be screwed up and twisted, after which they will revert to their original shape. The hats are shaped onto wooden moulds – today with mechanical presses, but in the past by hand, using a process of steaming and ironing. People in some areas prefer the plain undecorated hats, while others opt for patterned weaves which incorporate the various dye colours into geometric designs. The Wayuu tribes of La Guarija in Columbia are famous for their decorative, woven sombreros, called *womo kots*, with patterns based on their basketry traditions.

Although the men's straw hats are referred to as 'sombreros' they are smaller than the 'cowboy' type, but still have a distinctive crown, dented in the middle top and a brim that curls upwards at the sides. They are ubiquitous wear in most parts of Mexico and Guatemala, but can differ in shape according to the particular style adopted by the individual communities. The men of Todos Santos Cuchumatan in the Guatemalan Highlands wear a Panama hat with a modest brim and a series of eyelet holes let into the indented crown to ensure good ventilation. A decorative hatband wrapped with an extra braid is common to all these hats, only the colour of the wrapping showing any individuality. Many communities embellish their hats at festival times and in Mexico, the women garland the tall crowns of their straw hats with flowers and feathers, at times looking like a walking flower garden.

An alternative method was to plait the fibres to make into braids, which could be sewn round and round in circles to form the hat. In the past these were sewn together by hand, but nowadays a sewing machine is used. Dyed fibres are plaited into long, patterned braids with anything from twenty to forty palm leaf fibres included. Circular mats are braided in a similar way, while in Guatemala grasses are used to make little baskets by coiling bundles of grasses and securing with cotton over-stitching.

Costume Accessories –
Carrying Cloths and Bags

The method of wrapping goods in a cloth for transportation is common to all areas. The two pairs of opposite corners are tied together around the contents and there are a variety of ways of securing this, with woven straps to the back or with a band around the forehead. At times the straps are dispensed with and the corners are tied diagonally across the shoulders, although many Guatemalan women carry the wrapped bundle on their heads. Alternatively, a basket or a brightly coloured plastic bowl will hold the vegetables or trade goods, sometimes perched on top of the folded *tzute* cloth. On market days the cloth is opened up and spread on the ground, by the side of the road when selling goods to tourists, or even on the station platform as at Machuu Pichu where the travellers are forced to walk along the track.

For personal use, there is a great variety of carrying bags designed for every practical purpose. These range from large woven bags supported with a shoulder strap, to the little *ch'uspa* coca leaf bags used in many areas of Bolivia and Peru. In the past the coca leaves were reserved for the priesthood and the shamans, helping them in their predictions or incantations. When the Spanish took charge, their overseers made the coca leaves available to all and encouraged the slaves and manual workers to chew the coca leaves as this tended to stave off hunger and they would produce more, for less food consumed. This habit was taken up by the miners, who needed a stimulant as their lives were in constant danger – the work was extremely hard with many of the deep-pit mines accessed by a series of rickety ladders up which the spoil was carried on their heads in open baskets. These little *ch'uspa* bags are beautifully made in the double-weave technique, incorporating symbolic designs in the patterning. A plaited cord forms the handle and the bottom is decorated with tassels or pom-poms. Coca leaves were much in evidence at weddings and the bridegroom's bag would be filled with leaves as a sign of plenty.

Shoulder bags have been used by the men from the earliest times, a necessity when the costume did not include any

The men of Todos Santos Cuchumatan all carry bags, many of them self-made in crochet threads.

pockets. Even in Guatemala today many of the trousers are made without pockets. The men of Todos Santos Cuchumatan each carry a woven or crocheted bag, which appears to be an essential part of their costume and the one item of dress that allows them to express their individuality. Originally the men would crochet these bags purely for their own use, but they have become very popular as sale items for the many tourists who come to visit the area. The women also use these bags, but small items are often secreted into the pouch made by the *huipil* where it bulges over the skirt. Beadwork bags are now made as items for tourist sale, rather than as a useful fashion accessory, although the little neck purses, which are decorated with symbolic motifs, can also function as containers for protective amulets.

Belts

The woven belt has great significance, with the symbolic meanings within the patterning giving it a magical property. The decorative elements might also denote status and rank or as in our contemporary society, sporting or military achievements. Perhaps the encircling quality of the belt was in itself something special, giving the wearer a sense of safety when held within the bounds of its protection. In Peru, the Quechua word for belt is *chumpi*, used to describe belts of different widths, each having a series of significant signs and symbols woven into the patterning. These symbols transferred their magical properties to the belts and they themselves were used in a magical sense as a link between humans and the gods. Special matrimonial belts were woven at the time of weddings, which in the Lake Titicaca area were all celebrated at the same time of year, in May, when the planet Venus was in an auspicious alignment. On Taquile Island the man would wear a wide red belt. Sometimes several narrow belts are sewn together to make a wider sash which would possibly be easier to weave than an intricately patterned broad belt. Women are said to have given birth on a *chumpi*, which might then wrap the baby itself. The *chumpi* belt accompanied the wearer through all the stages of life, sometimes worn hidden as the carrier of auspicious amulets, or worn outwardly to celebrate religious ceremonies and family festivals and eventually used in connection with funerary rites.

A combination of belt and bags is worn by the men of the Huichol tribes of western Mexico. A series of little fabric bags are strung together or fixed to a waist cord. Made from oblongs of woven cloth with traditional floral designs embroidered in patterned cross-stitch, these bags are folded in half and sealed at the top. They are decorated with wool tassels at the bottom corners and are said to contain magical

properties. Larger, but similarly decorated bags are open at the top and used for carrying more practical items.

In the Amazon area of South America, the belt was often the only item of costume worn by the men. This took on a special significance and the wearing of a jaguar pelt was regarded both as a symbol of power and of status, while feathered armbands worn by the Kamayurá tribe took on an equally symbolic role as the projecting feathers enabled the men to 'fly' during the dance ceremonies. The men of the Waiwai tribe wore belts of woven seed beads, with hanging tabs inserted at intervals, decorated on the ends with macaw breast feathers, of a similar technique to the bead weaving on the women's aprons.

A mother and boy wearing traditional costumes. The woman has tied a bright red sash beneath her brocade-weave huipil – *from Todos Santos.*

Political and Economic Constraints Affecting Costume Today

In a modern society used to an escalating pace of change, it is comforting to realize that there are still people who adhere to their traditional modes of dress. How long this will be possible to maintain is open to question. The pressures of modern living and political oppression in several of the countries in the areas of both South and Central America have eroded much of the indigenous way of life. In many cases the wearing of traditional clothing has been seen as a threat, even as a sign of rebellion against authority. The repression of dress is a two-edged sword, for in prohibition a new sense of identity can be born.

A variety of garments is worn in Chichicastenango market, including modern cardigans, with one even folded as a head cloth.

Modern Adaptation of Costume

In the big cities of both South and Central America, modern dress is the normal wear for both sexes, although a poncho or *sarape* of varying length and design is often worn over the shirt and trousers by the men. Although the many villages of the Guatemalan Highlands still take pride in the wearing of their traditional costume, especially at times of religious celebration or for local festivals, it is the men who are more likely to adopt factory-made clothing. This is partly due to the discrimination shown to the indigenous population, both in the workplace and in the cities where the *trajé*, or traditional clothing, is indicative of a lowly status, with the wearers regarded as simpletons or 'country bumpkins'. In certain instances the men will leave the village wearing their national dress, but change to reveal a polyester shirt and trousers, or the modern uniform of T-shirt and blue jeans before they reach the town.

However, in many of the mountain areas of Guatemala, there is a general adherence to indigenous dress. Apart from their forays into the weekly markets, many of the country women seldom leave their remote villages and are far less likely to abandon their sense of identity with regard to dress. They still wear the decorated *huipil*, the wrap-around skirt and a variety of headdresses, together with the ubiquitous *tzute* cloth that both covers and carries everything. At times modern printed fabric is substituted for the hand-woven pieces, but this is generally used for the aprons that cover their traditional clothing.

In the larger cities the local women have adapted to modern dress, especially when working in hotels or manufacturing, but at certain times the tourist industry demands the wearing of national costume, where hotel and restaurant staff are sometimes dressed in a glamorized version of the local costume, in order to conform to the expectations of the clientele. The greater the intensity of the tourist industry, the more elaborate the costume becomes. This is especially the case in coastal areas of Mexico, which has a more substantial tourist industry than many of the inland areas.

This does not apply to the carnival costumes of Brazil and the West Indies, where the inhabitants celebrate what were once the 'free' holidays granted to the original slave population. For one day only, the slave might become 'King', while his Master was demoted. Originally, costumes were based on the rituals of the syncretic religions of West Africa, when the women wore long white robes and made sacrifices to the sea. Later, the ceremonies were intermixed with local pagan concepts and costumes became far more exuberant. While the carnival in Rio is the most famous, the festival of Sâo Jâo, which takes place in the north-eastern Brazilian town of Cachoeira, once an important river port for the export of sugar and tobacco, is equally colourful. The area surrounding the capitol, Salvador, was inhabited by a succession of African slaves who managed to preserve their culture through religion, a mixture of Catholicism and Candomblé. Spirit possession and the cult of death went hand in hand with exuberant singing and the veneration of Catholic saints. The women wear flounced, white skirts held out with hoops and tie white turbans around the head.

Although the carnivals are a tourist attraction, the people take part as an expression of a self-identity, which escalates into competition with rival groups to produce the most elaborate costumes and the best decorated floats, all of which have taken many months to construct.

7

Embroidery and Appliqué

Spanish Influence on Surface Embroidery

Surface stitching was taken to the New World by both the Spanish and the Portuguese, by the wives of the original settlers and by the convent nuns who wished to teach the converted their particular type of fabric decoration and at the same time provide religious vestments for the Catholic clergy.

The Spanish had inherited a rich tradition of embroidery from the Moorish Arabs, their rulers for over 800 years. The 'Blackwork' counted-thread embroidery, so long associated with the Spanish and ultimately with Catherine of Aragon, was based on the geometric Muslim tradition which had its roots in third-century Egypt, Persia and neighbouring countries. This type of embroidery was later found in Moorish Morocco, where the Fez embroidery is a coloured version of Spanish Blackwork, while descendants of Portuguese invaders brought Italian – inspired Assisi-type embroidery to Azemmour on the Moroccan Atlantic coast. Over a period of time these European influences were to cross the Atlantic and find fertile soil amongst communities already well versed in the textile arts.

Floral embroidery of a non-figurative type took a firm hold in the imaginations of a people at one with their nat-ural surroundings, where knowledge of agriculture and the uses of plants for both medicine and dyestuffs was essential for their survival. Persian designs were already well established as part of the Italian brocade weavers' repertoire and had influence on Spanish church embroidery. The Silk Road was a channel for design ideas as well as for goods and pattern concepts from Central Asia, India and ultimately from China, which found their way to the West and eventually to Europe and the New World. When sea-trade became established on the Pacific coastlines of Central America, a more direct to route China and also to the Philippines was to have a considerable influence on trade and textile production.

The women of the conquered countries of the Americas, who were already proficient in the art of inlay and brocade-

OPPOSITE PAGE:
Chain-stitch embroidered panel showing scenes of rural life in the high-altitude areas round Lake Titicaca – the potent sun motif peeps from behind two mountains in the background.

Two young girls from Chichicastenango work coloured embroidery for tourist sale.

A boy's shirt collar from San Antonio Palopó is stiffened with stripes of chain stitch on the wrong side, probably worked with a hook. The edges are bound with coloured, cotton threads.

weave techniques, soon embraced the concept of free stitching, aided by the use of the newly imported steel needles brought over by the Spanish. Under the influence of the convent nuns, the working of the different types of embroidery gradually spread from those areas originally converted by the missionaries. These would of necessity be the ones easiest to colonize and to reach geographically. The more accessible areas of Central America were the first to benefit and the art of embroidery still flourishes here today. In South America there was already an ancient culture in which the decoration of cloth of was of prime importance and gauze-weave embroidery had reached the status of a fine art.

Central America

Satin and stem stitch are both simple stitches where the embroidery thread is worked as an over-sewing stitch that passes completely round and through the background fabric, so that it looks almost the same on both sides. The Spanish introduced many other surface stitches including chain stitches and the knotted stitches for which the Spanish are famous. Coral stitch, herringbone, fishbone and variations of feather stitch were combined with backstitch and seeding to give a rich repertoire of stitching. The looped stitches, like velvet stitch, were used in some areas to decorate the *huipils* with borders of textured pile. These looped-pile stitches might also be worked with a small punch needle, in a similar manner to the working of rugs with a large-scale punch

needle. Not all of these stitches would be used at the same time; a limited selection was included as embroidery on the *huipils* and their use became identified with specific areas.

Certain counted-thread stitches that were already in use are similar to pattern darning, so were soon accepted as they too have their equivalents in weaving and in time came to supplant many of the weaving patterns. When a line of equally spaced darning stitches is filled in on the return journey, the technique is called double running, sometimes referred to as Holbein stitch, one that is frequently used in Spanish black work. Cross-stitch and long-armed cross became very popular and were incorporated as decoration on costume. Although hand embroidery freed the workers from the constraints of the warp and weft of the woven fabric, factory-produced cloth gave them less satisfaction as a vehicle for individual expression. The worker was not in charge of the complete process, which in the past combined the construction of the fabric together with the integral decoration. The result was a profusion of embroidery, as if the worker wanted to make up for the time saved in having forsaken the complexities of traditional weaving.

In time there was also a greater selection of embroidery threads, a change from the hand-spun cotton and wool that had been available earlier. Today, few can afford real silk threads, but mercerized cotton, artificial silk and rayon threads were eventually imported, followed more recently by a large range of synthetic threads. Contemporary embroiderers prefer the lustrous threads and the bright colours of modern dyes, which do not look at all out of place in the brilliant sunshine. Thin woollen threads or a synthetic substitute are still used for much of the satin-stitch embroidery. The Huichol people of north-western Mexico take commercially spun wool apart and re-spin for their own use, or divide or multiply the strands to satisfy their own particular needs.

Ecclesiastical Embroidery – Convent Nuns as Teachers

The nuns taught not only embroidery, but also fine sewing – one of their objects being to see the native population clad in clothing that complied with their own concepts of decency. Originally, schools were set up by the friars for the purpose of converting the population to Christianity, but when the nuns followed, they began to teach the arts and crafts they had learned in their convents back in Spain. The pupils were taught first to make samplers of stitches for practical fine sewing and only later for decorative embroidery.

The nuns introduced metal thread embroidery to be used for ecclesiastical vestments, altar cloths and later for making image dresses to clothe the statues of the Catholic saints that had displaced the idols of the pagan religion. Gold and silver metallic threads are held onto the fabric surface with couching stitches. The gold thread, which usually takes the form of a core of silk or cotton thread around which a flat strip of metal is wound in a spiral formation, could not be taken through to the back of the fabric surface without deformation. Other gold-thread types such as heavy cords or decorative wires were also couched down with tiny spaced stitches in a matching thread colour. These were complemented by the addition of spangles and sequins, which would catch the light of the candles in the dimly lit churches.

This love of rich decoration was to be translated to fiesta costume, some of which followed the Spanish bull-fighting tradition where the Matador's suit was heavily padded and encrusted with metal threads and layered sequins which formed some protection from the bull's horns. In the Los Reyes state of Mexico, *La Danza de los Cuadrillas* is performed by the men dressed in richly embroidered suits. Satin or velvet fabric in black or red forms a background for the exotic gold and silver thread work, with areas of padded and raised work, together with the addition of spangles and sequins, worked in designs similar to those found on the Church altar frontals, but with the addition of symbols such as a crayfish or birds of prey, dispersed among cornucopias of flowers. The men wear a wax mask with a beard attached and all is topped by a large, embroidered felt sombrero hat.

Whitework Embroidery

Whitework embroidery has always been a feature of church needlework, following the tradition of fine linen, woven in the spirit of a religious offering. Flax was only grown in the central parts of America for a short period as the Spanish feared competition with the home-produced linen industry and finally banned the American product. Finely spun and woven cotton cloth can be substituted for the linen, but nothing can replace the sheen that is one of the special qualities of natural linen. Surface stitching in white thread was a common form of decoration, with padded satin stitches giving the designs a raised appearance. The embroidered cloths were used as covers for the altar top, often with a decorative border or lace edging overhanging the heavily worked altar frontal. A square cloth would be used as a 'chalice veil' to cover the offertory cup. Eyelet embroidery was a nineteenth-century innovation, rather like a poor man's lace, and was taken up not only by the Church, but also by the women to decorate their petticoats and collars.

This drawn-threadwork handkerchief from Panama has an ink written message 'Balboa, Canal Zone, 1912' and was possibly sent home as a souvenir.
(Jeri Ames Collection, Maine, USA)

Drawn and Pulled Thread Work – European Origins

Although this type of embroidery was also worked by the nuns, it was originally a European tradition based on a rural society that had little money to spend on rich embroidery. Natural hand-spun linen fabric was used both for the background fabric and to provide the embroidery thread. In 'drawn-thread work', linen threads were withdrawn from parts of the fabric to leave spaces and these threads were then used to produce patterns by drawing together and binding the remaining ground threads. In 'pulled-thread work' – normally worked on a loosely woven fabric – no threads are withdrawn and the decorative effect is achieved by pulling together the ground threads to achieve an openwork pattern. The *Mestizo* and the colonial Spanish ladies used drawn and pulled-thread work on cotton fabric to make ornamental mats in a domestic context, while in areas of Mexico and Guatemala it was used to embellish parts of the costume of both men and women. Although the original tradition was for white embroidery on a white fabric, a love of colour prompted local women to adopt coloured embroidery threads as binding agents.

Needle weaving is a drawn-thread embroidery technique of European origin. Here, the weft threads in a selected pattern area are withdrawn from the centre of the motif. Ends can be worked back into the sides or cut off and held with buttonhole stitches. The vertical threads that remain are

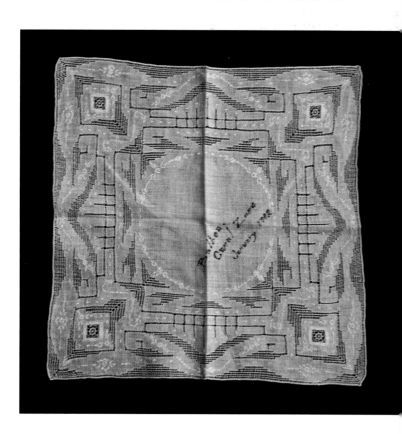

embroidered with needle-woven or needle-wrapped stitches to form openwork patterns that completely fill the area with geometric patterns. These counted-stitch techniques were favourites of the Mayan women who were used to counting the threads in pattern weaving. Embroidery in a single colour was preferred for the edges of the underskirts worn in the Yucatan peninsula, but several colours were incorporated into narrow bands to decorate the front and shoulder areas of the men's shirts.

Openwork in Pre-Conquest Peru

At first there may appear to be no connection with the drawn-thread work of European origin and the gauze weaving of the ancient Peruvian cultures. The link is in the type of embroidery stitches used to decorate the openwork of the background fabric. Although one fabric is altered by the withdrawing of threads and the other has the openwork dictated by the weaving process, both will ultimately provide a similar type of fabric base for the addition of the embroidery.

In his book *Textiles of Ancient Peru and their Techniques*, Raoul d'Harcourt gives exact details of the stitches used on the open spaces of network, pointing out that they are exactly the same as the stitches used on filet, or darned net as worked by embroiderers today. The Peruvian ground fabric is not a network made of a continuous thread, but rather a weave construction where the weft threads are woven independently around the spaced warp threads, thus forming a square mesh. Herringbone and *Point de Reprise* as well as darned circles and wheels appear on the mesh of the network. This similarity, which at first seems surprising considering that the area in question had no contact at that time with any other foreign lands, can be explained by the fact that there are only so many ways in which a decorative element can be combined with a certain fabric structure. What is surprising, is that this isolated society had reached such a peak of textile technology at so early a time.

Floral Embroidery in Guatemala and Mexico

While there are many delightful examples of floral embroidery worked onto the *huipils* of Guatemalan women, they are less common than those of neighbouring Mexico where a veritable flower garden of embroidery decorates the traditional *huipils* and the blouses that are now worn in so many parts of the country. The reason for this may be one of climate where, in the comparatively cooler temperature of the Guatemala mountains, woven garments are still more practical, or that their tradition of inlay-woven floral designs still holds sway. The use of the lighter cotton fabric in the hotter areas is an ideal base for these exuberant designs, which over the years have attained the status of a folk art.

In Guatemala, in the Quiche area of Chichicastenango, floral embroidery is worked onto both male and female garments. Ceremonial *huipils* from Patzun were decorated with a mixture of floral and geometric patterns that surrounded the round neck opening to form a circular yoke.

Embroidered huipil *from Patzun with floral stitching worked across the central* ruanda *seam.*

Detail of the flower embroidery showing the shaded stitches.

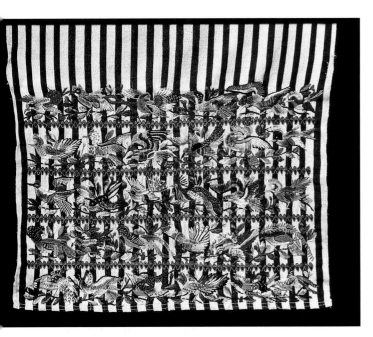

The lower section of a man's trouser leg with embroidery featuring little birds worked across the stripes – from Santiago Atitlán.

Detail showing the colourful satin and stem-stitched bird motifs – c. 1990–1994.

The embroidery covered the central front and back joins of the vertically striped hand-woven fabric. Floral satin stitch embroidery in cotton threads is worked round the neckline of a *huipil*, which comes from Patzun, but is very similar to one worn by a weaver in San Antonio Aquas Calientes. The slightly padded stitching is worked over the top of the front and back central joins of the striped fabric to form a semi-circular 'collar'. To some extent, the design differs on the front and the back, an expression of individuality showing the embroiderer did not wish to repeat herself. In some sections, shaded threads are used, in others the embroiderer has cleverly mixed the differently coloured threads to suggest the streaked lines on the flower petals. The work is mainly in satin stitch, but stem stitch in a darker colour is used to outline some of the flower edges and the central veins of the little leaves.

Santiago Atitlán is famous for the embroidered trousers of the men. They were worn as everyday dress at one time, but are now more likely to be reserved for festival time. The trousers are made from vertically striped woven fabric and are distinguished from those of Solola, where the decoration is part of the inlay-weave technique. An array of delightful little birds is embroidered across the stripes in satin stitch with some outlines in stem stitch. These stitched outlines, which are worked in a darker thread, emphasize certain areas such as the wings, beaks and tails, giving a definite feeling of vibrancy to the embroidery. Similar embroidery is worked onto the striped *huipils* worn by the women, and separate panels of the embroidery are now worked as sale items for the tourists. It is interesting to note that the embroidery on a pair of trousers purchased in 1994 is far finer than that on similar embroidered panels, purchased in 2004. The same lovely little birds are depicted and the embroidery technique is of a similar standard, but the scale of the new work is almost twice that of the original.

In Mexican Oaxaca, the blouse tops and full skirts of the women from the Tehuantepec area, especially at fiesta time, are almost covered with hand-stitched floral embroidery – apart from the deep lace frill at the skirt hem. Flowers are large and florid, worked in contoured bands of satin-stitch embroidery in brilliant reds, orange, blues, yellows and mauves onto black satin or dark velvet fabric. Occasionally, selected areas only are embroidered, featuring large floral sprays or deep bands of flower patterning. This type of embroidery is reminiscent of the embroidered and fringed shawls, popular in Spain during the nineteenth century, which were eventually imported into Mexico. Roses are a favourite flower, often worked in ombré silk or rayon threads, while further south, in the state of Chiapas, the *Mestizo* women embroider roses onto their net skirts.

Flowers are the main subject choice for everyday wear, but here the floral embroidery does not necessarily cover the entire background of the fabric, taking the form of floral motifs positioned on the front, sleeves, necklines and at times the hems of the blouses or dresses. Unlike the gala costumes, the embroidery is worked in cotton threads, sometimes as a soft cotton cord or more frequently in the form of stranded threads. The white blouses are embroidered along

A little girl's dress in dark blue cotton is decorated with flower embroidery – Teotihuacán area, Mexico.

Although not finely worked, the design is lively, satin-stitched in cotton embroidery threads.

the yokes and neck areas, with additional embroidery on the sleeves and cuff edges. Little girls' dresses, sold in tourist shops, still have imaginative hand-worked floral motifs embroidered onto dark coloured cotton cloth, showing that craftsmanship still endures.

Free Stitches

Some of the various embroidery stitches introduced by the Spanish and Portuguese were taken up in different areas and became connected with a particular region or section of the community. It has already been mentioned that the men belonging to the *Cofradias* of Chichicastenango embroidered the side flaps of their ceremonial breeches with chain stitching. The small-scale chain stitch would be worked in a fine thread, covering most of the fabric ground. Sunray patterns were considered to be auspicious, indicating by association the strength and importance of the wearer.

Chain stitches, in the form of a detached chain, or lazy-daisy stitch, were used in Mexican embroidery to simulate the long petals of circular flowers, radiating out from the centre. These were worked on their own to cover a background, or mixed with other surface stitches, including French knots and variations of feather stitch and herringbone. French knots are combined with pile-work, probably using a punch-needle rug technique, in a piece of Mixtec embroidery echoing the stepped brick-fret motifs on the temple walls at Mitla, near Oaxaca.

Brazilian Embroidery

The embroidery stitches used would be those that the nuns were familiar with. Some found greater favour with the indigenous population than others. Bullion-knot embroidery was probably introduced into Brazil and neighbouring countries by the Portuguese. Today, it is popular in the USA and in Western countries and takes the form of raised stitching, mainly depicting floral designs. According to the Brazilian Dimensional Embroidery International Guild, based in the USA, 'Brazilian' embroidery was developed by Elisa Hirsch Maia during the early 1960s. Unable to obtain floss thread in suitable colours, she began to dye the locally available wood-pulp cellulose threads for her own use. Eventually, an industry was set up in Brazil, producing multicoloured rayon threads for use with the 'Vari-Cor' embroidery. Soon the craft became known as 'Brazilian' embroidery, taking its name from the origin of the threads, which being smooth, were excellent for bullion-knot stitching.

Maria A Freitas, who was born in Brazil, took up this embroidery and her talent led to teaching. In the late 1960s, she and her husband moved to the USA and started a business manufacturing the variegated rayon threads. The bullion knot is worked by twisting the embroidery thread from an average of seven to twenty times round the needle end that protrudes from an incomplete stitch, which is the estimated length of the finished knot. The remaining thread is drawn through the twists to form a coiled knot around the embroidery thread. The completed stitch can lie flat or, worked at a shorter distance, can be curved or form a loop. The knots were sewn to resemble flower petals or stamens, leaf shapes or flower centres, sometimes grouped to form raised shapes.

Bullion knots appear early on in Western embroidery and even feature on the little 'slips' embroidered onto even-weave linen during the sixteenth century. As late as the mid-twentieth century they were also included in ecclesiastical embroidery tuition in the Italian convents, forming part of the education of novices and young girls. When worked in metallic golden cords, the knots would form a rich decoration and this may be the origin of the name 'bullion' knot. This type of embroidery travelled across the world as far as the Philippines, where it is worked onto little smocked dresses made for the export trade. It is far more likely that bullion-knot embroidery reached these Pacific islands from the Americas, than from west to east, and today it is worked as a leisure pastime in Japan.

Cross Stitch and Counted-Thread Embroidery

A different interpretation of flower patterns is seen in cross-stitch work where a geometric rendering of any naturalistic design is the inevitable outcome of working on an even-weave fabric. Italian brocade-woven fabrics were imported into Central America from Spain during the eighteenth century and the designs were transferred into weaving patterns, which in their turn were interpreted in counted thread embroidery, including cross-stitch. These floral designs take on a different aspect when worked on the plain, white cotton ground of a full-length *huipil* from the Oaxaca area. A greater proportion of white background fabric gives the large, open flower patterns a more delicate appearance. They are interspersed between rows of geometric stitching reminiscent of crenulations or Greek key patterns. Red is the favoured colour, having magical significance, followed by yellow, blue, orange, mauve and green.

Many of the weaving patterns which are interpreted as cross stitch or as pattern darning, are placed onto the *huipils* or blouses in the position that was once held by the woven inlay designs. The Huichol tribes use a mixture of cross stitch, long-armed cross, darning and double-running stitches to decorate garments and bags with designs of flowers, birds and little animals. Peacocks, eagles and little figures may be shown individually, or are included as part of a geometric border pattern. Their stitching is especially fine, and is worked onto fine white cotton for the men's shirts and the women's *huipils*.

Cross-stitch and long-armed cross, where one leg of the cross stretches over its neighbouring stitch, are used in several areas of Mexico to embroider both the blouses and the covering *quechquémitl*. Although many of the patterns were derived from the indigenous weaving tradition, the twentieth-century importation of commercial cross-stitch patterns introduced foreign design elements, which gradually became incorporated into the local repertoire.

Smocking

Smocking is the one European embroidery tradition that did not find great favour in the Americas, but there are examples from some areas of Mexico. The neckline frill of a blouse from Tojobales in southern Mexico has little pleats held with embroidery stitches. This is not worked in the traditional smocking technique where the 'reeds' or gathers are held with tacking threads that are removed after the surface stitching is finished. English smocking stitches are based on a stem or oversewing stitch that is worked on top of the 'reeds', holding them together to form an embroidered pattern, and some of the Mexican blouses in the collection of the Metropolitan Museum of Art, New York are finely embroidered with these traditional smocking stitches.

A different smocking technique is worked on a blouse from Tlaxcala in central Mexico. The gathering on the blouse front is worked as a type of smocking where the 'reeds' are held with a series of running stitches that keep the gathers in place, while at the same time delineating the design. This smocking is based on Portuguese work where the contrast-thread running stitches are passed over the gathered 'reeds', or under and through them to form the positive and negative elements of the design. Coarse versions of this traditional work are found in Portugal today and take the form of gathered bag handles, apron tops and tourist blouses.

The gathered front bib area of the Tlaxcala blouse is decorated in counted running stitch to form patterns reminiscent of Assisi-type embroidery where the negative parts of the design stand out from the darker, filled-in background. The original Assisi work shows winged beasts placed either side of a Tree of Life, or a fountain – a design that originated in ancient Assyrian stone relief carvings – while in some Tlaxcala embroidery, a similar central motif is flanked by birds representing the eagle and serpent device, the national emblem of Mexico. The background filling of the original Assisi embroidery is normally worked as long-armed cross

ABOVE: *Pieces cut from discarded brocade-patterned huipils and cloths are re-assembled to make patchwork bedcovers for tourist sale in Chichicastenango market.*

RIGHT: *A winged creature embroidered onto fine cotton cloth in herringbone stitch, possibly worked by the Huichol tribes of north-west Mexico, but purchased in the Teotihuacán area.*

and this stitch was commonly used by Mexican embroiderers to work similar motifs of mystical beasts adapted from the Italian designs.

Embroidered Pictures and Wall Hangings – Guatemala and Mexico

The production of pictorial embroidery for tourist sale in Chichicastenango market has increased greatly during the last ten years. This type of embroidery is worked onto a background fabric of white cotton in brightly coloured embroidery threads, mainly in cotton but with some synthetics. Although there is evidence of embroidery on the long sashes or head coverings, the main output is for pictorial cloths and for little picture panels, either sold on their own or combined to make a patchwork bedcover with plain fabric borders. The subject matter shows scenes from local life, with little people, animals, flowers, houses, fields and agriculture. Churches, religious symbols and even the gravestones, carved to resemble the ancient stele stones, are shown. The larger pictures may include a variety of subjects, rather as if the embroiderer wanted to record the life of the entire area in one go. A favourite design shows the 'flying men' who descend spirally around a pole from ropes tied to their feet. Once part of a religious ritual, they are now a source of entertainment for both local inhabitants and the tourists.

In Patzun, Guatemala, a type of satin-stitch embroidery, originally worked in silk threads, entirely covers the surface of the factory-produced white cotton background fabric. A rectangular cloth embroidered with religious symbols such as the cross, doves of peace, stars and animals and curved lozenges, was used at marriage ceremonies. Colours include purple-blue, red, orange, green and yellow. The cloth would be attached to a veil and form part of the wedding headdress. A similar type of embroidery design, using religious and secular symbols, was worked in thin wools as a political expression by poor or persecuted women in areas of Guatemala.

The Huichol tribes of Mexico's north-west use a different stitching method to make little pictures embroidered onto plain white cotton fabric. The bands of stitching are worked in stranded cotton threads using a close herringbone stitch which reverses to double backstitch, only the outlines of the embroidered bands being visible on the wrong side of the embroidery. Some of the pictures depict little animals, though the type of animal is not always easy to identify, appearing to be a mixture of several creatures, occasionally sprouting wing-like protrusions. These may be mythological creatures connected with the naturistic religious beliefs of these people, who refused to be fully converted to Christianity, preferring to worship their own gods while still paying lip service to the Catholic Church. Once again, these little pictures are sold in tourist outlets, but they originate from a people who have an excellent reputation for embroidery and whose traditional costume is a display canvas for a whole raft of embroidery designs and motifs, often worked as cross stitch.

Chain-Stitch Embroidered Pictures in Bolivia and Peru

The wall hangings embroidered in chain stitching onto hand-woven woollen cloth are found in the area around Lake Titicaca where the bowler-hatted women sit in groups by the lakeside. The embroidery is worked with a metal hook, something like a small crochet hook but with a sharper point at the base of the hook. The yarn is always held beneath the background fabric and the hook is used to draw the thread through from the back of the fabric to form a chain loop on the front surface. This stitching is worked as a continuous line and is a coarser version of the fine tambour-work embroidery found in India and the Middle East and later worked in Europe onto fine muslin fabrics as a form of lace.

The hook passes through the slightly open structure of the woollen fabric, which allows the thread to be drawn up through successive loops to make the chain-stitch lines. However, if the hook is withdrawn from the loop, it will pull undone and so will all of the previously worked chain stitches. For this reason, fastening on and off is important. The yarn used is generally made from undyed natural sheep's wool in shades of brown, fawn, grey and white, but occasionally a purchased yarn in similar natural shades may be added to give more variety to the work.

Much thought is given to expressing the design elements as a series of continuous lines that not only outline but also fill in the interior of each motif. The pictorial subjects of this type of embroidery are nearly all familiar scenes from the surrounding area, especially those showing reed boats with the double-ended prows, the tied reed bundles and the decorated square sails. The familiar flamingos, fish and frogs, as well as the reeds that border the lake, all are shown in charming detail. Agricultural scenes of ploughing, together with birds, small animals and often the sun motif, will complete a picture that is a record of the everyday life of this lakeside community.

It is not known if this type of chain stitching evolved from tambour work and the chain-stitch crochet introduced by the Spanish, or whether there is any link with the chain-stitched embroidered Peruvian textiles of the Pre-Columbian era. Although it is possible that much of the very fine 'stem-stitch' Paracas embroidery was worked on the loom, most larger-scale chain stitching could only be achieved as hand

Bowler-hatted women sit working their chain-stitch embroidery on the Peruvian shore of Lake Titicaca.

stitching, quite probably with the use of a hook in the same manner as the tambour chain stitching, which is almost indistinguishable from hand embroidery. A pre-Columbian indigo-dyed, woven tunic in the Birmingham City Museum collection is decorated widthways across the hem with several rows of chain stitching. In comparison with the fine stem stitching, these stitches at about 6mm (¼in) in length, are quite coarse. The chain stitches could be worked with a needle, but a hook inserted vertically would be far less likely to bend and distort.

Embroidery as a Political Statement

The **Paños** *of Guatemala*

Paños, or embroidered yarn pictures, similar to the embroidery from Patzun in Guatemala, were made originally to make a political statement, but are now more likely to be sold to the tourist trade to generate much needed income. In Portuguese, the word *Paño* refers to the plain tabby weave of the background fabric. A picture purchased in the Solola area in 1994 is embroidered with black, fawn, mustard, orange and yellow synthetic yarns. Apart from a voided area on the borders of the white cotton cloth, the entire surface is covered with stitching in bands of closely worked herringbone stitch. Motifs show two animals with spots on, presumably jaguars, a chalice and a series of rainbow-type arches. A typed note was attached to the embroidery, with an official-looking stamp of the *'Comite del de Ayud a Refugiados Guatemaltecos'.* The note states as quoted:

> in one region of Guatemala, women traditionally embroider yarn pictures called paños during their pregnancies. Now a group of widows make them in order to support themselves and eighty-three orphans. These women and children lost their relatives in massacres carried out by government forces in their villages. Some of the paños have the more traditional symbols concerning the church and pregnancy. The colours reflect happiness, sadness, or hope of the women. The chalice signifies the body and blood of Christ. The animals await the birth of the child to give him/her a home. Other paños contain symbols that reflect the present [sic, 1994] situation of the country and the spirit of struggle in Guatemala. In these squares, the arches are explained as representing the people, the Quetzales (a bird with long tail and feathers) liberty, the doves peace, and the tigers evil or the army and the government.

It is not clear from the above whether this particular *paños* purchased in 1994 was political or religious. The chalice is symbolic of the Church, the animals may be benign, but also could be interpreted as 'the tigers of evil' and the arches obviously represent the people.

Arpilleras *from Chile*

The word *arpillera* originally meant sackcloth, or as known in the USA, burlap. This was the only fabric available to the

A yarn picture or paño *worked in a close herringbone stitch shows motifs that could be religious, or project a political statement.* (Purchased from the Solola area of Guatemala, 1994)

poor women of Chile who in 1974 used stitching to express their feelings in an unbearable political situation. The Pinochet dictatorship was a time of repression where the ordinary citizens lived in a climate of perpetual fear, exacerbated by the 'disappearance' of many of their closest relatives and friends.

The first *arpillera* workshop was set up under the sponsorship of the Vicaría of Solidarity during March 1974, a year after Agosto Pinochet came to power and overthrew the existing socialist government. Unfortunately, the new regime was a change for the worse with civil rights abandoned, political parties and trade unions prohibited and hundreds of people, mainly men, arrested each month. This left the women without providers, often forcing them to find some way of supporting their large families of small children. The Catholic Church, at length feeling that it must respond to an increasingly desperate situation, set up the Vicaría of Solidarity in order to denounce these violations of human rights and their resulting consequences. As the

Catholic Church was acting within its own ecumenical laws, the government was powerless to interfere.

Fourteen women are said to have taken part in the initial scheme. All had lost a close relative and had met each other previously while searching for their loved ones, thus forming a common bond. Initially, pieces of fabric from old clothing were gathered by the Church organizers and given to the women to make into little pictures, which would eventually be sold abroad to bring in at least a subsistence income. This could not be done officially and the *arpilleras* were exported in secret, which in itself was a hazardous undertaking.

At first, the working of these *arpillera* pictures was a way for the women to convey their anguish. The subjects would be chosen carefully, often showing scenes of everyday life, but always with a pictorial message that might be encoded within the representation, or with the addition of a slogan such as *'Donde estan?'* meaning 'Where is he?' Gradually the women gained confidence, even taking part in political marches, protesting outside prisons and demonstrating while wearing photographs of their missing relatives pinned to the front of their clothing. The government officials took little notice of the women – in a macho society women were not considered of any importance apart from their domestic role in family life. Although some officials were aware of the existence of the *arpilleristas*, they were not aware of the importance of the embroidered messages that

In Peru, this little square picture is called a Cuadro, *a name which originally referred to political statements made by the poor women – Lima c.1990.*

were finding their way out into the world, and thus influencing public opinion.

The technique used to make the *arpillera* is a mixture of applied patchwork with three-dimensional padding for the little 'dolls' or figurines. The backing of burlap forms the first layer, onto which larger pieces of fabric are laid to represent either outdoor scenery, mountains and sky, or the walls of houses and other buildings. These pieces are tacked down before sewing to the background, either with blanket stitches in contrasting colours, or with the fabric edge turned under and hemmed. The little figures have padded faces with embroidered features and the women have free-flowing hair made of woollen threads. Hands and feet can be padded, or left free as additional pieces. Skirts, with embroidery on, are added, together with hats and for the men, ponchos and trousers. As time went on, the embroidery and decorative elements of the *arpilleras* became more elaborate, no doubt catering for the expectations of the tourist market.

It is said that the movement started by the women who made the *arpilleras* was the foundation for future resistance that led eventually in 1989 to the first free elections since the coup of 1973. The resulting democracy meant that the *arpillera* workshops lost the sponsorship of the Vicariate and in 1992 they were closed officially, their role as carriers of political statement being no longer considered necessary. However, the women continued to make these little pictures that had become part of their way of life, as well as providing a livelihood in a still depressed community. The subjects portrayed were now an expression of their lives and surroundings, but without the political overtones that at one time gave these decorative embroideries a hidden but sombre element. Their evolution through the years gives us an insight not only into the development of the women's awakening political awareness, but also the record of a period of history that should not be forgotten.

Arpilleras *from Peru*

Similar little embroidered pictures made in impoverished areas of Peru are often referred to as *cuadros*, meaning 'squares'. A number of co-operative workshops have been set up in the shanty-town areas around Lima, the capital city on the west coast of Peru. In many instances there is no other way for poor families to earn a living. Villagers come from the high mountain areas looking for work and a better life, only to be caught up in a poverty trap. The finished embroideries are collected by the convent nuns who then export them for sale abroad.

Contemporary *cuadros*, which are made to a high standard, are more elaborate than ones available during the 1980s. They include a greater proportion of embroidery

stitches and show a more sophisticated approach to the making of the little three-dimensional figures. No longer limited to the traditional square shape, modern *cuadros* are made as oblong wall hangings and even take the form of Christmas stockings. It is possible that the convent nuns have directed the subject matter, for one Christmas stocking shows a Nativity scene. The 'Inca'-type stone wall of the stable has a thatched roof and the baby Jesus lies on a pile of bright yellow wool, representing corn, while a group of llamas surround the crib. Mary has a bright blue *llilica* cape and Joseph a poncho in minute-scale weaving. The scene shows the mountains of the High Andes silhouetted against a starry sky, with the Star of David having a comet tail. Elaborate stitching outlines the trees, bushes and flowers.

A rural landscape is the subject matter of an impressive wall hanging that combines three scenes, descending from the Andes Mountains. The first shows three alpacas, each with a woven saddlecloth, grazing on the high pastures while a magnificent condor – unmistakable with a red head and white neck ruff – soars high above. In the middle layer little people, men and women, dressed in bright clothes and little crochet hats, sow seeds on the foot-ploughed fields. Below is a weaving village complete with a back-strap loom tied to a tall tree. The detail is amazing. The loom contains actual weaving, while other women are shown fluffing up the wool or cotton, ready for spinning. Some spin with a distaff and tiny spindle, or are shown carrying bundles of spun and dyed wool. The padded faces appear to be covered with fabric from old tights, each one embroidered with minute features. All have arms and legs made from wool-wrapped wire with changes of colour for arms, hands, legs and feet. Embroidery stitches include satin, stem, blanket stitch and couching.

The wall hanging is lined with cotton calico and a small pocket has been added to the back. A pencilled 'Verina Slejos' gives us the name of the embroiderer, while a paper in the pocket lists the contents of the design in Spanish. Similar embroidered pictures are made in Colombia, where they are called *gobolinos*.

Embroidered Dolls

The tradition of making little fabric dolls, first encountered in the grave goods from Chancay on the western coast of Peru, has found a modern interpretation in the production of embroidered and weave-decorated dolls for the tourist

Little doll figures, dressed in local costume, are made for sale by the women of the Ayacuche area of Peru.

trade. This is a fairly recent innovation and may be a development of the little three-dimensional padded figures represented on the *cuadros*. The dolls are not intended as toys, but are faithful replicas of both the people and the various costumes found in the Cuzco areas of Peru. Although they are available in tourist venues such as Cuzco and Machuu Pichu, they are also exported to other countries, probably under the direction of the nuns who export the *cuadros*.

The dolls are beautifully made. Although sold as 'family groups' tied together with brightly coloured synthetic wool, each doll is an individual. They are firmly made, with wool wrapping around the arms and legs and minute features embroidered onto the fabric-covered faces. The woman invariably has a baby held on her back by a shawl and is accompanied by her children – a little boy and a girl. The mother wears several layers of black fabric skirt, with each hem decorated with a narrow woven braid. Bright pom-poms are tied to her ankles and to the ends of her woollen plaits and onto the points of both her son's and

husband's knitted *ch'ulla* hats. Braid decorates the large, flat *montera* hats and borders the poncho of the man, who also caries a woven *ch'uspa* bag into which a typed note is slipped, stating that the figures are representative of the Ayacuche area.

These dolls are so popular that they have become part of a rural industry, providing work for women in areas of the High Andes normally dependent on an unreliable system of agriculture as their only way of earning a living.

Another basic doll type, more in keeping with the ancient ones from Chancay, is also available in tourist outlets. Called *rusticas*, they are made in one piece from old fabric and banana fibre, shaped slightly to the neck. Clothing is simple, made from woven cloth for the skirt, while a knitted fabric might cover the head and provide a base for the embroidered features. Although the cylindrical figure lacks arms and legs, a baby tied to the front appears to be indispensable. These dolls are probably versions of actual dolls, played with by the poorer children.

The Kuna women used the reverse appliqué technique to make the front of a mola *blouse. Chain and stem-stitch embroidery has been added to the faces of these twin lions or jaguars.*

Reverse Appliqué – of the San Blas Islands, Panama and of Columbia

The hand-stitched appliqué panels that form the front and back of the Kuna women's *mola* blouses are not only a decorative element, but also an expression of their daily lives. These islanders, who have for so many years lived in a secluded society, have a different concept of the universe and a firm belief in the forces of nature. Although their religion is now adapted to Christianity, they follow their own interpretation and would appear to have accepted much of the outside twentieth-century influences without altering their basic way of life.

A matriarchal society brings the women together, both to share domestic tasks and ideas. When a girl marries, her new husband moves in with the mother-in-law and becomes part of the bride's extended family. Tasks are allocated according to age and status. The older women elect to do the cooking, others busy themselves with household chores, some look after the children, thus leaving the younger women with time to work on their *mola* designs. The way a woman looks, the quality of her embroidery and her choice of colours and jewellery, all contribute to the respect with which she is regarded and this also reflects on her family. The skill with which she sews the designs, the careful working of the hem stitching and the quality of any additional embroidery will all be taken into consideration when she is to be chosen as a bride.

The pattern for a new *mola* may be the sole choice of the individual worker, but often a group of women will discuss suitable subjects. Many of these include household items and scenes from everyday life as well as of the spirit world and the very important puberty ceremony where the young girl is admitted into adult society and prepared for marriage. Modern *molas* are influenced by illustrations in magazines, books and adverts on TV. The division of labour allows the women to spend many hours working on their *mola* blouses. The portability of the embroidery means that it can be worked when the women are in groups, between chores, or when out visiting other families.

When the pattern and the order of the layers of coloured cloth have been chosen, the design is drawn onto the top layer of cotton fabric. Next, all the design lines are tacked (basted) using a contrasting thread. Using a pair of sharp, pointed scissors, the worker makes a narrow cut parallel with either side of the design line. This free fabric edge is then stroked under with the needle and hemmed with hidden hemstitches beneath the fold, securing it to the layer of cloth below. This technique is repeated for any subsequent layers, thus revealing the colours beneath in narrow bands.

There can be anything from two to four layers of cloth. A one-colour *mola* has a base cloth and one colour above it, originally referred to as a 'Grandmother' *mola*. This method was one of the earliest forms and is the simplest to work, the design often including geometric patterns with black, red and yellow continuing to be the favoured colours.

A method giving inverted colour formations is called 'oblagated', meaning colour change. A pattern is cut at the same time from two pieces of fabrics in different colours. These are separated, and each contrasting colour is inserted into the space left by the other one. Each counter-change set is placed onto a differently coloured backing and all the edges turned under to reveal the background colour, thus producing two separate appliqué panels.

The areas of plain cloth between the design lines are slit and the edges turned under, revealing the layer beneath. Apart from adding a decorative element to the design, these slits, called *tas-tas*, form a practical purpose by making the thick layers of the cloth more supple. This elasticity prolongs the life of the garment, makes it smoother and the narrow seams less liable to come apart and fray. At one time, little additional decoration in the form of embroidery stitching was added, but now it has become more popular. In some instances it has resulted in the reduction of colour layers, making the *mola* less stable and the protruding embroidery stitches more likely to abrade. Stitches are worked with the same fine sewing cotton used to hem the lines and slits. Rows of minute chain stitches echo the slit patterns, while running stitches in different colours fill in the larger spaces of unsecured areas within the design.

Molas with few layers may have additional pieces of coloured cloth inserted to produce a more intricate design. Very few of the early *molas* have survived due to the tropical climate. Some small pieces of indigo dyed and painted cloth exist, but most of the cotton cloth from the early twentieth century onwards was imported, at first bartered for with produce and craft goods and in later years by the selling of completed *mola* panels for the tourist trade.

Assembling and Decorating a Mola Blouse

The top yoke for the front and back of the blouse is cut from two rectangular pieces of commercially printed cloth, the length being the same measurement as the *mola* width. Often, vibrantly coloured patterns are chosen which, to our Western eyes, are at variance with the *mola* designs. The shoulder seams are joined together for about 5cm (2in) at either end of the rectangular yoke. This leaves a wide, horizontal opening for the neck, with a few gathers at the centre front and back. This top area is decorated with applied bands of coloured cloth, occasionally with a saw-tooth edge of cloth triangles, called *dientes* or teeth, peeping from beneath. These are made by taking a narrow band of fabric and slitting upwards on one side only at regular intervals. The fabric cuts, which penetrate less than half way, are then stroked under with the needle on both sides to form a triangle shape, which is sewn down with invisible hem stitches.

The neck is bound with fabric in a contrasting colour. A fabric band is applied to cover the seams that join the *mola* panel to the yoke, often with the addition of ric-rac braid and a second set of cloth triangles in a contrasting colour. The sleeves are cut as rectangles from the printed fabric. The sleeve top is gathered at the shoulder crown, also at the cuff

Free-stitch machine embroidery is worked onto a red felt hat by a member of a co-operative workshop set up in the Chivan area of Peru.

end to form a small, puffed sleeve, once again finished with an applied band decorated with purchased ric-rac and a row of little cloth triangles. The sleeves are set in below the upper level of the *mola* panel to provide greater ease as the *mola* blouse has gradually become more fitted. Side seams are also covered with a fabric strip and a narrow frill in a contrasting colour is added to the base. This helps keep the *mola* blouse in place when covered by the wrap-around skirt.

Machine Embroidery

A people who over the generations have learned to adapt to a variety of rulers, changes of religion and way of life found no difficulty in accepting the sewing machine. There is no feeling that machine work is in any way inferior to hand embroidery. Since the basic sewing machine is merely a mechanized needle that only comes to life in the hands of the operator, it is judged by the results that are achieved, not compared with any other form of embroidery.

In the hands of a competent machinist, the results are indeed something to be marvelled at. The treadle-operated machine allowed the worker to use both hands and thus guide the embroidery more freely. Modern workshops have been set up in various areas, in both South and Central America and here electric sewing machines can give the same facility, although the treadle machine still holds sway in most places.

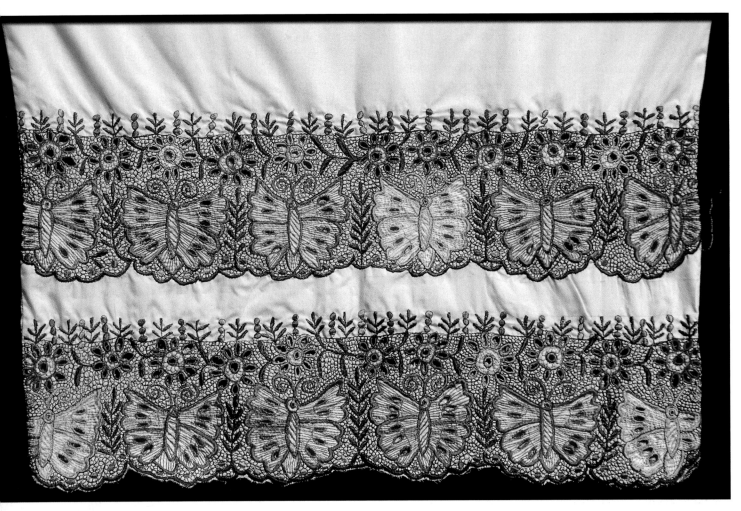

Free machine embroidery has taken over from hand work to decorate the hem of a cotton huipil *from the Yucatan peninsula, Mexico.*

Peru

Today, straight-stitch free-machine embroidery is worked in the Cuzco region of Peru. The little teeth that normally feed the cloth forwards beneath the machine needle are put out of operation, either by lowering these feeder 'dog' teeth, or covering them with a plate. This allows the worker to sew in any direction – backwards, forwards or round in circles: flowing designs give the best results, where the embroiderer does not have to keep starting and stopping. A good operator has complete control of the machine and is in effect, drawing with the needle. These machines are all lock-stitch machines which use two separate threads, one threaded through the needle on the top of the fabric and one thread held in a shuttle or bobbin beneath the feed mechanism. The two threads are combined by the bobbin-race point to interlink and form a locked stitch that is the same length on both sides of the fabric. This means that two different colours can be used, the top contrasting with the bottom one, or they can be the same, producing similar embroidery on both sides.

Items are made in the co-operative workshops for both the tourist trade and local consumption and the Chivay embroidery has a distinctive look, setting it apart from that worked in other areas. Bright red felt hats with bowler-shaped crowns are highly prized and are worn by the women, children and even the little babies tied onto their mother's backs. The embroidery on these hats is a *tour de force*, for they are stitched with the same colours on both sides and it is difficult to decide which is the right or the wrong side. The embroidery covers the entire brim area, divided into horizontal bands, each band filled with a different set of motifs, flowers, little fish and birds with exotic tails. The colours chosen are white, red, blue, pink, yellow and green in fine machine embroidery threads. The embroidery is even worked onto the band round the crown that is integral with the hat, as the stitching goes right through both surfaces. Thus the brim of the hat will look equally well when worn turned up or down.

A belt worked in a similar way has a background of blue fabric bordered with red supported by a layer of interfacing. As the back of the belt remains unseen, the underneath thread is in white, while the same white, red, blue, pink, yellow and green colours are used on the surface to portray the flowers, fish, bird and rabbit or guinea-pig motifs. The Chivay embroiderers wear their finery as part of everyday dress. The machine-embroidered panels are attached to the side-fronts of their jackets and used as a central panel on the blouse front. Smaller motifs may be applied to the skirt hems, combined with woven or purchased braids. Even the little dolls made for sale in this area have machine embroidery to decorate their tiny skirts.

Mexico

Free-stitch machine embroidery is now used in the Yucatan peninsula or south-eastern Mexico by the Maya women to decorate their long, *huipil* blouses. This takes the place of the original hand-stitching, but looks most effective worked in coloured threads on a white cotton ground. The areas covered include the square section around the neck that forms a decorative rather than an actual yoke. On a modern *huipil*, purchased recently near Merida, two scalloped borders also embellish the lower section and hem.

It is still possible to see the pencil lines that have been drawn to define the pattern areas. The machine embroidery is worked over a single layer of the firm cotton fabric, almost filling the design areas with both straight-stitch and satin-stitch embroidery. The satin stitch is most probably worked on a machine that has a swing-needle capability. These machines came into general use during the mid-twentieth century and were the forerunners of the automatic pattern machines, which eventually led to electronic pattern control.

However, it is possible to work satin stitch, which is a closely worked wide-width stitch, on a straight-stitch or treadle machine. The width of the stitch is achieved by the worker moving the cloth, generally held in a frame, rapidly from side to side. This needs expert control. The embroidery on the Mexican *huipil* features both straight-stitch embroidery, worked as a series of continuous circles as a background fill and the satin-stitch embroidery to outline the main pattern motifs. Butterflies with large coiled antennae are filled with a mixture of straight-stitch lines and satin stitch, which outlines the oval holes that imitate patterns found on the wings. The central areas of circular and oval shapes are later cut out, as well as the scallop-edges that border the hem and the inner neckline of the yoke top. The bright colours of the machine embroidery thread – blue, orange, pink, yellow and green –

are tempered with the used of black thread for the circular infill and the straight-stitch outlines of the motifs.

Machine embroidery on purchased cotton fabric developed from the use of narrow borders on both *huipil* blouses and the wrap-around skirts, to full-scale decoration. Another fashion is for the use of purchased ribbons, which are applied and held with machine stitching to decorate various surfaces of the clothing. These ribbons can border the hems of wide skirts, or cover the joins in narrow ones, or in a festive context, are arranged as frills on necklines and sleeve edges.

In both Mexico and Guatemala, machine-embroidered bags and small items sold at tourist markets are very similar. Floral designs are worked to cover almost the entire surface with satin-stitch embroidery, often in ombré machine-embroidery threads – the range of shades within one colour giving the embroidery a richer feel. Whether the design of these bags is common to both countries is not clear; it is more probable that they are produced in one area or workshop and exported as a commercial enterprise.

As the way of life has changed and women who work for a living spend less time in the production of cloth for their own garments and for domestic use, it is inevitable that alternative methods for the decoration of clothing will be found. Those women who have become expert machine embroiderers are fulfilling a need and in doing so are continuing to promote the creative textile arts and, at the same time, still preserve their traditional pattern motifs.

Two very similar bags, machine embroidered with ombré threads, probably come from the same workshop – although the pale one was purchased in Mexico City and the other from Guatemala.

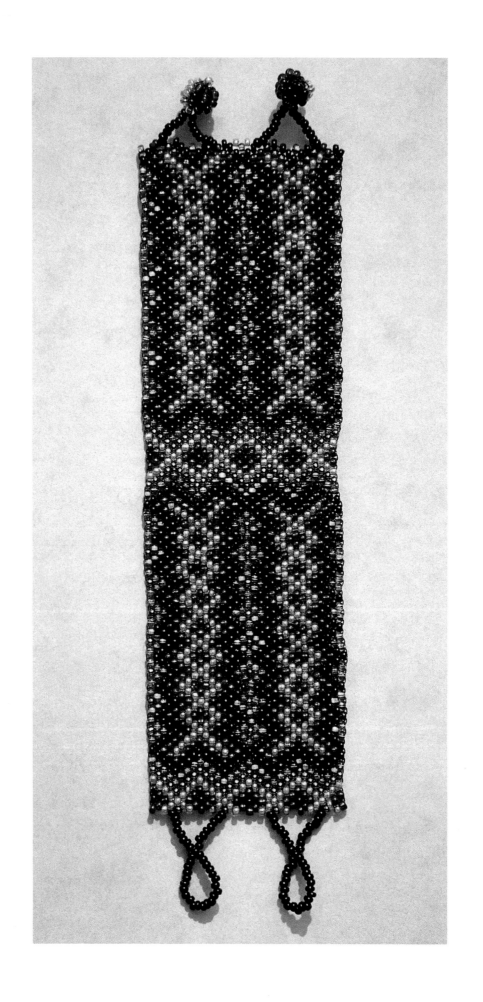

8

Beads and Beadwork

Beads before the Spanish Conquest – Seeds, Shells and Stones

There would appear to be a compulsion by people all over the world to adorn themselves with both natural and mineral objects that have nothing to do with the body clothing that normally provides protection from the heat or cold of our varied climates.

These objects may take the form of amulets, lucky charms or magical talismans. They can be items of regalia, religious symbols or badges of rank. However, they are far more likely to be worn as 'jewellery' in the sense of bedizening the appearance of the wearer. This adornment in itself can be the signal of status, wealth and achievement, while a string of animal teeth and carved bones would also proclaim the prowess of the hunter. The intrinsic worth of the object is inconsequential; it is the rarity, the degree of difficulty in finding or making the object and the amount of workmanship required, that makes it desirable.

In most primitive societies, seeds, nuts and fruit kernels were gathered, pierced and strung about the neck. Initially this may have been a method of food storage and only later used for ornamentation. In the tropical climates of the Amazon Basin, little in the way of clothing was needed. The various tribes used feathers and seeds as decoration, either in the form of necklaces, or sewn onto bark or vegetable fibre as body ornament. Seeds, later to be replaced by trade beads, were incorporated into bead-woven aprons and included with feathers in the various headdresses that distinguished one tribe from another. The Wayana-Aparai women made beaded aprons with intricate patterns based on the men's twill-woven baskets. Small seeds and seedpods were pierced, but larger vegetable shells were drilled to make discs that would be pierced and threaded as a series of flat beads to make long necklaces. Circles, cut from coca-nut shells by the Wayuu people of northern Columbia and Venezuela, are oiled to enhance the colour and sometimes covered with gold.

Shells were gathered and they too were to form the basic material for some of the early beads. Snail shells were pierced to form bead necklaces as early as 7,500BC in southern Mexico. Many types of seashell were differently coloured on the inside, enabling the bead maker to work with several gradations of colour. The orange and red *Spondylus* shells of the spiny oyster, which came from the coastal areas of Ecuador, were held in high esteem and beads and ornaments have been found among the grave goods of the Chavin and Moche cultures in Peru. The shells were imbued with magical rainmaking properties and although inedible, were deemed to be the food of the Gods. The coastal waters of Peru and Chile were cool, at the mercy of the cold Atlantic current and the spiny oysters were found only in the warmer waters of the more northerly tropical regions. The island of Puna is said to have been the centre of a vast export trade for these valuable shells, with fleets of sailing-rafts taking them to the Ecuadorian mainland and from there to Chimú and Chincha states, which were in power before the Incas expanded their territory throughout Peru and the Andes in the early fifteenth century. The trade in the shells was far-reaching, for the Maya in Central America used these highly regarded red *Spondylus* beads as currency.

Pottery Beads

As soon as it was discovered that clay fired to a high temperature would produce watertight pots for carrying water and for cooking, the firing technique was transferred to other objects made of clay. Who knows if the art of making

Contemporary necklaces from Guatemala, 2004. A wide, network necklace is shown, together with one threaded as a spiral helix.

fired clay beads was first discovered by a happy accident? The potter may have rolled surplus bits of clay and used them as test pieces in the kiln. It was only one more stage to make a hole in the middle, enabling the clay ball to be threaded. Holes were made by piercing the damp clay with pieces of grass or a narrow stalk. This vegetable matter would burn away during the firing, leaving a perfectly formed narrow hole. Beads were decorated by incising lines or impressing hard objects into the damp clay. Alternatively, pattern moulds were made into which the clay was pressed. Beads were painted with contrasting clay-slip before firing, or decorated afterwards with mineral colours and glazes.

A modern bead-making industry is now established in the area around Cuzco, Peru. The small pottery beads, which were at first made entirely by hand, do not have any link with the past. They developed from the larger sized pottery toggles made for tourist sale, used on bag-thongs and to secure cords on garments. They are now exported in great quantities, generally cylindrical in shape with painted and glazed designs reminiscent of 'Inca' patterns. Necklaces made from these beads are advertised for sale in mail-order catalogues, or they can be purchased separately and threaded as required by the wearer.

Stone and Mineral Beads

Pebbles with holes in could also be strung and this eventually lead to the drilling of holes and the carving of stone and other minerals. Some of the early discoidal stone beads are flat with roughly shaped edges. Later, round beads were carved with decoration similar to that used on the pottery beads. These stone beads are similar to the stone spindle-whorls, but are normally spherical in shape, with a smaller hole drilled through the middle. Some very small beads found in Columbia have two holes drilled through, possibly intended for sewing onto a garment. Semi-precious stones, including obsidian and jade, provided black and shades of green as early additions to the colour repertoire. During the period AD800–1500, rock crystal, onyx and carnelian were worked in northern Columbia by the *Tairona* people who were famed for their skill at making stone beads. Unlike woven textiles, beads do not deteriorate and are evidence of an extensive trade enterprise ,originally set up by the Olmecs of Central Mexico, that stretched well down into the areas of South America.

The Maya inherited the love of jade from the Olmecs and considered it their most precious stone. The fact that it had to be imported from Guatemala made it even more valuable. As these stones were hard to incise and drill, it was necessary to use some type of abrasive in conjunction with fluid to aid the work. The Olmecs are said to have invented the technique of cord-sawing which enabled the workers to make round or angled cuts. Jade was cut using a bowstring of agave fibre, coated with abrasive. Unwanted parts of the jade stone would be ground away to reveal the best colour and the final results polished with beeswax. Holes were drilled using a pointed, hollow tube or bamboo cane filled with fine sand or other abrasive powder. A simple drill could be rotated within the hands, but this must have been somewhat limiting. The bow drill, where a cord was wrapped round the drill to give a reciprocal movement, or the pump drill which was moved up and down like a ratchet screwdriver, were both used in many of the early cultures.

The Mixtec people of the Oaxaca region of western Mexico preferred to use turquoise for their beads and jewellery. As turquoise is found naturally in desert areas, it was easier and cheaper to obtain than the imported jade. However, the Mixtec craftsmen are famed for mixing their beads, and multi-type necklaces have been found in tombs of the late fifteenth century in the site at Monte Alban. They combined gold beads with those made from shells, rock crystal, jade, amber, coral and jet. Modern necklaces made with commercial beads still follow the same patterns today.

Gold Beads

There were two types of goldsmith – those who made jewellery for wear and decoration and those who made golden articles as votive objects for the glory of the gods. Gold especially was connected with the Sun god. Gold was called 'The Sweat of the Sun' and silver was known as 'The Tears of the Moon'. Gold was found as nuggets in many riverbeds of both South and Central America. The early gold workers in the coastal areas of Peru of about 500BC used a hammering technique to make flat sheets of gold that were then formed into the various objects. Tools were simple, made from stone, obsidian and copper as the use of iron was unknown before the Conquest. Although gold casting was perfected by the early centuries AD in Columbia, the Chimú goldsmiths still preferred to use the hammering techniques. They made round, hollow beads by forming the flat sheets over a half spherical shape and then joining the two parts together. As they did not use solder, it is thought the beads were held together with natural glue. Sadly, next to nothing remains of the early golden artefacts, apart from those found in more recently excavated tombs, for nearly all was melted down by the Spaniards.

Silver Ornaments

The metal silver has long been mined in both continents and is in continuous use up to the present day. It is said that the Spanish preferred silver jewellery and ornaments to that made of gold, but it is not recorded if this was a fashionable choice influenced by a tradition of Spanish silver-work, or if the more precious gold metal was reserved initially for export as gold bullion to fill the coffers of the Spanish Court, thus setting a precedent.

The pin that is used to hold together the corners of the *manta* cloak in Ecuador, or the *lliclla* in Bolivia and Peru was normally made of silver. Silver beads, discs, pendants and earrings were worn as part of the costume of the women and to some extent, of the men of many areas of Central and South America. This depended to some extent on the proximity of the silver mines, or of an established trading system. Apart from the decorative element, this was visible wealth where a person carried their fortune about the body and, in some instances, this display would advertise a woman's suitability for marriage.

Trade-Beads and Sequins

Glass beads were introduced by the Spanish and Portuguese as trade items to barter for precious metals and jewellery. As the craft of glass-making was not known in either South or Central America before the Conquest, the original inhabitants thought the glass beads were made from jadeite and rock crystal, both precious materials that were difficult to work. The Spanish did not enlighten them and walked away with a fortune's worth of gold and semi-precious stones. In post-Conquest times many beads were imported by the Spanish from Bohemia and Italy, the multi-coloured glass beads from Venice being the most popular. Jewellery continued to be made by the indigenous craftsmen, as many of their techniques could not be bettered. Over the years they began to incorporate Spanish designs, but these were amalgamated with the ancient motifs that were part of their inherited tradition.

The little round beads known as *rocailles* were imported in vast quantities. Eventually they were to supersede the use of seeds for both sewn and strung decoration, bead weaving and network and they are still very much in use today.

Although many modern types of bead are moulded, the original glass *seed* beads were made by the glass blower drawing out a narrow tube of glass, hollow in the middle. This was chopped up into small sections to make the beads. These small sections were tumbled in containers filled with abrasive until they became rounded. Beads can be square or faceted and the holes in the middle coloured to give contrast. The variety would appear to be endless. Bugle beads are made from narrow tubes cut to different lengths and although they are normally sewn as bead embroidery, they are often incorporated with strung beads as part of a necklace or bracelet.

Other imports were sequins and spangles. The Spanish, like wealthy people in many other European countries, loved to include tiny spangles on their embroidered clothing. The first spangles were made by joining a tiny coil of wire into a circle and then hammering it to form a small, flat disc. Later, these discs were stamped from a flat metal sheet and first became known as *paillettes*. For the decoration of special garments, the *paillettes* were stamped from thin sheets of silver and colour tinted to match the embroidery.

Buttons

A practical method of holding separate parts of a garment together is with the use of buttons slotted into buttonholes, or buttons held with loops formed with thread, fabric or with strung beads. These buttons can be utilitarian, made of wood, leather, cloth, bone, pottery or carved stone. Those made from gemstones or precious metals take on a secondary role as jewellery worn for display. Lucy Davies and Mo Fini, writing in *Arts and Crafts of South America*, give details of the silverwork included in their costume by the Gauchos of Uruguay. Engraved silver buttons were worn as part of an elaborate silver display, which included their knives, belt buckles, spurs and horse trappings.

The patterning on this belt shows various motifs, including a horse, worked in a network of brick stitch –
Mexico City, 2002.

Originally, elaborate shapes that were pierced by more than one hole were referred to as *sequins*. In the course of time, the name *sequin* was transferred to the simple disc and this is how they are known today. They can be flat or faceted with a single hole in the middle, or cup-shaped when they are called *couvettes*.

Nowadays they are made of a shiny, coated plastic in a variety of plain and iridescent colours and, as well as their lavish use on festival, carnival and dance costumes, are included as part of the decoration of everyday garments. In Mexico the Nahua women add sequins to the embroidery on their skirts and *quechquémitl*, while the women of the Cuzco area, Peru, add zigzag rows of sequins to the edges of the frills that border their hats and incorporate them with machine embroidery, woven bands and machine-made ricrac to their jacket fronts. Sequins add sparkle to lives that in the rural communities are often hard, with a demanding and often unending workload.

Buttons, especially those made from the 'mother-of-pearl' shell, have long been used throughout the world in a decorative context that is divorced from the purely practical one of holding the garment sections together. Sometimes the original purpose for using a fastening is no longer necessary, but the buttons are still included as part of an ongoing tradition. This can apply to costume adapted from military uniforms and is found in some of the jacket and trouser decorations of Guatemalan costumes. These buttons are not used as substitutes for beads, but rather as a decorative addition to identify what was once a serviceable closure.

The Abalone shell, which has an iridescent secretion on the inside surface, comes from a species of marine snail found in several parts of the world including the coasts of California and Mexico where commercial fisheries still exist today. The lustrous sheen of the 'mother-of-pearl' buttons must have made them very attractive. These buttons were cut from the shells as flat discs by drilling with a circular drill. In the past this would be with the use of a hand-operated drill, but in a commercial context, power drills are used. This is a delicate operation, for although the shell is tough, at the same time it is apt to splinter. After drilling, the remaining shell would look like a sieve or colander and the spaces between the holes would be used to cut discs for smaller buttons. As the shell is concave, no button is ever completely flat and this adds to the way the surfaces catch the light. Either two or four sewing holes would be made afterwards with a fine drill.

The pattern on this Mexican network collar is similar to those found in the graves of the Chimú culture.
(Purchased from Mexico, 1984.)

The Peruvian inhabitants of the areas around Cuzco sew these pearl buttons to the earflaps and borders of the men's knitted *ch'ullo* hats. Decorative buttons feature on many of the garments worn by both men and women, especially at festival times. During the last fifteen to twenty years, even the everyday costume of the Cuzco area has become more elaborate. The basic costume has not altered, but the women love to add buttons, both mother-of-pearl and plain white ones, to their hats and fitted red jackets. These buttons are purely ornamental and are sewn in a variety of straight rows and undulating patterns onto the cuffs, cuff tabs, jacket fronts and pocket tops. They are often combined

with the brocade woven ribbon-bands that are sewn in vertical strips to the jacket fronts or used as hatbands. The increase of tourism in the area has made additional money available to be spent on finery and this in its turn engenders further tourism. The pearl buttons, originally imported at some cost, would form a substitute for the real pearls, the wearing of which had always been the prerogative of the wealthy. The true marine pearls were found off the Pacific coast of northern Columbia, but over a period of time the pearl beds were exhausted with over-fishing and glass beads or imitation pearls eventually took their place.

Bead Stringing and Network

Beaded network is formed from a single element of beaded thread that interlinks with itself to form a structure. This beading technique is used to make small articles, bags, belts, body ornaments, bracelets, necklaces and collars. It can be worked to form a close structure, or the loops of threaded beads interconnected to form an open net of joined meshes. These open meshes form the basis of network bead collars.

Netted bead collars are found in cultures all around the world. Unless the provenance of the exact location is known, it is difficult to tell whether a bead collar has been made by the Zulu of South Africa, the Inuit of northern Canada or by the Huichol people of western Mexico. As with a great number of other textile techniques, there are only so many ways of doing something to obtain a particular outcome. The joining together of strings of beads to form a network was simply the next stage in the development of the craft. The only difference is in the beads used, their colours and the order and size in which the meshes of the bead-net are constructed. Originally a strong thread was made from agave fibre, but nowadays, synthetic threads are available for the bead threading and network.

The methods that are still in use by bead workers today may have been the result of experimentation when the first meshes were made by joining a string of beads, at intervals, to make little circles of beads. This would form a more elaborate version of the plain strung necklace and variations would include a larger or more important bead, held within the circles. The next stage would be to link a row of beaded loops below the first horizontal row of beads. Subsequent rows of bead loops are in their turn, linked to the one above. This allows for the shaping of the necklace by the inclusion of extra beads on the outer rows.

Beads that are sewn together closely in linked rows, but without the spaces that form the open meshes, will form a stable but slightly pliable construction. A given number of beads are strung for the first row, plus three extra for turning the corner, after which an additional set of beads is linked into the alternate beads on the first row which lies above. The beads of each subsequent row slot into the spaces between the ones above, rather like the staggered rows of seats in a theatre. The beads will lie with the holes facing horizontally across the work. This method of stringing is referred to as *Peyote* stitch. If the bead holes lie vertically, then it is called brick stitch, as the bead formation resembles that of the alternating bricks in a wall.

Beadwork items sold at tourist outlets follow both traditional motifs and modern fashion. This beadwork belt was one among many displayed on a market stall in Mexico City, 2002.

There are many variations in the way that beads can be sewn together. Rows of beads that lie directly beneath each other are sewn in double rows with the thread interlacing in a figure-of-eight formation. Additional bead rows are linked to the first in a similar way. Other methods include sewing the rows together in varying sequences of threaded loops. As long as all the beads interconnect in one way or another, a stable beaded fabric will result. Beads can be sewn to form tubes and spirals, or combined to make spiral helixes and these methods are used today to make necklaces on a commercial basis.

Similar types of stringing were used in the ancient cultures to make netted collars or bibs, using a variety of differently coloured discoidal beads. A bead-netted bib from the Chimú culture, dating from AD1000–1470, includes discs of orange *Spondylus* combined with purple and white shells and green malachite to form a design featuring little people, possibly priests, with raised hands. A deep, circular netted collar, also from the Chimú culture, features an elaborate zigzag pattern formed from beads made from the red and orange *Spondylus* shells, light coloured mussel shells

and the contrasting black of jet. The outer border is finished with a mother-of pearl fringe of lozenge-shaped pieces, with rounded edges at the bottom. Today their descendants, the bead workers of Ecuador, produce elaborate bead-netted collars, with patterns of shaped motifs linked by a series of bead strands in contrasting colours.

Beadwork Decorations of the Huichol People, Mexico

The availability of the brightly coloured trade beads, which were even in size and shape, made it comparatively easy to work patterned designs in the beaded network. It was simply a matter of counting and threading on the beads in the correct order, either following a pattern chart as is the custom today, or by adapting the traditional geometric weaving patterns. The same method is used to make bags and purses, belts and bracelets. Little network bracelets, all made to a similar pattern, are found in many other countries – often separated by vast distances. The technique is the same for the Piro Amazon people of Peru, the Kalash women of Pakistan's mountain valleys, or a young Romanian girl from the farmlands of northern Moldavia. The only basic difference is in the method of fastening. A favourite in some places is to add pearl buttons onto one end and thread or bead loops to another.

These little network bracelets are very similar, but were purchased from different countries. The outside pair comes from Guatemala, while the central one was found in Merida, Mexico.

The bracelets found in Guatemala and Mexico have special bead-formed buttons and bead loops incorporated within the beadwork structure. Although similar bead buttons are made by modern bead workers, the original use would appear to be unique to these countries. These bracelets are about 5cm (2in) in width and 14cm (6in) long excluding the fastenings, large enough to go round a medium to small-sized wrist. Network bracelets purchased in a street market in Merida, Yucatan peninsula, Mexico during 2002 are exactly the same in size and shape as two bought in Guatemala during 2004 and variations of the zigzag lightning patterns are common to both sets of bracelets. The only difference is in the netted stitching: the ones from Merida are worked in a fine *Peyote* stitch, while those from Guatemala are in a slightly more open network. Little beadwork keyrings in the form of animals, birds and fish, purchased in Merida, Mexico in 2005 are exactly the same as those bought in Guatemala the previous year.

It is more than probable that the bracelets and other small beaded items sold at tourist outlets all come from the same source. One bracelet from Guatemala is exactly the same as one illustrated on a Mexican Internet site which lists these bracelets for sale under the heading of 'Huichol and Tepehuano Art'. The Huichol tribes, who for well over 1,000 years have lived in secluded areas of the Sierra Madre Mountains in west-central Mexico, have long been famed for their expertise in beadwork and embroidery. Today, pectorals and bracelets of netted beadwork with decorative patterns created by the use of coloured beads form an important part of the festival costume, worn by the men as well as by the women. The Huichol men decorate their hats with bead-netted bands and are equally famous for their sashes and bead-work bags.

The Huichol are among the purest of the indigenous tribes, with a culture and religion close to that found in the pre-Columbian era. Until recently, their language was not transcribed in a written form. All tribal knowledge was passed down through the generations by the telling of stories, the performance of rituals and ceremonies and the use of symbols to encode their spiritual beliefs through the various forms of their art. These included the bead-decorated gourds, called prayer bowls or *jicara*. These bowls were carved from the nut of the Huaxtecomate tree which is indigenous to the Oaxaca area. When the bowl has been hollowed out and the surface smoothed, it is coated with a thin layer of beeswax and pitch pine. Today, patterns are made with little coloured beads which are pressed into the surface, covering the wax completely. In the past, pressed seeds, stones and shells were used to form the patterns that included symbols of religious significance, for these bowls were made to contain offerings to the gods.

During the mid-twentieth century this method of making patterns by pressing objects into wax was transferred to the so-called 'yarn paintings'. Pictorial scenes and designs were made by pressing coloured yarn into a beeswax foundation in the same way that was used for the beads. Also called 'Huichol Thread Art', these pictures vary in size from about 30–60cm (12–24in) square, with circular discs up to 120cm (48in) across. The designs, like those on the beaded gourds, are very colourful with circular, Mandala-type patterning, many of them containing the bird and animal symbols that define their culture. These pictures are said to represent the visions of the Shamans and were developed from the small objects once offered in supplication to the gods. A collection of the beaded gourds, beaded artefacts and yarn paintings is on display in the Anthropological Museum in Mexico City.

Bead-decorated gourds, originally used as prayer bowls for offerings, are still made by the Huichol tribes who make patterns by pressing beads into a wax-covered surface.

It was the availability of the trade beads that formed the basis of the Huichol beadwork industry. Glass beads were first introduced by the Jesuit priests and gradually replaced the seeds and shells that had been used previously. The vast majority of these people still live as subsistence farmers, scraping a living from an inhospitable landscape. As members of an isolated section of the national community, the Huichol formed a society based on self-help, setting up *ranchos* where individuals share group responsibilities. The function of the *ranchos* is not only one of work organization, but rather the overseeing of religious ceremonial that is based on the natural cycle of seasons and crops. The Shamans, who fulfil the role of leader, soothsayer and healer, play an important part in the ordering of the *ranchos*.

Today, more of the young people are moving to the towns in the hope of seeking a better life, but the ability to work as a group has enabled the villagers to set up beadwork co-operatives. The range of beadwork goods produced for sale has increased over the last few years. Apart from the traditional beadwork craft items such as the beaded gourds,

jaguar heads and contoured masks, they have branched out into making bags, belts and necklaces, Christmas tree ornaments and key rings. Many of these smaller items, such as the key rings, take the form of the animals, birds and reptiles that are part of the Huichol pattern heritage. Little beaded eggs, varying in size from hens' eggs to quails' eggs, echo the patterns pressed into the wax-coated gourds, but this time as convex articles, with the beads coating the outer surface. There would seem to be no end to the ingenuity of these gifted people.

The Huichol people produce a great variety of beadwork items. These include little padded motifs covered with beaded network, sold in the form of key rings featuring birds, animals, reptiles and traditional symbols.

Bead Weaving

The technique of bead weaving differs from that of beaded network in that the strings of beads form the weft element of a warp-based fabric. This requires the warp threads to be set up on some type of loom. The simplest form is the bow loom where a narrow beaded braid is woven from threads strung between and tensioned by a bow-shaped piece of wood or cane. This method is common to other countries and similar bow looms are found amongst the hill tribes of Thailand. The bow loom is used for weaving narrow braids when a row of beads is incorporated to lie on the outer edges of both sides of the woven band. These beads are first threaded onto the outside warp threads and pushed down one at a time to be held by the change in the warp shed each time the plain weft thread passes across. This beaded process can also be worked on any narrow loom, whether a braid loom or the simple back-strap loom tensioned by the foot or big toe. These narrow, bead-bordered braids are woven by people from the Cuzco area to serve as chin straps or ties for their hats, as well as for hat bands and extra decoration for their clothing.

In bead weaving, where continuous bead rows sit in between the warp threads, it is necessary that these threads are supported and tensioned on a small loom or a specially made beading loom. This can be of the simplest form – children often make a loom by taping upright combs to either end of a cardboard box and winding a continuous thread between the two ends. Similar methods were used for making the basic looms to produce small items. Those made especially for the purpose, allowed for the length of the warp to be wound onto rollers placed at either end of the loom. The back-strap loom and small, braid loom were equally suitable for the purpose, allowing the bead weaving to be combined with traditional weaving.

Beads for the first row are threaded in pattern order onto a length of weft thread, using a long needle that is fine enough to pass through each bead twice. To secure the beginning, the end of the beaded weft thread is fastened to the outer warp thread of the first row. The needle is passed beads lie in rows directly above one another and do not stagger.

Bead weaving is used to make bags, belts, earrings, flat necklaces and chest ornaments, the sale of which brings in an essential income to help the local economy of the countries of Central and South America. The peoples of Mexico, Guatemala, Nicaragua, central Panama, Columbia, Guyana and Brazil among many others, all practise the art of woven beadwork.

Beaded Aprons

In a different context, bead weaving is one of the favoured techniques used by the tribal people of the Amazon Basin, Guiana and Columbia. In the past, before the importation of trade beads, seeds were pierced and woven to make the aprons worn by the women. These items of prestigious clothing formed a frontal covering to the lower part of the body, which was naked apart from a profusion of bead and feather ornaments above the waist. Seeds could be oval in shape, but round beads were chosen by the Waiamiri-Atoari women to make the small aprons that were worn as a *cache-sexe*, leaving their buttocks bare. Most aprons are decorated with feather tassels and strings of seed beads, according to the customs of each area. Women were allowed the shorter feathers, the long plumes being reserved for the men.

A miniaturized back-strap loom is used by tribes in the Brazilian Amazon to work diagonal bead weaving, while the Waiwai women weave their aprons upside down by starting from the bottom at the waist and work upwards to finish the hem at the top. A different method is used for an apron from the Amazon area, once in the collection of the Museum of Mankind, but now in the British Museum. This shows a central panel of bead weaving inserted as part of the woven fabric structure where the beaded section shares a common warp with the conventional weaving. Once the mid-point of the woven cloth is reached, the areas at the sides are woven separately and when completed, the bead weaving is inserted into the warp threads of the unworked central section. Finally, normal weaving is resumed and closes all sections with a cloth panel above the beadwork.

A second apron was shown as work in progress. The loom was formed from a pair of long, pliable canes, tied together at each end and sprung apart in the middle by two crossways rods, with their ends tied securely to the side canes. The bead-weaving warp was secured to one crossway rod as a selvedge. The free ends of the warp were rolled round and tied in groups to the second rod, where they could be released as the bead weaving progressed. A geometric key pattern of dark on light beads was completed at the beginning end, with the work proceeding upwards.

Bags are always a popular product. These, purchased in Guatemala in 2004, vary in construction, as the miniature bag is worked in Peyote stitch, while the large one is bead woven on a small loom.

under the warp threads and the beads are pushed up and manipulated with the fingers so that one bead lies between each of the warp threads. There will be as many beads as there are warp spaces. On completion of the row, the needle is passed back, but this time going *over* the warp and *through* each bead in turn. This ensures that each bead is secured in place between the warp threads so that the

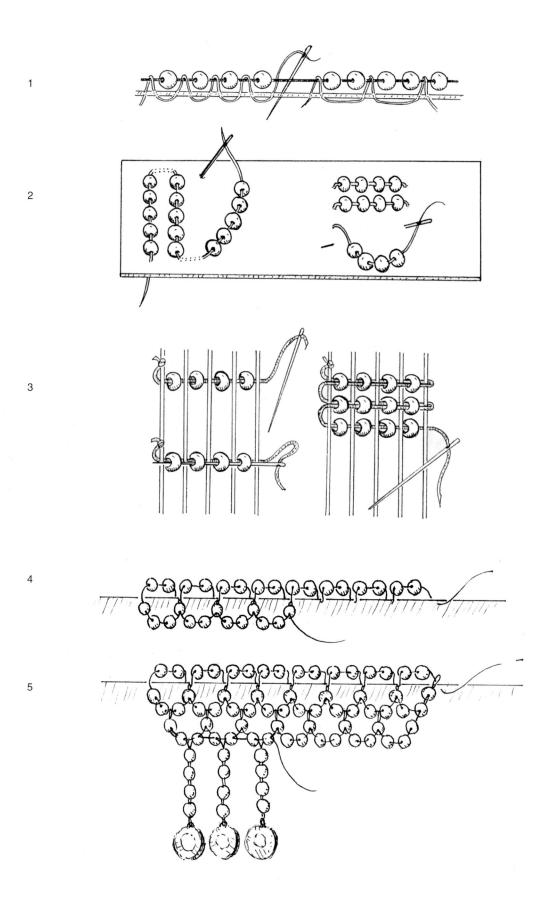

1

2

3

4

5

Beadwork of the Kuna People

The Kuna women from the San Blas Islands off the coast of Panama have a great love of beads, necklaces, earrings and of golden ornaments in the form of chest-plates. These beautiful ornaments are made from flat, hammered gold formed into symbolic motifs with the addition of flat drops and appendages in a variety of shapes. Gold rings are worn according to current fashion, but the most striking piece of jewellery worn by the Kuna women is the nose ring. The nose is considered to be the most attractive part of a woman's face and although the nose ring is less commonly worn today, the women still accentuate their noses by painting a vertical line down the centre. In the past these golden nose rings were large, but gradually reduced in size until those worn today are quite small. Coin necklaces and necklaces formed of many strings of beads have always been popular and they are still worn in profusion. Little bead bibs are made in the beaded network technique using the modern round beads. They can be finished with a fringe formed of bead loops each one ending in a silver coin.

A fashion for bead-threaded arm and leg bands originated before the introduction of trade beads, but the evenly sized beads in a variety of colours allowed the women to form a series of intricate patterns. Beads are threaded in a pre-determined pattern order onto a continuous length of strong thread that is long enough to complete the pattern when wound round the arm or leg. This winding of beaded thread can reach from the ankle to the knee, while the arms are covered from the wrist to the elbow. The resulting patterns can be quite complicated and the threading has to take into consideration the swelling of the calf and the alteration in arm size. The winding appears to be very tight, but this is possibly the only way that the pattern can be kept in order, for if the beaded thread slips sideways, it will be out of sequence. Patterns are made up of a series of plain bead bands, or of geometric patterns that echo some of the designs on the *mola* blouses. Sometimes, several separate bead bands are worn with gaps in between. The combination of beadwork, gold jewellery and beaded leg bands together with the intricate designs on the *mola* blouses and the brightly coloured headscarves, gives the Kuna woman a distinctive appearance that reflects both her self esteem and innate love of craftsmanship.

OPPOSITE PAGE:
1) Bead couching.
2) Lazy bead stitch.
3) Stages in bead weaving.
4) Beaded network, first two rows.
5) Beaded network, subsequent rows and
*   bead-fringe ending.*

Bead Embroidery on Clothing

The introduction of trade beads and sequins, together with the availability of fine sewing needles, heralded an explosion of beadwork on costume, religious garments and ceremonial clothing. This soon extended to festival wear and has found an ultimate expression in the theatrical dress made for the Carnivals. To some extent the addition of beadwork to a garment is determined by the cost. According to Chloë Sayer, the Nahua girls from Chilac, in Mexico, wear heavily beaded blouses at fiesta time. Floral motifs composed of beads are sewn to the gathers that control the front fullness of the *huipil* blouse, but the expense entailed can limit their use. The one advantage of beading over embroidery is that the beads can be re-used, for they seldom deteriorate.

The love of ornamentation in both Central and South America stems from the craft expertise of the early inhabitants. The inclusion of beads, shells, feathers, gold and silver ornaments and other decorative objects, either within the weave structure or as an addition to the finished cloth, was part of a natural progression that took place over several hundreds of years. The availability of comparatively cheap beads and sequins after the Spanish Conquest must have provided a tempting alternative to the labour-intensive production of the carved mineral and wooden beads, or to the expensive gold jewellery that was the exclusive province of the high-ranking goldsmiths.

The nineteenth century saw a definite increase in the general ornamentation of costume. The inclusion of beading on articles of dress varied according to the different classes of the people. The wives and families of the Conquistadors followed European fashion and traditions, which were adapted and copied by the *Mestizo* women. The costumes of the indigenous people were often decorated according to the original placing of the design motifs, so that the bead embroidery would occupy those areas formerly worked as weave patterning. Any garments directly influenced by the Spanish occupiers, for instance the cotton blouses in Mexico, which replaced the woven *huipil*, were more likely to be decorated according to the European country of origin.

The Peruvian people from the area around Cuzco are now adding beads and sequins to borders and areas once occupied solely by intricately woven bands. It is to be hoped that machine-made ric-rac, decorative buttons and sequins do not entirely supplant the time-consuming craft of brocade weaving. However, there is hope for the future, in that the art of weaving is actively encouraged by the Centre for Traditional Textiles in Cuzco.

9

Manipulated Thread Crafts

Unlike weaving, which is a multi-element thread construction, many of our manipulated thread crafts are formed from a continuous, single element of thread. Looping, netting, knitting, crochet, tatting and to a certain extent needle lace, all come under this heading. Continuous knotting is tied into a single element of thread, but knotted fringing, *macramé* and bobbin lace are all multi-element thread crafts, but without the addition of a transverse weft thread as in weaving.

Looping

One of the earliest forms of single-element thread construction is looping, a mixture of netting and knitting. The various looped openwork fabrics do not have the same elasticity as knitting, but are less likely to unravel as the thread is locked together in a different way. The net looping was worked with a needle, probably made of bone, using a plied thread of cotton, hair or vegetable fibre. The Peruvians used net-looped techniques to make both heavy-duty nets and carrying bags as well as network of a much finer scale to be included on clothing or to cover various articles.

Raoul d'Harcourt, in *Textiles of Ancient Peru and their Techniques*, describes two types of simple looping. The first method starts at the right-hand side with the thread loop fixed to a foundation rod or string. Working downwards, subsequent loops are threaded in figure-of-eight formation to each one above, forming a vertical column. At the bottom, the figure-of-eight loops are worked upwards alongside the first column, with each loop linking into the sides of the ones on the previous column. A series of loop columns, worked alternately upwards and downwards, will form a stable loop-net fabric, the change of direction of the working thread ensuring that the finished textile will lie flat and not curve or distort.

In the second method, the initial row is made by forming a series of thread loops across a foundation rod or string, working from left to right. All subsequent rows of loops are worked into the curved loop spaces of the ones above, linking the entire structure together. The loops will not sit underneath one another, but will form a construction of staggered loop-rows. A greater stability can be given to this

OPPOSITE PAGE: A young boy wears his best ch'ullo *knitted hat at Pisac Sunday market, Peru.*

RIGHT: The exact origin of this small pot is unknown, but it is an excellent illustration of simple network looping, worked in a vegetable fibre to cover the pot closely.

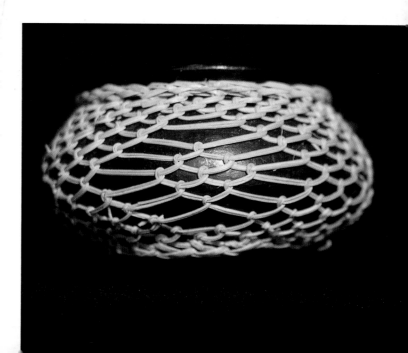

looped structure by placing a horizontal thread across each row. This thread is incorporated with the looping which encloses both itself and the loop above. Needle-lace makers will recognize this as *Point de Venise*, when worked to a much finer scale.

Cross-Knit Looping

This looks rather like knitting, but the loops are not formed by looping within each other as a sequence of looped elements as in knitting, but by linking in with each other, so that each loop is connected to the one directly above, as well as to its neighbour on either side. Once again, the looping is started on a supporting string or former. The top row of loops is worked from left to right. Subsequent rows are worked into the loops above, but this time, instead of looping into the curved thread between each loop, each loop is linked around the base of the loop already formed above. Thus the loops on each row do not stagger, but lie directly beneath one another. This makes a very stable openwork fabric as the vertical lines of linked loops hold each other in position and any damaged fabric will not unravel to the same extent as in a knitted textile. Annemarie Seiler-Baldinger refers to this technique as 'encircled looping' in her book *Textiles, a Classification of Techniques*. There are sections on a whole series of linking and cord-looping methods, as well as knotting, twined and bound methods.

A variety of looping techniques were found on a mantle from a pre-Inca tomb in the Paracas area, including woven-pile looping. Little three-dimensional figures are attached to the four outer edges of the rectangular cloth. Raoul d'Harcourt gives detailed descriptions of these figures and their symbolism. This superior garment must have belonged to a very important priest or ruler, as the realization and the workmanship are of the highest order. We are lucky that this textile survived in a presentable condition. It is now in the keeping of the Brooklyn Museum, New York.

Netting

The difference between 'netting' and 'looping' – both of which are openwork constructions – is that the meshes of network are knotted to hold them in position. In pre-Conquest Peru, examples of net work have been found which show a variety of meshed fabrics, some with tufted fibres and feathers incorporated within the meshes. An excavation in the Chimú Valley revealed twined, looped and network fabrics made from cotton and vegetable fibres dating to well over 3,000 years' ago.

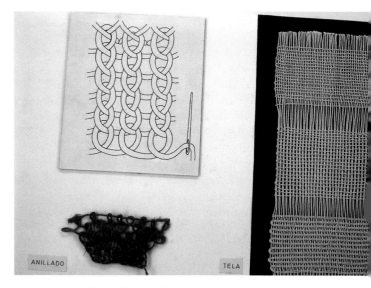

An example of cross-knit looping, together with a sample of simple weaving techniques.
(Pachacamac site Exhibition, near Lima, Peru)

Most types of net work require the use of some kind of former to keep the mesh size constant and some type of tool to hold the length of thread while the meshes are being made. Although the early netting could have been formed with the fingers, it was most probably worked with a bone needle or wooden shuttle of the correct size to pass easily through the meshes.

According to Raoul d'Harcourt, the simplest type of Peruvian knot used in the formation of network was the overhand knot. This knot is inclined to move across the mesh it is intended to hold and although the completed textile can be strong, during constant use the instability of this knot can result in the distortion of the finished network. The Peruvians used the overhand knot to make many kinds of net, both practical ones and lighter ones. A stable fabric could be made by making the meshes so small that the knots lay alongside one another, thus preventing them from slipping and a pliable, close-meshed fabric would result.

The next type of knot was formed from two half hitches, making a 'clove hitch', which was more practical and provided a semi-stable fabric. The threads used were agave, cotton or wool and, when worked closely, a fabric was formed that was suitable for making fine, woollen caps. This is not the true netting knot, used by fishermen to make their nets, but looks very similar and can be worked in different combinations of mesh size to produce a variety of patterned textile fabrics that once again, are proof of the expertise of the ancient Peruvian craft workers. An example of this type of netting can be seen on the lower part of a Nasca feather headdress, dated to between 200BC–AD100, in the collection of the University of Cambridge Museum of Archaeology and Anthropology.

European Netting

The so-called 'true' netting knot, which was not found in ancient Peru, is also known as the 'sheet bend'. This knot, which is quick to undo, is used by sailors to make their ropes secure. Whether it was first used in a sailing context and later developed for netting, or the other way around, is not known. Meshed nets are used all over the world, the most familiar being fishing nets, at one time all made by hand. Both the Portuguese and the Spanish, being maritime nations, were familiar with this type of netting.

Although the scale of the netting and thickness of thread used can differ, in order to avoid too many joins a considerable length of working thread is needed. The tool used to hold the thread is called a netting needle and can take a variety of forms, the most common being that of a flat netting needle, made from wood or from metal, or shaped out of wire. It has a pointed end at the top and is of the correct width to pass easily through the chosen mesh size. The thread is wound round a central spike that sits in the middle of and is integral with the needle. A figure-of-eight winding formation keeps the working thread in place and allows it to be unwound when more thread is needed.

The use of a gauge, or former, is necessary to make meshes of an even size. The gauge is shaped from a flat strip of wood or similar material, the correct width for the net size. The formation of the completed net mesh is a diamond one, so the width of the gauge will measure twice the length of one of the four diamond sides. A row of loops is set onto a string or rod for the first row, using the netting needle to make the loops over the gauge. To make the following row, the netting needle thread is taken through the first loop from behind and then round the gauge which is held beneath, before making a knot round the intersection where the two loops meet. The gauge is removed, the knot pulled tight and the process repeated across the rows. This results in a very stable fabric and the knots will not move or come undone. The diamond shape of the mesh is pliable, so that a net can be held together or stretched out and still retain its original shape.

An example of a typical network mat with needle-darned and looped patterning – early twentieth century.

Embroidered Net

We tend to think of netting as a coarse, practical construction, but nets can be made to a much smaller scale and fine nets form the basis of darned-net embroidery, or filet. This type of embroidery, where thread patterns are made on the net by darning or looping the embroidery thread through the net meshes, probably originated as ecclesiastical embroidery in Italy and was then taken up by the Spanish convents. Apart from use on Church textiles, it became a popular type of needlework in the New World, especially in Mexico where it was used to make lacy borders for costume as well as for little mats and doilies.

Knitting

The Spanish brought the art of knitting to their conquered lands. Like many of the other thread crafts, knitting of one type or another is though to have originated in the Middle East. European knitting had reached the status of a fine art by the end of the fifteenth century, with elaborately patterned jackets worked in silk thread worn by royalty and the aristocratic classes. Knitting requires the use of long, pointed needles to aid in the manipulation of the stitches and support the work in progress. The diameter of the needle determines the size of the finished stitches. Normally, two needles are used to make a flat type of knitted fabric, but four needles or more can be used to make a circular construction.

A continuous thread forms the first set of looped stitches, cast onto one of the needles by taking the working thread in turn through each formed stitch to make a new stitch with the aid of the point of the second needle. The work is turned for each subsequent row with the new stitches worked in turn into the ones of the previous row. If the needle is taken into the front of the stitch, a *plain* stitch will result, if the needle is taken into the reverse of the stitch, a *purl* or slanting stitch will be formed. These two stitches form the basis of all patterning methods, with variations made by winding the thread more times round the needle, or working two or more stitches together to make holes and a lacy type of pattern.

Knitting, South America

Knitting found greater acceptance in the High Andes regions of both Bolivia and Peru where warm clothing was needed. Knitting is used for many articles, including hats, a variety of bags and the little purses that hang from the waist belt. Although hand-spun yarns of alpaca, llama and sheep's wool are still used in parts of Bolivia and Peru today, factory-spun and dyed yarns have now taken over. The use of alpaca is restricted to the areas around Lake Titicaca, the highlands of Bolivia and northern Argentina. Sheep's wool is commonly found in highland areas of Columbia, Ecuador, Peru and Venezuela. Cotton knitting threads are a more likely choice for warmer climates and are popular in northern Chile, Columbia and the lowland areas of Peru.

A hat and a pair of socks from the Cuzco area of Peru, knitted on five needles to form a circular construction.

Men's ch'ullo knitted hats from Cuzco. The one on the left is decorated with pearl buttons and woollen tassels. Both show diamond patterns – c.1985.

Pisac Sunday market, situated in the upper valley of the sacred Urubamba River near Cuzco. Peru is famous for knitwear and craftwork.

The areas around Cuzco and Lake Titicaca are famous for the men's conical knitted hats, called *ch'ullus* or *ch'ullos*, which the men knit themselves in a variety of dazzling patterns, mainly geometric. This tradition dates back to the last part of the nineteenth century and is still very much in evidence today. Janet Willoughby has made a video film entitled *Peruvian Knitted Hats*, in co-operation with the *Centre for Traditional Textiles of Cuzco*. This film shows how the craft of knitting flourishes in these areas and gives an in-depth description of the techniques used in the mountain villages above the Sacred Valley of the Urubamba River and of the island villages in the middle of Lake Titicaca. Both men and women knit, following the patterns and shapes that are part of their traditional costume, each one unique to their particular village or area.

In the high altitude village of Accha Alta, the men knit their distinctive round, skull-cap-shaped hats, which are worn under a round felt hat. They use dyed, hand-spun wool or natural-coloured alpaca yarns for the hats, which are knitted in a circular formation with four thin needles to hold the sections of the circle, plus a fifth needle which is used for the actual knitting. Although some commercial needles are available today, the wire spokes from bicycle wheels are still used to make the needles, sometimes with a small hook formed at one end. The main knitting yarn is always tensioned around the neck, but additional colours are often wound as small balls of thread that hang down

until each in turn is used to form the different colours of the pattern. The knitting is always worked from the inner, wrong side of the hat, enabling the worker to control the change of yarn colour more easily.

A slightly different method is used in Chinchero, where an elderly man is the only one remaining to work the traditional knitting. Here, the circular hat narrows into a funnel shape at the top, which then branches out to form three long, knitted tassels decorated with pom-poms on the ends. These hang down at the side of the head in wear. All the differently coloured threads are tensioned around the neck and each new colour is interwoven at the back, or inside of the work, by twisting with the previous thread. The Centre for Traditional Textiles in Cuzco is conducting research into the designs and patterns in order to preserve them for future generations. The Centre is a non-profit-making organization set up in 1996 to aid the survival of traditional Andean textiles. Quechua weavers and their families are given help to combine their skills and develop marketing opportunities in the region.

There are various methods for beginning or finishing the edges of the hats. In Pitumarca, crochet is combined with knitting to make the initial border. A band, the correct length for the circumference of the hat, is worked in double crochet for a few rows before making a series of picot-bobbles at intervals along the bottom edge. The crochet is worked with a long hook with the thread tensioned round

This man's knitted cap from Lake Titicaca shows many of the typical weaving symbols including ducks, a horse, zigzag snake, pecking hen and floral, cross and hooked motifs.

one side of the head. Although there is a tradition that a father will knit caps for himself and for his sons and daughters, a boy will start to learn to knit by the time he is ten years old and make his first hat with a white end, called a *ch'ullo Santa Maria*. When he is old enough to marry, or takes a partner, then he will wear the patterned hat with a plain, red end. To keep the patterned area from fading in high-altitude sunshine, the hat is often worn inside out, to protect it. In the video, a man is shown casting on stitches for the hat in two colours, dark and light, that alternate. This is to make the initial band at the bottom of the hat, before the main patterning starts.

Knitting is regarded as a male or a female occupation, according to the custom of the particular community. Even in the villages where the knitting of caps is the prerogative of the men, women also knit other articles, such as patterned arm-warmer bands for their husbands and caps, gloves, stockings, ponchos and sweaters for the tourists.

On the island of Amantini, it is the women and young girls who knit the men's caps, using their own particular method. Here, the two earflaps are knitted first, starting at the point and working upwards. The top edge is then cast off, later to be picked up along the top and incorporated with the initial cast-on circle for the hat. The entire hat is then knitted upwards as before. The mothers on this island and on the western shores of Lake Titicaca knit little ruffled caps for their daughters, a style at one time worn by the adults.

Although one side of Lake Titicaca belongs to Peru and the other to Bolivia, the area around the lake is still inhabited by

the neck, unlike European crochet, where the thread is tensioned over the fingers. Knit-stitches are picked up along the straight edge of the crochet band to form the beginning of the hat. When the main body of the hat has been worked, stitches are picked up again on the lower edge to make an earflap on each side. The earflaps are worked downwards to end in a point. In wind-swept Chalvatiri, as in Pitumarca, the men wind small balls of thread for the pattern colours and tension the main colour only around the neck. The coloured threads are joined in by tying round the main thread with a slip knot and hang down while the work progresses.

The reed-surfaced islands of high-altitude Lake Titicaca are home to a race of expert knitters. Once again, it is the men who take a pride in knitting their own hats. They still work to the fine, traditional patterns, but produce coarser, although well-made versions, to provide an income from tourist sales. On the Island of Taquile the unmarried men wear conical hats with a long, white end that hangs down

Socks, with a pattern of little dolls holding hands, are made for tourist sale by the women of the floating reed-islands on Lake Titicaca.

people who share similar craft traditions. In the past, similar Bolivian hats were knitted on very fine needles to make a close fabric that when washed, would become slightly felted, thus making it impervious to the bitingly cold wind at high altitude. The traditional symbols and patterns are worked at a fine gauge of from 30–38 stitches per 5cm (2in) to produce a fabric that can sometimes be mistaken for weaving. The knitted, conical caps are worn on their own, or under a felt hat that varies in shape according to the different village origins. They can have plaited or braided ties and the earflaps are often decorated with tassel ends or pom-poms.

A finely knitted man's cap from the La Paz area of Bolivia. After washing, the slightly felted fabric helps to keep out the bitter winter winds – mid twentieth century.

A rare, late nineteenth-century example from the area around La Paz, the high altitude capital of Bolivia, shows the use of openwork lace knitting to make a cone-shaped cap with earflaps. This child's cap, which has blue seed beads incorporated into the knitting, is part of the collection of the Musée de l'Homme, Paris. A white or fawn cotton thread is chosen for the lace patterns, reminiscent of those on Shetland or Russian lace shawls, with the holes formed by knitting selected stitches together and then increasing stitches on the following row. This openwork was probably convent inspired, as lace knitting is used occasionally on the borders of altar cloths.

Purses and Knitted Dolls

Money purses, called *monederos* and drawstring bags called *bolsas* or *bolsitas*, are knitted by the highland people of Bolivia and Peru in a great variety of shapes and sizes. A little knitted *monedero*, or money purse, purchased in Cuzco in 1986 has an opening near the narrow top wide enough to slip a coin in – where it will fall inside the pouch – but which necessitates the upturning of the purse to take it out. The outside is decorated with fringing and at the top, a cord is used to tie it to a belt or waistband.

The knitted bags can be both practical and decorative, some having a series of differently sized pouches incorporated within the large one. Many of these purses take the form of animals, or birds, while others are made as three-dimensional figures of little people, their hollow arms and legs providing further compartments within the purse. These figure-purses possibly had their antecedents in the knitted silk purses that took the form of an animal or a doll and were carried by fashionable Peruvian ladies during the mid-nineteenth century. This is not a European tradition and may, in its turn, be linked to the little embroidered figures found in the graves of the Chavin culture. Today, little knitted dolls, very similar to the cloth ones, are for sale at tourist outlets.

This knitted mondero, *or money purse, has a narrow opening near the top and is decorated with a series of wool tassels – Cuzco, mid 1980s.*

In Peru and certain areas of Bolivia, knitted masks are made by the women, for the men to wear at festivals and at various religious ceremonies. These knitted masks possibly had their origin in the carved wood, metal or *papier maché* festival masks. According to Cynthia Gravelle LeCount, writing in *Andean Folk Knitting*, an unusual Bolivian example is called a *passamontana*, meaning 'mountain crosser'. This was obviously some type of Balaclava helmet which covered most of the face, but leaving slits for the eyes and the mouth and would protect the wearer in high altitudes. The Peruvian festival masks vary in shape, all covering the face except for the slits, with shaping for the nose and chin. Some have earflaps and several have a neck extension.

Knitting, Central America

The hot climate of Mexico and other countries of Central America meant that knitting, especially with the use of woollen fibres, was not taken up to any extent. A certain amount of fine knitting with the use of cotton threads was promoted by the convents, but craft workers preferred drawn-thread work, filet darned net, bobbin lace and Sol lace. A certain amount of knitting was worked in highland mountain areas where the climate was more temperate, but in Guatemala, the men prefer to use crochet for their carrying bags. In more recent times, the knitting of garments in synthetic threads has been taken up as an income source. At the Mayan site of Ichimché near Antigua Guatemala, an elderly man was knitting articles for tourist sale, using a pair of fine needles to work factory-dyed yarn.

Crochet

Crochet is another single element craft made from a continuous thread. The basis of crochet is the formation of a chain stitch that is looped through itself in various combinations to form an elastic stitch construction. Like knitting, this is one of the thread crafts where the thread is easy to unravel, which has both advantages and disadvantages. A hook, made in a

ABOVE: *A crochet lace border is designed to show beneath the* huipil *hem worn in the Yucatan peninsula, Mexico.*

LEFT: *This stall holder at the ancient site of Ichimché knits using fine needles. He is wearing the wool* ponchito *skirt and carries a woven bag, bearing the Quetzal symbol.*

The men of Todos Santos Crochet their own shoulder bags and hats, as well as little purses and herb-stuffed balls for tourist sale.

A mask from Chichicastenango, Guatemala, worked in crochet, using synthetic threads – early 1990s.

variety of sizes, is used to form the chain stitches according to the thickness of the working thread or yarn. Wool or synthetic wool substitute is used for garments where a degree of warmth is necessary. A fine white cotton thread was used for working fine-scale crochet for lace-type articles such as church altar furnishings, mats and doilies. The elaborate lace collars from Oaxaca region and the deep lace borders on the embroidered *huipils* worn in the Yucatan peninsula, Mexico were frequently worked in crochet. Coloured threads were incorporated on the cuff borders, seam edges and insertions which embellished the embroidered blouses and *huipils*.

In the highlands of Guatemala, it is the men of Todos Santos Cuchumatan who crochet their shoulder bags in brightly coloured threads. As they do not have pockets in their distinctive costume of striped trousers and black over-pants, the bags play an important part in carrying everyday necessities. They also crochet the little round hats, often sold to the tourists, while they themselves prefer to wear the Panama hat with a woven band. Many other small objects, such as little balls stuffed with herbs, are also made for export and look very decorative with a series of striped cro-chet and zigzag patterns. In the market at Chichicastenango, crochet head masks are for sale, worked in a dark thread with contrasting colours to outline the eyes and mouth, echoing the style and shape of the *papier maché* masks, worn at fiesta times.

Crochet in fine cotton thread is popular in many areas of Mexico and was used originally by the *Mestiza* women to make doilies and other articles. According to Chloë Sayer, crochet was later taken up by the indigenous women to decorate their clothing and the uses included crochet yokes that featured animal, bird and floral motifs. In some areas, crochet lace frills border the neck and sleeve openings and crochet bands were used as insertions to join dress sections together and for the seams of the *quechquémitl*. Crochet borders were often used to decorate the sides of the hammocks.

Macramé Knotting

Macramé was an Arabian craft, introduced to Spain during the Moorish occupation. Once again, the Arab weavers found this an excellent way of finishing the warp ends. As a multi-element technique formed of a sequence of vertical threads which all inter-reacted with themselves, it was possible to set a separate number of threads onto a rod or holding cord and work these as individual pieces to make bags, belts, mats and cords. There are two basic *macramé* knots, the overhand knot and the half hitch. These two knots are combined to form the variations found in *macramé* work. All of the vertical threads are linked together by one or other of these knots, to form a close-worked lattice or a more open mesh. This linking will vary according to the chosen pattern. Overhand knots that are worked in two stages over sets of four threads, with the first tying from the one side and the second tying from the opposite side, will form a flat or square knot. This is also known as the cow hitch. An openwork mesh is made by dividing the threads across the row and borrowing two of the four-set threads from either side to tie a new set of knots in a staggered row beneath the first one. A 'braid' is made by tying a continuous set of these square knots in sequence over four threads, while a spiral braid is made by tying the overhand knot in one direction only.

The half hitch knot is formed with the introduction of a separate working thread, secured to one end of the work. This working thread is used to tie a knot around each vertical thread in turn, from above. Patterns are made by tying a sequence across a number of threads and then returning with the same knots tied in reverse from the opposite direction. A half hitch knot and a reverse half hitch knot tied together form a clove hitch and this knot is used both in patterning and when setting the initial threads onto the rod or string. For convenience sake, many workers wind the individual threads round a small bobbin, or wind as a figure-of-eight around the fingers before securing. Whichever method is used, the winding starts at the end nearest the work in order to allow the working thread to unwind freely. *Macramé*, which has similarities with the various types of pre-Conquest knotting, was used as a decorative way of finishing woven items as well as for the sides of the sprang-constructed hammocks.

Plaited Braids

The plaiting of groups of thread lengths may well have pre-dated weaving, for in plaiting techniques the threads can perform the function of both warp and weft by the interchanging of threads at the selvedge sides, crossing and interweaving at an angle of 45 degrees. This angle will depend to some extent on the openness of the work. We are all familiar with the braiding of hair, which is practised in many countries across the world and is never completely out of fashion. Three is the smallest number of single elements that can be formed into a simple plait, while an uneven number of threads can be added to work a wider form of the 'flat' plait. Raoul d'Harcourt lists two types of plaiting or braiding worked by the people of ancient Peru, dividing the types into those where the working ends are free and those with fixed ends where the plaiting takes place within the structure.

When the threads are plaited in different colour combinations, these flat braids take on a new dimension of pattern sequence that adds vibrancy to the finished article. The variety of braid patterns used by the Peruvian craftspeople would appear to be endless, but all patterns are worked within the limitations set by the chosen technique. There are many instances of the interchange of coloured threads and the changing of thread direction. In the Nasca culture, two sets of flat plaits lying parallel to one another are combined by sharing the working threads at intervals. Another Nazca method involved the division of threads within the work so that sometimes one colour showed on top, at other times it was hidden beneath the working thread. This allowed the most complex of patterning in several colours to be made with half shades produced by the proximity of different colours, giving an effect akin to pointillism. Groups of up to four threads were combined and worked in one direction as a thick thread and then divided to work in the opposite direction. A thick thread, after passing through several pairs of thin threads, would on the opposite direction itself be divided into thin threads, reverting at the next turn to become once again, a thick thread. This is like, but not the same as, ply-split braiding and produces similar distinctive zigzag patterns.

Recent research into the ancient Aymara language of the Andes by Rafael Núñez, a cognitive scientist at the University of California, San Diego, has resulted in the discovery that those who speak this language regard time in a different way to our European concepts. To the Aymara, the past time stretches in front of them, all the way to the distant horizon. The future lays physically behind them – it has not yet happened. Is there some possible relationship with the early crafts of net work, plaiting and braiding, which long preceded weaving? All of these crafts are worked from the top, downwards. Unlike weaving, the completed work thus recedes forwards, away from the worker and may have influenced their way of thinking.

Plaited 'Sprang'

Some of the plaiting methods that are worked between two holding cords are similar to plaited sprang, which originated in ancient Egypt. Here a continuous thread is wound between the two holding cords, which are held apart under tension at a determined distance. Using finger manipulation, the elements of the wound thread are crossed over each other in turn to form the first set of plait crossings. On the second row, the threads are crossed over the opposite way. A similar set of crossed threads appears at both ends of the work, as a mirror image. The work is continued until no space is left in the middle, when a central thread holds all in place. A Nazca coca-bag in the Museé de l'Homme is worked in this method and shows the change in pattern direction at the centre.

Hammocks

When the Portuguese invaders set foot on the coast of Brazil in the year 1500, they were amazed to see that the native inhabitants slept in 'nets' attached to the beams of their houses. A fire lit beneath kept them warm and free from both predators and demons. The Portuguese called these hanging beds *rede de dormir*, or nets for sleeping. However, in the Mayan dominated countries these hanging beds had long been known as the *hamaca* or *hammoca*, the name taken from the Hamac tree that originally provided the fibres. In later years, the more abundant sisal fibres were commonly used. The Spanish Conquistadors were happy to adopt the hammock, but eventually preferred the use of the more absorbent cotton thread.

It is difficult for people who live in a temperate or a cold climate to appreciate the importance of the hammock. In the hot and humid areas of Central and South America, the open-type netting or meshwork from which the hammock is formed allows for the circulation of the air. The hammock has many other advantages. The main one is that it can be set up easily, whether in a dwelling or out in the forest, as long as two uprights are capable of supporting both the hammock and the weight of the occupant. It is simple to take down, can be rolled up and is easy to transport. A hammock is measured by its width, which determines how many people it can accommodate, the widest ones measuring up to 3m (approximately 10ft) or even wider when stretched out. They were adopted by the British and French sailors for use in their ships, but the British Navy used a woven, canvas cloth for single hammocks which could be rolled up during the daytime.

The fixed-end plaiting method of sprang was used in the tropical parts of Mexico and Central America and most of the Amazonian areas of Brazil and Venezuela. The advantage of this method was that the construction was very elastic, allowing the meshes to form to the body shape while keeping the sides taut enough to prevent the occupant from falling out. In the Yucatan Peninsula, vertical frames were used to plait the hammock fabric in absorbent cotton threads, while in other areas a variety of vegetable fibres or plant lianas were used by the tribes of the Amazon forests. The towns of Timbauba in northern Brazil and San Jacinto in Columbia are famous for their hammock making, each producing intricately patterned fabric, distinctive to their particular areas. The Wayuu people of north-eastern Columbia also worked their plaited hammocks on vertical frames, each community

Hammocks, showing the 'sprang' meshwork, fringing and wooden spreader, are slung outside a shop in Mitla, western Mexico.

priding themselves on the designs and colours used. The Paraguayan tribes from the Chaco region made their hammocks using fibres from a variety of bromeliad plant. These fibres are spun by twisting on the thigh and are dyed with natural dyes from bark, roots and seeds. A sprang woven-fibre hammock with added feather decoration was collected during the 1830s by Johann Natterer. Originating from the River Negro basin, this hammock is a rare example that has survived the rigours of tropical climate and is now in the collection of the Museum für Völkerkunde, Vienna.

Much of the social life of these tropical people was based around the hammock, as it was also used for sitting in, when social or shamanistic gatherings took place. At one time the Kuna women from the San Blas Islands off Panama made the hammocks that played such an important part in their tropical communities, but nowadays they are far more likely to be purchased ready made from Columbia. The Kuna mothers sang to their small children while swinging the hammocks, like rocking a cradle. Meanwhile, the elders of the tribe would retire to their hammocks when officiating during the puberty ceremony for a young girl. The cycle of chants took many hours to perform, even running into a period of several days. The Great Spirit Wind would be called up by the chanters and when it was considered to be blowing, the hammocks were swung violently to and fro while the chanting continued unabated. When a girl married, the bridegroom would be 'forcibly' brought into the mother-in-law's house to share the bride's hammock. Herta Puls, in her book *Textiles of the Kuna Indians of Panama*, tells us that if the bridegroom escapes and is brought back three times, the marriage is void. If he stays, the couple must talk all night and the marriage might well be consummated later in the quiet and privacy of the jungle. At the end of life, in the death ceremony, the corpse is placed in a hammock and kept in the house for a day and a half. Afterwards the corpse is buried, still in the hammock and offerings to the spirits are placed on top of the covered grave.

Today, there is a thriving hammock-making industry in the Yucatan area of eastern Mexico. Most of these hammocks are made from cotton, but modern fibres such as polyester and polyester-cotton are machine twisted into cords that are then formed into the hand-worked sprang technique. It is said that each hammock takes up to 3.2km (2 miles) of cord and between forty and ninety hours to complete. Nicaraguan hammocks are more closely worked as the climate is cooler, while Columbian hammocks are made from a mixture of wool and synthetic Orlon and have the added feature of a 'spreader' bar at the top, which gives greater stability in use. The sides or 'verandas' of the hammocks can be decorated with a deep, hanging fringe of crochet or *macramé*, ending with a row of tassels. This fringe is sometimes referred to as the 'veranda.'

Cord Braids and Slings

Both square and round-shaped cords or braids were made using an even number of strands. Many of the Peruvian plaited cords are similar to the Japanese *kumihimo* braids, the main difference being in the method for the

A contemporary sling from Peru is evidence of a continued practical use over the centuries.
(Lent by Betty Ballard, Spinners and Weavers Association)

construction. The Japanese use a stand called a *Maru Dai* to support the threads and keep them in order, while the Peruvians and Bolivians always work in the hand. Many of these braids, which among other things were used to make slings, were found in the Peruvian graves of the Nazca cultures dating from 900BC–AD650. Today, similar slings are still in use in the highland areas of Peru and have not altered in design or workmanship as the shape could not be improved on. The slings played a very important part in the ancient culture, being used for both ceremonial and practical purposes. According to Rodrick Owen, writing in *The Big Book of Sling and Rope Braids*, the slings are still made by the men who use hand-spun alpaca for the ceremonial slings. A more serviceable, coarse llama wool is used to make herding slings to protect the llamas and alpacas and the flocks of mountain sheep from predators. In the past they were obviously a fearsome weapon in the right hands, for not long after the Conquest a Spaniard wrote: 'Their chief weapon is the sling. With it they can throw a large stone with such force it could kill a horse'.

The sling braid itself can be worked in a variety of patterning methods, but the construction requires a loop at one end and an open pouch area partway down the length. The loop is made by splitting the braid, working on two separate narrow sections, which are then rejoined into the main body of the braid. The sling pouch can be an extension of the braid with added threads, a split area with flattened sides or a separate entity joined afterwards, the method depending on where the sling is made.

Examples in the collection of the Ethnographic department of the Birmingham Museums show these different techniques. One with a complicated braid-work pattern has a plain area with added threads worked as series of flat braid strips to form the pouch. A sling made in coarser fibres expands as a woven area, then contracts to reform the braid. Rodrick Owen tells us that ceremonial rope braids were made without pouches, but that they were decorated with tassels and shorter braids.

A variety of cords and braids were made to serve many purposes. *Bolas*, made from three stones attached to joined lengths of llama tendons, was used by the Incas as a weapon of war. When thrown, the *bolas* would twirl round the legs of a warrior to disable him and it was used to bring down both horse and rider when the Spanish Conquistadors invaded. Eventually, the *boleadoras*, made from leather cords to which three iron balls were attached, was used by the Gaucho horsemen of Uruguay and the Argentinian Pampas to hobble their cattle. The Gauchos were equally accomplished with the lasso, which was thrown to entangle around the horns of the cattle and secure it. The Gauchos were experts in the use of cattle hide cut into strips, plaited and used to make clothing as well as saddlery and stirrups.

Bobbin Lace

The open-ended plaiting methods are the same as those used for the plaited patterns worked in bobbin lace. The only difference is that for convenience, the fine threads are wound around bobbins and the positions where the threads cross are held with a pin set into holes in the pattern drawing or 'pricking'. The lace pattern is secured to and supported by a 'pillow' or a 'bolster', in the past stuffed with straw of similar vegetable fibre. The pillow has to be very firm to keep the supporting pins in position and under tension. The various lace-making areas of Europe used differently shaped pillows. In Flanders the pillows were round and flat, in Spain and Portugal, cylindrical bolster-shaped pillows were preferred, and it was this type of pillow that was eventually transferred to the New World.

Although the bolster pillow was the most popular, there are many variations of shape and size. In some areas the cylindrical bolster is placed upright with the pricking pattern round the circumference, in which case the heavy wooden bobbins will hang down the length. If the bolster is placed horizontally, it requires some sort of support, either in the form of a separate stand, or a small-scale cylindrical bolster is set into a second pillow with a flat surface to support the bobbins. This latter type is of French origin, but was sometimes used by the Portuguese. The lace bobbins have a short 'neck' at one end around which the lace thread is wound, topped by a 'head' to prevent the thread from falling off. The lower end of the bobbin takes many shapes, but is generally bulbous to give weight to the thread and ease of handling. Large bolster pillows with heavy bobbins are still in use in Bolivia today, for the production of a coarse type of lace.

A line of pins is set at the top of the work, the bobbins are wound in pairs and the centre of each double thread in turn is looped over a pin. Two pairs of bobbins are necessary for making the two basic lace stitches, 'twist' or 'half stitch' and 'plait' or 'whole stitch'. Twist is worked with two threads, while whole stitch, sometimes referred to as 'cloth stitch', is normally worked over four threads at a time. Cloth stitch makes a plait if worked downwards over the same set of four threads, but forms a weaving stitch if continued across the row. The varied combinations of these two stitches form the patterns in bobbin lace.

Bobbin lace was taught first in the convent schools and was later produced in workshops as a commercial product. Initially it was much in demand for church lace, but gradually took over as a fashion product. In time, the indigenous lace making came to supplant the imports from Spain and Portugal, but the industry declined during the early part of the twentieth century, when machine-made lace gradually took over.

Ñanduti and Sol Lace

The word *Ñanduti* means 'web', an excellent description of the filmy, open-work construction of these little needle-stitched lace circles, or 'sun' shapes. There are differing opinions as to whether this type of lace was imported into the southern continent by the Spanish Jesuit priests as a church lace, or whether the Portuguese Conquistadors brought it as a form of traditional decorative drawn-thread work from the home country. The *Sol* or 'Sun' lace had developed from the Spanish mediaeval drawn-thread work, which was the forerunner of needle lace. Both horizontal and vertical threads were withdrawn from areas of fine, linen fabric to form an openwork grid. The remaining threads were held together with darning and knotted stitches before the ground fabric was cut away from behind the motifs to create an airy design. Gradually this pattern area increased and the large rectangular spaces left in the corners of the cloth were filled with diagonal lines to form circular shapes. Eventually, the circular elements of the design took over, so that the *Ñanduti* motifs became joined to one another. The angular shapes left between the circles were themselves incorporated into the lace work, with stitches laid at right angles making an intervening grid pattern.

The *Ñanduti* lace from Paraguay is famous for its fineness and delicacy of workmanship. The stitches used were fairly simple and included the darning stitch – which is like a miniature version of weaving – and knotted stitches that joined the radial lines of the circles to the spokes of the web.

The fine, muslin fabric was stretched onto a rectangular wooden frame, called a *rastidor*, that was used as a support during work. The circular patterns were marked onto the fabric with a hard pencil and these outlines were then defined with lines of running stitch. Next, the spokes for the wheels were laid across the circles, linking into the running stitch outlines. Finally, the darning and knotted stitches were worked and when all was completed, the background fabric was cut away to reveal the circular web designs set within the cloth. Similar versions of *Sol* lace were made in Mexico and the other areas of Central America. Its popularity may have been due to the comparative simplicity of the stitches and the portability of the embroidery frame, thus having an advantage over bobbin lace with the more cumbersome pillow and stand.

The Paraguayan *Ñanduti* lace is often confused with a similar type of lace from Tenerife in the Azores. At some stage it was decided to do away with the supporting fabric and frame. Instead, the web for the rounds of lace was made by lacing threads across a wooden former with circles of holes drilled at intervals. Alternatively, pins were stuck into a circular pattern supported on a small, hard pillow. The rounds of lace were removed from the pillow when completed and later joined together to make the lace, which is always referred to as 'Teneriffe' lace, with a double 'f'. Originally, the little lace circles were worked in fine thread and included a greater variety of stitches, but in recent years, a coarser version of these lace mats continues to be produced for the tourist industry.

Colonial Lace and European Influences

South America

The Conquistadors, who set up a flamboyant vice-regal court in Peru during the sixteenth century, endeavoured to emulate the riches of their homeland by embellishing both furnishings and clothing with increasing amounts of lace, as if this alone was a mark of their attainment. Lace was worn as a fashion accessory during the seventeenth and eighteenth centuries, especially by the *Mestizo* classes that eventually were to form an increasing proportion of the population.

According to Florence Lewis May, writing in *Hispanic Lace and Lace Making*, the wearing of lace of all types was equally prevalent in most of the areas conquered by the Spanish and the Portuguese, with the costumes differing very little from those worn in Europe. In Columbia, the women wore mitre-shaped linen caps, covered with lace, while in areas of Panama, lace decorated the wide sleeves of the women's shifts and the hems of their petticoats were bordered with deep lace that showed beneath the outer skirts. In Ecuador, fine-quality lace was sewn to the linen garments, while the women of Lima in Peru wore short skirts in order to display their lace finery. Initially, Flemish-type bobbin laces were preferred, but vast quantities of the coarser *torchon* laces were exported from Spain to fulfil the need. The *torchon* bobbin laces were based on a geometric grid pattern and were comparatively quick to work. These imports eventually led to the passing of sumptuary laws to regulate the use of black and white lace, but as usual, with little effect.

Lace was made in the convents and at the convent schools and enough was produced in Argentina at the end of the nineteenth century to affect the amount of lace imported. Schools were set up in orphanages, for both lace and embroidery, during the early part of the twentieth century and the money earned by these girls was set aside for when they became old enough to leave. The only type of lace that continued to play an important part in the South American lace industry, was the *Ñanduti* lace made in Paraguay. This was used on costume as collars, for mantillas and shawls, as well as for decorative mats and to add to church linen.

A South American festival fashion, worn by the Gauchos, is for trousers that flare out at the hems, with a vertical slit at the hem that opens out to contain a triangle of lace frills. These are worn over heeled riding boots and look very decorative when the Gaucho is mounted on his horse. Originally, the lace was worn on long, cotton under-trousers, also trimmed with fringing and embroidery. These were worn under and protruded from, the wide trousers. The fashion is echoed in the lace-frilled petticoats of the women, whose Spanish-style dresses are designed to spread out over the back of the horse when they are seated behind the Gaucho at fiesta time.

Central America

Apart from the production of cotton laces, both gold and silver laces were made in Mexico during the nineteenth century. The gossamer *blonde* laces were as popular in Central America during the early to mid nineteenth century as they were in Europe, while black or white silk was used for the *rebociño* or mantilla, that acted partially as a veil.

Lace ruffles even became part of the liveried uniform of the indoor slaves of those plantation owners who wished to copy European models. Apart from lace worn by the *Mestizo* women as an expression of fashionable dress, lace also played an important role in the costume of the women of the indigenous tribes and it was used to decorate the yokes of the Mexican *huipils*, the European style blouses and the borders of petticoats that were worn to show beneath the outer skirts. Lace was also worn on the men's costume, both as decoration and as a sign of wealth.

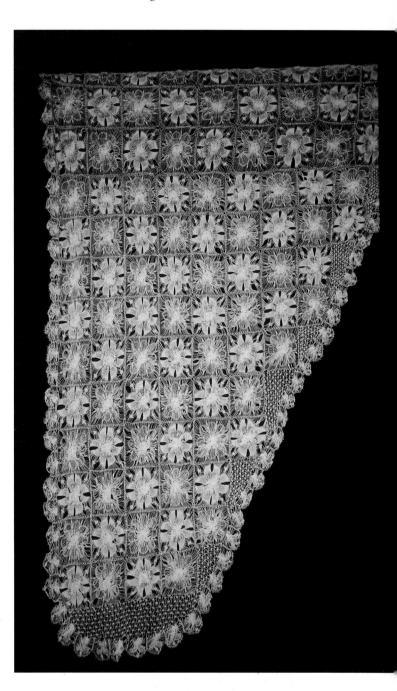

The rounded end of a Ñanduti lace stole, probably worn by a woman of the Mestizo class.
(Jeri Ames Collection, Maine USA)

10

Decorated Finishes, Fringes and Tassels

Gold Appliqué

The gold appliqué tunics of the Peruvian Chimú culture, dating from about AD1200–1400, are astonishing in their use of hundreds of little gold platelets, made from the beaten metal, covering the surface of the garments. Sometimes the tunic is completely covered with the gold rectangles, or they are used to form a band within the borders of a tapestry woven garment. The tiny gold rectangles have a hole drilled into each of the four corners and these holes are used to attach the squares, either with a strong thread or a thin wire. Alternatively, pierced discs carved from shells or rectangles formed from precious metals were included within the woven weft using the pre-threading method. These discs and plates, pierced only at the top, could lie separately or form overlapping rows that would provide a rich but supple fabric for the gold-covered tunics and bags, reserved for the king or a high-ranking official. These garments would be worn on important occasions together with items like a pair of ceremonial boots, which apart from the soles, are completely covered with the platelets.

The gold workers of the Chimú Empire were renowned for their art in making ornaments from sheet gold, which they hammered out using polished stones, possibly of obsidian. Gold was not used as a form of currency; its value was an intrinsic one, the warm, lustrous glow symbolizing divinity and power reserved only for royalty and the priesthood.

OPPOSITE PAGE:
Fringes and bobbles decorate a selection of woven and knitted textiles from Bolivia.

RIGHT: On Almlonga market day, a Guatemalan woman wears a cluster of tassels to decorate her folded tzute *headcloth.*

Featherwork

The construction method of attaching feathers to lengths of thread possibly originated in the tropical forests to the east of the Andes mountains and was used by the indigenous tribes as part of their decoration on ritual costume. The tribes of the Amazon Basin are famous for their feather-decorated headdresses, which have been worn during their elaborate dance ceremonies over a period of many generations. The headdresses were constructed in sections so that they could

be taken apart for storage. Most of these headdresses have disintegrated in the humid tropical climate, but Chimú carved effigies at Chan Chan show chieftains wearing very similar feathered headgear. The headdresses and feathered breastplates were worn during the 'Ant Dance Ceremony'. Fire ants, vicious stinging insects, were inserted into the woven basketry formation of the breastplates and these were applied to the bodies of young warriors to inflict pain during the initiation ceremonies. The Wayana tribe's ant or wasp shield was used and decorated in a similar way. Not all of the feathers are sewn, many are glued in place onto the basket-woven shields as well as on the carved wooden masks worn by the Shamans. These take symbolic forms and depict the jaguar, the anaconda snake and various birds.

ABOVE: Multi-coloured wool tassels decorate a narrow, woven purse or musical pipe bag – from Cuzco, Peru.

ABOVE LEFT: This brocade-patterned sash, worn as a headdress in Chichicastenango, Guatemala, is finished with plump tassels on both ends.

Tassels, Bobbles and Pom-Poms

These decorative additions are very popular in all the areas of Central and South America. They are generally used to embellish costume, especially on hats and belt ends, but also perform a function as a talismanic decoration on animals. At festival times and for religious processions, the llamas are decked out with an excess of brightly coloured thread tassels fitted onto their harness or tied to their ears and hair.

Traditional tassels, combining multicoloured threads, are used to finish the ends of the headdress sashes worn in Chichicastenango, Guatemala. The woven end of the sash is turned up to form a mitred corner to which is added three thread plaits worked in a variety of colours to support the tassels. The six plump tassels add a striking effect to an already decorative headdress. Multicoloured wool tassels are threaded into the sides of a long, narrow woven purse or carrying bag for a musical pipe from Cuzco, Peru and groups of thread tassels are added at intervals to a knitted *monedero* purse. Cascades of differently coloured thread tassels hang down from the top point of the conical knitted *ch'ullo* hats and are tied to the pointed ends of the earflaps.

Pom-Poms

Pom-poms take many forms and entail different construction methods. The Quiche hair-tassel pom-poms from Zunil in Guatemala decorate the ends of a tapestry-woven patterned braid. Vertical stripes of plush threads are formed round a core in the same way that bell-pull ropes are made, by slotting the cut threads into position on a narrow loom. Long tassel threads, which dangle below the pom-poms, hang down the side of the face when the band is wound round as a headband. This method of pom-pom making is used in many areas of the world. Smaller, but similar thread pom-poms are found on a little woven *ch'uspa*, coca-leaf bag from Bolivia. They are included on three finely braided cords that hang from the lower edge and divided to make six pom-pom ends.

A different type of pom-pom is made to finish the twisted cord ends of a hair band from Antigua Guatemala. Little circular disc shapes, possibly tap washers, are bound with thread which is wound round the disc and through the

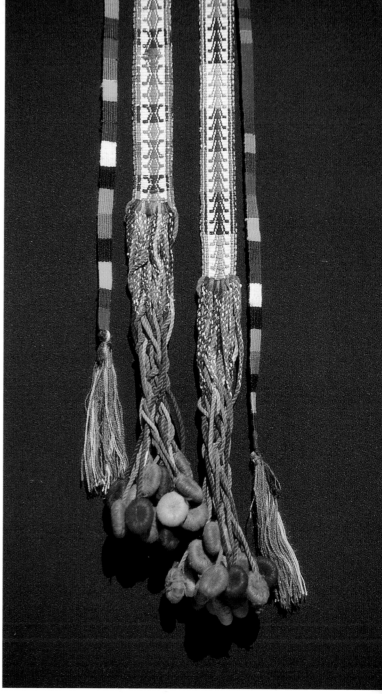

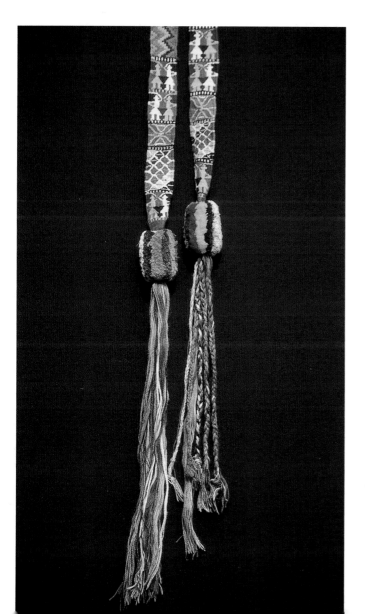

ABOVE: *Thread-covered circular discs are suspended from the ends of a hair band – from Antigua, Guatemala.*

LEFT: *A tapestry-woven head braid from Zunil in Guatemala has striped, plush pom-poms worked above the plaited thread ends.*

central hole until it is completely covered. The cords are loosely plaited together and the pom-pom discs are fixed firmly to the cord ends. They hang down in multicoloured groups of twenty or more.

Little stitch-woven bobbles make an unusual edging on a man's sash from Todos Santos Cuchumatan. The sash is worked with the four-selvedge method, thus finishing in the middle where there is a slight difference to the pattern. Each end of the warp is worked over a narrow rod, which when removed, leaves loops of threads. These loops of thread are woven over in groups, in coloured wools, using a needle-weaving formation.

A technique similar to the Todos Santos sash bobbles is used on the ends of a double-faced woven *wincha* or head-band, purchased in La Paz, Bolivia. The warp-end threads of about 5cm (2in) in length are divided into nineteen narrow groups. Each thread group is woven in and out, using a needle and a variety of coloured wools to cover the threads entirely. All of the woven thread groups are held together at the bottom with a piece of wool braid.

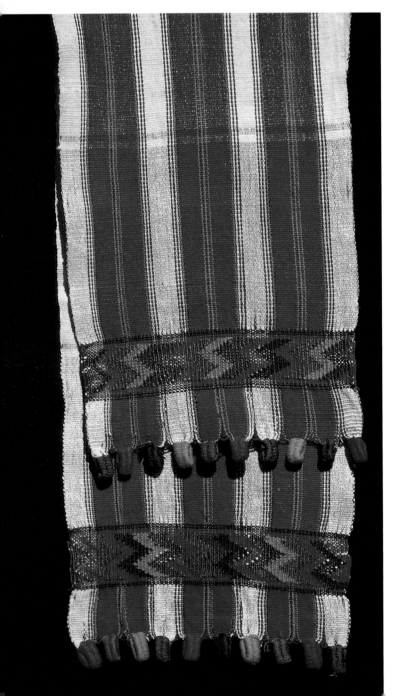

Little stitch-woven bobbles make an unusual edging on a man's sash – from Todos Santos Cuchumatan, Guatemala.

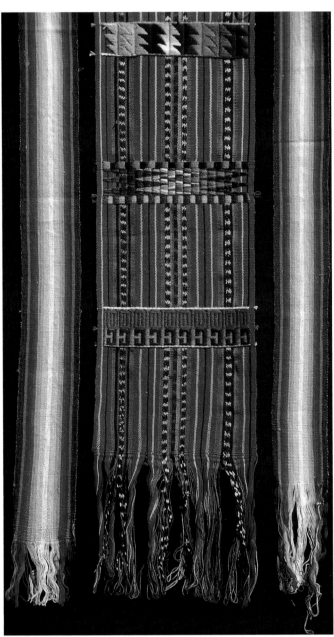

A red ikat-woven belt from the Guatemalan Highlands has a fringe of uncut, surplus warp-end loops. A striped belt from Panama is finished in a similar manner.

Fringes and Shawl-Ends

Any woven textile that was not finished with the four-selvedge method would need some way of securing the warp thread ends when it was removed from the loom. In some instances these ends would be tied off and sewn down as a hem, but the warp ends provided an additional element for decoration. Some of the methods were indigenous to the American continents, but others were imported from Spain

A fringe of twisted warp ends decorates the edges of a sash. Double-faced brocade motifs include peacock birds, jaguars and serpents – from San Juan Sacatapéquez.

side, while a space the width of the fringe is left before the selvedge threads are set on at the right-hand side. This leaves a section unworked at the right with the weft threads crossing the empty space, before they are held at the right-hand selvedge. These horizontal weft threads will form the fringe when taken off the loom and are cut free from the selvedge.

Knotting

The Spanish had long used knotting to hold and decorate the ends of their silk shawls and *mantillas* and the fashion was taken up by the post-Conquest settlers, especially in areas of Mexico and Guatemala. The Portuguese introduced similar fashions into Brazil, Paraguay and Argentina. At first the warp ends themselves were used for knotting, but the shawl fabric could be finished with a hem and groups of knotting threads introduced, often in a heavier weight of silk thread. Overhand knots were used, with the patterning formed by dividing and alternating the groups of threads. Thus the knots would form a lattice of meshes that altered in size and frequency across the rows. Once trade was established across the Pacific to the West, imports of goods from China to Mexico during the nineteenth century included Chinese silk shawls with knotted fringe ends, thus completing the circle, as the Spanish had first been influenced by trade goods from the Eastern silk routes.

Macramé

In Mexico, the Nahua men from the Puebla region worked an elaborate pattern sequence in *macramé*, knotting onto both ends of their sashes. The pointed ends of Vandyke triangles supported a series of tassels making it a rich accessory. The knotting was often used to finish the ends of the ever-popular *rebozo* shawls, with the decorative elements used to identify the varying types and qualities. An *ikat*-woven *rebozo* shawl from Pauline Milne's collection, purchased in Mexico during the early 1980s, has an elaborate fringed border formed from alternating segments of blue and black silk threads. These are passed through one another in various combinations using ply-split, *macramé* cording, oblique plaiting and twisting techniques so that the colours interchange to make diamond patterns.

The warp ends of a little woven bookmark from Zunil in Guatemala are finished with several rows of *macramé* knots. An even more important areas was the fringing that was added to the outer sides of the hammock. Although

and Portugal. A basic way of dealing with warp ends was to twist them in groups across the width of the fabric and hold the ends with an overhand knot. An *ikat*- woven belt from the Guatemalan highlands is finished this way. A wider belt from the same area makes use of the long, uncut looped ends that are removed from the two bars of the back-strap loom when the weaving is finished.

Separate fringes are woven on a narrow-width loom. The warp is set on as a series of close threads at the left-hand

A bag from Brazil, woven from soft, cotton cords has the warp stripes finished as a series of plaits with tassel-thread ends.

together at the ends. Thread tassels are slotted into the braids at intervals.

Most of the Peruvian belts are finished with sets of little finger-looped braids. These braid-groups are nearly always tied together at the ends. A belt from the Lake Titicaca area has thread slotted through the plait ends that are finished as loops. The loop plaits on the end of a woven belt from Chile has each of the multicoloured ends tied into a rough knot, leaving the plaits hanging loose. An older belt from the Charazani region of Bolivia ends with a series of twelve loop plaits, all linked together at intervals to form a cohesive whole. The colours of the warp-faced double weave are echoed in the plaits, reversing their colours at intervals to make this a superior piece. A similar technique is used for the ends of a woven belt from Cuzco in Peru. These loop plaits are also linked together and reverse colour at the halfway mark. The ends are all held together in a point.

Borders can be worked with an additional set of threads, or by manipulation of the warp threads. These threads can

This young girl is joining two widths of woven cloth with an embroidered ruanda *seam – from San Antonio Palopó, Guatemala.*

network was popular, *macramé* proved to be a firm favourite. Knotting would perhaps provide a firmer border than an openwork of netting which would be subject to continual use over a period of time.

Finger Looping and Plaiting

Both methods are a popular way of finishing the long ends of belts, ties and sashes, either individually or as groups or sets of ends. If the warp ends of a wider, woven belt are cut from the loom, plaiting may be used to finish the ends. The end loops of a narrow, woven band are not cut when removed from the loom. These are plaited using the finger-looping method where the loops on one set of fingers are interchanged with the finger-loops on the other hand. This method is common to other countries around the world. A belt from Todos Santos Cuchumatan in the highlands of Guatemala has a pair of finger-loop plaits that are joined

be twined together in groups and twisted around one another, or pairs of threads can be worked as a combination of plaiting and weaving. See *Textiles, a Classification of Techniques* by Annemarie Seiler-Baldinger for additional combinations of twining and fringed borders.

The *Ruanda* Seam

The sewing together of narrow widths of cloth with decorative embroidery stitches was another pre-Conquest technique. The limitations of the loom width made this essential in the construction of any large garments or pieces of cloth. The name *ruanda* in Spanish means 'lacing' and refers to the joining stitches. These seams are found in areas of both South and Central America and only vary in the choice of thread colour and the type of lacing stitches used. It is believed that in the past they were sewn using needles made from thorns, or bone, or of annealed copper which had been treated by repeated beating and heating in order to make the needles hard enough for use.

The joining stitches are based on fishbone or herringbone stitch, which cross to either side with each alternate stitch, or with looped variations, once again worked on alternate sides of the cloth. The edges of the fabric to be seamed would first be turned under to provide a firm base for the stitching. The two flat pieces of fabric are then placed evenly

The decorative ruanda *seam used to join the sections of an* ikat-*woven skirt – from Junil, Guatemala c.1990.*

together so that the turned-under hems butt against one another. The workers always join the fabric lengths evenly, but often disregard any pattern matching of stripes or woven motifs. This does not appear to be of prime importance. Narrow-width woven cloths are joined in a similar manner today. Some modern *ruanda* seams are now stitched with a wide satin stitch on the sewing machine, but this is less pliable than the original hand stitching.

Bag Finishes

Bolivian bags, or *ch'uspas*, are finished with a binding of variously coloured synthetic threads to cover the ends of the central join on a four-selvedge construction. Occasionally this binding takes the form of a looped border. On a very small bag, it is not possible to finish off the central area of the weaving neatly, so this is possibly the reason for covering the ends, but to European eyes, the choice of synthetic threads in bright colours clashes with the superb quality of the woven portion of bags.

A Tarabuco coca bag from Bolivia has a superior method of finishing the bottom edge. A series of little wrapped cords

in colour sequence, are sewn over the edge to cover the end of the weaving. Additional decoration is in the form of wrapped thread cords with wrapped thread bobbles on the ends. A similar construction is used for the tab which is woven-in as part of the bag. The side seam decoration is a woven addition to the main work. This method is also used in the Cuzco area of Peru as a finish for woven articles. A very small loom, with a narrow width of warp threads, is set up alongside the completed side of the item to be decorated. A coloured pick-up pattern is woven on the little loom, using a long needle. This needle is taken through the fabric at the side of the weaving, as a sewing stitch, each time it is passed as a weft through the loom warp. Thus the woven braid pattern becomes integral with the side seam of the woven cloth or bag. An alternative method is to combine finger-looping and sewing where one person plaits the finger braid while the other inserts the holding stitches at the required intervals.

The amount of work and weaving expertise needed to make the small Bolivian bag cannot be appreciated until it is examined closely. These people, for whom future time does not exist in the present, are happy to spend as many hours as necessary to produce an article that is both useful and at the same time, very beautiful. It is to be hoped that the indigenous craft workers of both Central and South America keep their ability to make these lovely items and continue in the traditions of their ancestral heritage.

Glossary

Spelling varies from place to place, as many of the words are adapted from the Quechua, Aymara and Central American languages. Most weaving and embroidery terms are dealt with fully in the relevant chapters.

Agave A sub-tropical plant grown throughout the world to produce hemp fibres

Aksu Rectangle of cloth worn as a belted tunic by Inca women – Peru

Allwi masi Older Peruvian woman who guides a younger woman through intricate weaving patterns

Alpaca (*Lama pacos*) a slender bodied, long-limbed lamboid descended from the wild guanaco and the vicuña

Alpaka A Peruvian symbol meaning Secret Earth

Altiplano High-altitude area of Bolivia and Peru, with limited sustainable plant life

Amaru Alternative name for the two-headed snake god who originally lived in a lake

Arpilleras Fabric pictures first worked by the women of Chile as a political statement

Bayeta Plain, woven woollen cloth, generally cream – Bolivia and Peru

Bolas Three stones attached to lengths of llama tendons, used by the Incas as a weapon of war

Boleadoras Leather cords with three iron balls attached, used by the Gaucho to control cattle

Bolsas or **Bolsitas** Drawstring bags – Bolivia and Peru

Bombachas The wide-cut trousers worn by the Gauchos on horseback

Calzones Loose cotton drawers worn for work by the slaves or the native lower classes

Capiaxy Long, shirt-shaped woollen outer garment with open sides and decorative sleeves worn in the highlands of Guatemala

Carreta Mexican wooden spinning wheel used to produce coarse string for mats etc.

Chamarros Oblong poncho with opens sides and fringed ends – Mexico

Chola or **Cholo** Indigenous people from the Andes who have adopted Spanish language and dress

Ch'ullo Knitted cap with earflaps – Bolivia and Peru

Chumpi Hand-woven belt – Bolivia and Peru

Ch'uspa Hand-woven bag, made to contain coca leaves – Bolivia and Peru

Coca A shrub native to the Americas, the leaves are dried and chewed as a stimulant

Cochineal Red dye obtained from a parasitic cactus-eating scale insect

Cofradias Brotherhoods representing both people and Church in Guatemala

Cuadros Little appliqué embroidered pictures made in impoverished areas of Peru

Encomienda System of forced native labour, set up by the Spanish Colonists

Gobolinos Embroidered pictures similar to those from Peru, made in Colombia

Guanaco (*Lama guanaco*) a territorial wild lamboid found in Southern Peru, Bolivia and Patagonia

Guayuco Loincloth worn by Wayuu men – northern Columbia and Venezuela

Heddles A system of string or metal guides set to lift alternate warp threads and form an opening or shed for weaving on a loom

Huichol Independent tribes who inhabit the remote northwest mountain area of Mexico

Huipil Tunic-type blouse worn by women in Guatemala and Mexico

Ik Mayan symbol for the wind

Ikat Asian name for threads tied and dyed to make a resist pattern for weaving

Indigo A shrub or a herb, belonging to the genus *Indigofera*, used to produce blue dyes in fermentation vats, the colour deepening with exposure to oxygen

Iraca palm Leaves used for weaving sombrero hats and mats – Columbia

Ixtle Agavaceae family (genus *Yucca*). Fibres often used for netted fabrics

Jaina Warriors from Campeche in Mexico, late classic period AD 600–900

Jaspe Resist system where the weaving threads are tied and dyed to form a pattern

Jipipapa hat Woven straw hat originally from the town of the same name, in Ecuador

Kemp The outer guard hairs of sheep, keeping out cold and rain

Kukulcan Mayan feathered serpent god, Mexico

Llama (*Lama glam*) originally bred from the wild guanaco in the Andes

Lliclla Rectangular woven cloth worn as a woman's shoulder cape – Peru

Maguey Stiff fibre obtained from *Agave cantala*, used for rope and cordage

Macramé Multi-element thread ends joined with a series of knots to form a fabric

Manta Cloth or cloak – South America

Mengikat Indonesian word from which *ikat* is derived, meaning 'to tie'

Merinos Fine-wool sheep breed, developed in Spain before the Christian era

Mestizos A mixed blood group of Spanish colonists and the indigenous people

Mola Decorated blouse worn by the Kuna women of the San Blas Islands

Monedero Money purses from Bolivia and Peru

Montera Wide-brimmed circular hat, varying according to location – Peru

Mordants A fixative for natural dyes so that the fabric does not fade or lose its colour

Murex purple Dye produced as a defensive mechanism by the *Murex* marine snail, which is a gastropod mollusc

Ñanduti Needle-stitched lace circles, or 'sun' shapes

Oblagated Counter change patterns on fabric appliqué *molas* of the Kuna, Panama

Pacha Mama Mother Earth goddess – Bolivia and Peru

Panama hat palm Stemless palm-like herb used for weaving hats and mats

Paños Embroidered yarn pictures with religious or political themes, Guatemala

Passamontana Protective Balaclava-type mask worn by high-altitude mountain people

Pintos, Los The bare-legged, painted men of Tarahumara, Mexico

Pollera Full, gathered skirt worn with petticoats by women – South America

Ponchito Shoulder cape still worn by the men of Tarabuscan

Poncho Rectangle of woven cloth with head opening – South America

Popol Vuh Manuscript history of the Mayan Quiche people and lists of their Kings

Quechquémitl A Mexican version of the poncho resembling a cornered shoulder cape

Quetzal A bird native to Central America noted for its brilliant plumage and long tail feathers. Also monetary unit of Guatemala

Quetzalcóatl The feathered serpent god of the Aztecs

Quipu System of knots used by the Incas to record and transmit messages

Qutun The old Arabic word for 'cotton'

Rastidor Rectangular wooden frame used as a support when making *Ñanduti* lace

Rebociño A lace mantilla, that acted partially as a veil

Rebozo Rectangular shawl worn by Mexican women since the time of the Conquest

Reeling Silk filament groups are gathered to adhere to a stick, then wound onto a reeling wheel

Rocailles Little round beads, originally imported from Bohemia, Europe

Roderillo A rectangular woven blanket worn over trousers by Guatemalan men. Also called a *ponchito*

Rolag Weaving term. Straightened wool is rolled up to form a cylindrical shape, ready for spinning

Ruanda A decorative seam joining two narrow lengths of woven cloth together

Rusticas A basic type of cloth doll sold in areas of the High Andes in tourist outlets

Sarape An oblong panel of weaving with a slit in the middle for the head, sometimes worn draped as a cloak – Mexico

Shed A weaving term given to the opening formed when an alternate set of warp threads are lifted, enabling the weft thread to be passed through

Sisal hemp Comes from the *Agave sisalana* plant – Central America

Spindle Shafted device for spinning yarn, shaped like an elongated spinning top

Spindle-Whorl A weighted disc or pierced ball placed on the spindle shaft, used to control the balance

Spondylus Shells of the spiny oyster that comes from the coastal areas of Ecuador

Staples Variable, discontinuous lengths that make up natural fibres – including cotton, flax, wool and hair

Throwing Reeled silk filament groups twisted lightly together to form a weaving thread

Trajé Traditional clothing worn by the original inhabitants of conquered countries

Tzute Cloth used for various purposes by both men and women

Unku Tunic-shirt or *ponchito* – Bolivia and Peru

Vicuña (*Lama,* or *vicugna*) Territorial member of the camel family from Bolivia and Peru which has never been domesticated

Watado Warp *ikat* – Bolivia and Peru

Wincha Woven headband, sometimes beaded – Bolivia

Womo Kots Sombrero hats woven by the Wayuu people of Columbia

Yucca Plant of the Agavaceae family, the spiny leaves produce fibre for netted fabrics

Bibliography and Further Reading

General

Crabtree, Caroline, *World Embroidery*, David and Charles, 1993

Dubin, Lois Sherr, *The History of Beads from 30,000BC to the Present*, Harry N Abrams, Incorporated, New York, 1987

Gillow, John and Sentance, Brian, *World Textiles, a Visual Guide to Traditional Techniques*, Thames and Hudson, 1999 and 2000

Hamre, Ida and Meedom, Hanne, *Making Simple Clothes, The structure and development of clothes from other cultures*, Adam & Charles Black, London, 1980

May, Florence Lewis, *Hispanic Lace and Lace Making*, Printed by order of the Trustees of the Hispanic Society of America, New York, 1939

Paine, Sheila, *Embroidered Textiles: Traditional Patterns from Five Continents*, Thames and Hudson, 1990

Paine, Sheila, *Amulets, a World of Secret Powers, Charms and Magic*, Thames and Hudson, 2004

Sensier, Danielle, *Traditions Around the World, Costumes*, Hodder Wayland, 1994

Thomas, Hugh, *The Slave Trade. The History of the Atlantic Slave Trade 1440–1870*, Papermac, an imprint of Macmillan Publishers Ltd, 1998

Central America

Enciso, Jorge, *Designs from Pre-Columbian Mexico*, Dover Publications, Inc., 1971

Hecht, Ann, *Textiles from Guatemala*, The British Museum Press, 2001

Mahler, Richard, *Guatemala, a Natural Destination*, John Muir Publications, 1993

Morris Jr, Walter F, *Living Maya*, Harry N Abrams, Inc., 1987

Puls, Herta, *The Art of Cutwork and Applique, Historic, Modern and Kuna Indian*, B T Batsford, 1978

Puls, Herta, *Textiles of the Kuna Indians of Panama*, Shire Publications Ltd, 1988

Rivera, Aldaberto, *The Mysteries of Chichén Itzá*, Copyright Aldaberto Rivera, Yucatan, Mexico, 2001

Salvador, Mari Lyn, (eds), *The Art of Being Kuna, Layers of Meaning among the Kuna of Panama*, UCLA Fowler Museum of Cultural History, Los Angeles, 1997

Sayer, Cholë, *Textiles from Mexico*, The British Museum Press, 2002

Thames and Hudson (eds), *Sacred Symbols, The Maya*, Thames and Hudson, 1976

Von Zabern, Philipp, *Webkunst der Maya aus Guatemala*, Roemer-und Pelizaus-Museum, Hildesheim, 1992

South America

Braun, Barbara (ed.) and Roe, Peter G (text), *Arts of the Amazon*, Thames and Hudson, London, 1995

Cahlander, Adele, *Bolivian Tubular Edging and Andean Crossed-Warp Techniques*, Dos Tejedoras, P.O. Box 14238, St Paul, MN 55114, USA

Cahlander, Adele with Baizerman, Suzanne, *Double-Weave Treasures from Old Peru*, Dos Tejedoras, P.O. Box 14238, St Paul, MN 55114, USA

Davies, Lucy and Fini, Mo, *Arts and Crafts of South America*, Thames and Hudson, 1994

d'Harcourt, Raoul, *Textiles of Ancient Peru*, Dover Publications, Inc, Mineola, New York. Reprinted 1962 from original 1934 editor.

Editors of Time-Life Books, *Incas: Lords of Gold and Glory*, Time-Life Books, Alexandria, Virginia, 1992

Feltham, Jane, *Peruvian Textiles*, Shire Publications Ltd, 1989

Fini, MS, *The Weavers of Ancient Peru*, Tumi, London and Bath, 1985

Franquemont, Ed., *The Andean Art, a hands-on exploration of Andean Textile Traditions*, AWASQA

Heckman, Andrea M, *Woven Stories: Andean Textiles and Rituals*, Albuquerque, New Mexico: University of New Mexico Press, 2003

La Farge, Henry A, Editorial Director, *Museums of the Andes*, Newsweek, Inc & Kodansha Ltd, Tokyo, 1981

Meisch, Lynn A (ed.), *Traditional Textiles of the Andes – Life in Cloth in the highlands – The Jeffrey Appleby Collection of Andean Textiles*, Thames and Hudson

McEwan, Colin, Barreto, Cristina, and Neve, Eduardo (eds), *Unknown Amazon, Culture in Ancient Brazil*, The British Museum Press

Mosely, Michael E, *The Incas and Their Ancestors: The Archaeology of Peru*, Thames and Hudson, 2001

Rowe, Ann Pollard, and Cohen, John, *Hidden Threads of Peru – Q'ero Textiles*, Merrell in assn. with Textile Museum of Washington, DC

Scott-Macnab, David (ed.), *Discovering the Amazon, Part 1, The Mighty Amazon;* and Allen, Benedict, *Part 2, A Journey into the Amazon Jungle*, The Reader's Digest Association Limited, London, 1994

Wasserman, Tamara E, and Hill, Johnathon S, *Bolivian Textiles, Traditional Designs and Costumes*, Dover Publications Inc., New York, 1981

Fabrics, Fibres and Threads

Clutton-Brock, Juliet, *A Natural History of Domesticated Animals*, British Museum Publications (Natural History), 1987

Collier, Ann M, *A Handbook of Textiles*, Pergamon Press Ltd, Oxford 1970, 1974

Hardingham, Martin, *The Illustrated Dictionary of Fabrics*, Book Club Associates, London by arrangement with Cassell Ltd, 1978

Miller, Edward, *Textiles, Properties and Behaviour in Clothing Use*, B T Batsford Ltd, London, 1968 and 1983

Mochi, Ugo and Carter, T Donald, *Hoofed Mammals of the World*, Copyright U Mochi and T.D.C. 1953, Charles Scribner's Sons, 1971

Rollins, John G, *Needlemaking*, Shire Publications Ltd, 1981

Wild, John Peter, *Textiles in Archaeology*, Shire Publications Ltd, 1988

Youcett, William, *Sheep, their Breeds, Management and Diseases*, Edward Law, 16 Essex St, Strand, London, 1862

Textile Techniques

Baines, Patricia, *Spinning Wheels, Spinners and Spinning*, Charles Scribner's Sons, New York, 1977 and 1979

Baizerman, Suzanne and Searle, Karen, *Latin American Brocades: Explorations in Supplementary Weft Techniques*, Distributed by Alison Hodge, Publishers, Cornwall, UK, 1980

Balfour-Paul, Jenny, *Indigo*, British Museum Press, 1998

Barron, Birgit Olson, *Knitting on the Loom – Techniques for producing knit stitches within the woven structure*, published by Birgit Olson Barron, P.O. Box 782, Escabana, MI 49829, USA, May, 1988

Bjerregaard, Lena, *Techniques of Guatemalan Weaving*, Van Nostrand Reinhold Company, 1977

Burnham, Dorothy K, *A Textile Terminology, Warp & Weft*, Routledge and Kegan Paul, London and Henley, 1964

Casson, M and Cahlander, A, *The Art of Bolivian Highland Weaving*, Watson-Guptill, 1976

Collingwood, Peter, *The Techniques of Sprang, Plaiting on Stretched Threads*, Faber and Faber, London, 1974

Dendel, Esther Warner, *The Basic Book of Fingerweaving*, Thomas Nelson and Sons Ltd, 1974

Emery, Irene, *The Primary Structure of Fabrics*, The Textile Museum, Washington, 1980

Freitas, Maria A, *The Art of Dimensional Embroidery*, EdMar Company, Camarillo, CA 93011-0055, USA, 2002

Goodman, Frances Schaill, *The Embroidery of Mexico and Guatemala*, Charles Scribner's Sons, New York, 1976

Goodwin, Jill, *A Dyer's Manual*, Pelham Books/Stephen Greene Press, 1982

Hecht, Ann, *The Art of The Loom, Weaving, Spinning & Dyeing across the World*, British Museum Publications Ltd, 1989

La Plantz, Shereen, *Twill Basketry, A handbook of Designs, Techniques and Styles*, Lark Books, 1993

LeCount, Cynthia Gravelle, *Andean Folk Knitting, Traditions and Techniques from Peru and Bolivia*, Dos Tejedoras Fiber Arts Publications, Minnesota, USA, 1990

Morris Jr, Walter F, *A Millennium of Weaving in Chiapas*, distributed by Alison Hodge, Publishers, Cornwall, UK, 1984

Owen, Rodrick, *The Big Book of Sling and Rope Braids*, Cassell, London, 1995, 1996

Sandberg, Gösta, *Indigo Textiles, Technique and History*, A & C Black Ltd, London, 1989

Sandberg, Gösta, *The Red Dyes, Cochineal, Madder and Murex Purple*, Lark Books, 1997

Sayer, Cholé, *Mexican Textile Techniques*, Shire Publications Ltd, 1988

Sayer, Chloë, *Mexican Textiles*, British Museum Publications Ltd, 1985, 1990

Seiler-Baldinger, Annemarie, *Textiles, a Classification of Techniques*, Crawford House Press Pty Ltd, 1994

Stillwell, Alexandra, *The Technique of Teneriffe Lace*, B T Batsford Ltd, London, 1980

Tacker, Harold and Sylvia, *Band Weaving, The Techniques, Looms and Uses for Woven Bands*, Studio Vista, 1974

Catalogues, Journals and Pamphlets

Carey, Jacqui (Designer and Curator), *Braids and Beyond, a Broad Look at Narrow Wares,* Braid Society Exhibition

Cheyney, Judy, 'Saltilo Sarapes', *Journal for Weavers, Spinners and Dyers*

Edwards, Liz, 'Brazilian Blend – Five hundred years after the Portuguese discovery', *Wanderlust, Issue 42,* October/November 2000

Franquemont, Christine, 'Watching Watching, Counting Counting' – adapted from an article of the same name by Ed Franquemont that appeared in *Human Nature, Vol. 1 No.3,* March 1979

Giordano, Carlos Romero, *Oaxaca, Archaeology – Colonial Art – Traditions,* Bonechi - Monclem Ediciones, Mexico City, 2001

Haba, Lois de la, 'Guatemala, Maya and Modern', *National Geographic Vol. 146, No. 5,* November 1974

Liu, Robert K, 'Spindle Whorls: Pt.1. Some Comments and Speculations', *Source unknown, c.*1970s

Miller, Mary, 'Maya Masterpiece Revealed at Bonampak' *National Geographic Vol. 187, No. 2,* February 1995

Museum of Mankind – leaflet, *The Gilded Image – Pre-Columbian Gold from South and Central America,* The Trustees of the British Museum, 1996

Pilkington, John, 'Llama Karma, Four Feet in the Andes', *Wanderlust, Issue 26,* February/March 1998

Reid, James W, 'Victor and Vanquished, The Icongraphic Mysteries of a Tapestry from Pre-Columbian Peru', *Hali, 135. 25th Anniversary Edition,* July/August 2004

Reid, Jane, 'The Dolls of Peru', *PieceWork magazine,* April 2004

Sernatur – Tourist Promotion Corporation of Chile

Solis, Felipe, *National Museum of Anthropology,* Bonechi-Monclem Ediciones, Mexico City, 2002

Speiser, Noemi, *Loop-Manipulation-Braiding – Basic Instructions,* Jenny Parry Publisher, May 2002, Braid Society

Spinney, Laura, 'How Time Flies – how different languages reflect, and shape, our conception of time', *The Guardian,* 24 February 2005

Reference

Encyclopaedia Britannica, 2003

Craft Video Films

Willoughby, Janet. Ends of the Earth Ltd
Traditional Peruvian Weaving – Spinning, Dyeing & Weaving around Cuzco
Backstrap Weaving – Traditional Weaving in Guatemala and Mexico
Peruvian Knitted Hats
www.endsoftheearth.co.uk

Selected Websites

'A Short History of the Mayan Hammock', *Hammock Jungle LLC;* http://www.hammockjungle.com/information.php?info_id=7

'Arpilleras from Peru', *The Folk Art Gallery;* http://www.thefolkartgallery.com/arpilleras.htm

'Brazilian Embroidery', *The Brazilian Dimensional Embroidery International Guild;* http://www.bdeig.org/BDEIGhome.htm

'History of Hammocks', *Ecomall;* http://www.ecomall.com/greenshopping/hammock.htm

'Patagonia History', *BBC – North West Wales History – Patagonia;* http://www.bbc.co.uk/wales/northwest/sites/history/pages/patagonia1.shtml

'Traditional Beadwork Sailing Traders', *Huichol Art Gallery;* http://www.sailingtraders.com/traditional/html

Museums with Textile Collections

United Kingdom

Birmingham Museums & Art Gallery
British Museum, London
Horniman Museum, London
Pitt Rivers Museum, Oxford
University Museum of Archaeology and Anthropology, Cambridge

Chile

Archaeological Museum, La Serena, Northern Chile (pre-Inca artefacts)
Archaeological Museum, Santiago (ethno-historical, Colonial to present)
San Miguel de Azapa Archaeological Museum, Arica (world's oldest mummies)

Mexico

Museo Rufino Tamayo, Oaxaca (archaeology)
National Museum of Anthropology, Mexico City
Regional Museum of Anthropology, Merida, Yucatan
Regional Museum of Chiapas
Regional Museum of Oaxaca

Guatemala

Museum of Archaeology and Ethnology, Guatemala City (traditional costumes)
Popol Vuh Museum, Guatemala City (pre-Columbian artefacts)

Peru

Archaeological Museum, Cuzco (mummy bundles)
Archaeological and Anthropological Museum, Lima
Amano Museum, Lima (Chancay weaving)
Museum of Contemporary Peruvian Folk Art, Lima
National Museum of Peruvian Culture, Lima (costumes)
Pachcamac site Museum, Lima coastal area

Europe

Göteborg Ethnological Museum, Sweden (Kuna Picture writing)
Museum für Völkerkunde, Vienna, Austria

USA

Brooklyn Museum, New York (Paracas textiles)
Cleveland Museum of Art (Nasca textiles)
Metropolitan Museum of Art, New York
The Textile Museum, Washington DC
UCLA Fowler Museum of Cultural History, Los Angeles

Index